LEGITIMACY
IN THE ACADEMIC
PRESIDENCY

LEGITIMACY IN THE ACADEMIC PRESIDENCY

From Entrance to Exit

Rita Bornstein

AMERICAN COUNCIL ON EDUCATION
PRAEGER
Series on Higher Education

Library of Congress Cataloging-in-Publication Data

Bornstein, Rita.
    Legitimacy in the academic presidency : from entrance to exit / Rita Bornstein.
        p. cm.—(ACE/Praeger series on higher education)
    "An Oryx book."
    Includes bibliographical references and index.
    ISBN 1–57356–562–8 (alk. paper)
    1. College presidents—United States.   2. Education, Higher—United States—
Administration.   3. Educational leadership—United States.   I. Title.   II. American
Council on Education/Praeger series on higher education.
    LB2341.B596   2003
    378.1′11—dc21   2003053616

Formerly ACE/Oryx Press Series on Higher Education

British Library Cataloguing in Publication Data is available.

Library of Congress Catalog Card Number: 2003053616
ISBN: 1–57356–562–8

First published in 2003

Praeger Publishers, 88 Post Road West, Westport, CT 06881
An imprint of Greenwood Publishing Group, Inc.
www.praeger.com

Printed in the United States of America

The paper used in this book complies with the
Permanent Paper Standard issued by the National
Information Standards Organization (Z39.48–1984).

10 9 8 7 6 5 4 3 2

For my husband, Harland, an incomparable presidential and intellectual partner, and for our children, Rachel, Mark, and Per, their spouses John and Anne, and our granddaughters Ariel and Hayley

CONTENTS

PREFACE

CONCEPTUAL FRAMEWORK

The central thesis of this book is that achieving and maintaining legitimacy is the sine qua non of a successful academic presidency. Without legitimacy, no president can advance an ambitious agenda. Without legitimacy, a presidency is doomed. Stakeholders grant legitimacy to a president they believe is a good fit with the institutional culture and an effective leader (Hollander and Julian 1978, 118–19, 148). In the process of gaining legitimacy, presidents develop relationships of trust and influence that build the social capital essential to strengthening and transforming institutions.

Unless an institution is in a crisis requiring immediate and drastic action, presidencies tend to develop in a cycle of three stages, generally wrapped around a fund-raising campaign. These three stages, which overlap, are gaining legitimacy, creating legitimate change, and assuring a legitimate presidential succession. For a presidency to be successful, each stage must be characterized by legitimacy.

Presidents come to their positions with the sense that their constituents expect them to significantly improve, if not transform, their institutions. On the other hand, boards, faculties, and alumni often feel that they must "protect" their institutions from presidential initiatives. To overcome resistance and gather support for change, presidents must assure that initiatives are viewed as legitimate by anchoring them in accepted norms and procedures. In fact, every aspect of a presidency depends on legitimacy for its success, including the presidential search, transition arrangements, administration, governance, planning, lobbying, resource acquisition, and institutional positioning.

My interest in presidential legitimacy has two roots. The first stems from years of observing the humiliation of presidents who lost or never gained legitimacy and the cost of that failure for those individuals and their institutions. As I saw good people terminated from their presidencies, I began to wonder whether they could have been saved and what could be learned from those experiences. The second source of my interest in this topic is the significant challenge to legitimacy I faced in my own presidency. By the spring of 1990, trends in society and higher education had made it possible for the board of trustees of Rollins College, a liberal arts college founded in 1885 by the Congregational Church and presided over initially by the local pastor, to elect me Rollins's thirteenth president: a woman, a Jew, and a fund-raiser, with a Ph.D. in education. Having traveled an atypical career path, I was not viewed as, and did not feel like, an insider until several years after becoming president.

The philosopher Hannah Arendt describes the outsider as a "conscious pariah," a marginal person belonging to more than one culture, fully accepted in none, who therefore develops a unique outlook on those cultures (1978, 27, 68). The writer V.S. Naipaul is such a person. Born in Trinidad to a poor Indian family, he migrated to England to become educated and was later awarded a Nobel Prize in literature. He writes, "Because my movement within this civilization has been from the periphery to the center, I may have seen or felt certain things more freshly than people to whom those things were everyday" (2002, 517). Similarly, the marginal status of women in the academy enabled feminist scholars to provide new insights on a wide range of taken-for-granted assumptions. In the course of overcoming significant obstacles to legitimacy as president of Rollins College, I viewed events as both insider and outsider, and developed a critical perspective on taken-for-granted aspects of academic leadership. I hope that this analysis of academic leadership and legitimacy will be helpful to presidents, aspirants to the presidency, trustees, and scholars.

ORGANIZATION AND SOURCES

Part I, New Roles for the New Millennium, analyzes the impact of the 1990s and the first years of the twenty-first century on the evolution of the college presidency. The legitimacy, value, and performance of higher education were called into question during this period, and respect for its leaders declined. The ebb and flow of the economy and the financial markets, changing student enrollment patterns, and extraordinary social stresses between the late 1980s and the early 2000s required that presidents learn to lead in good times and bad. The early 1990s were characterized by severe economic challenges to higher education, requiring presidents to manage with scant resources. The late 1990s brought a robust economy and skyrocketing stock market, and those presidents who focused on fund-raising and external relations built colleges and universities that were healthier and wealthier than ever before. A new emphasis on financial management, fund-raising, economic development, and government relations opened the academic presidency to people with nontraditional backgrounds and skills. During this period, presidents also led their institutions in crafting appropriate responses to the new millennium's emphasis on globalism, technology, and diversity.

Part II, Achieving Presidential Legitimacy, discusses the first stage in a presidency. Legitimacy, acceptance of an incumbent as "our president," is a necessary precursor to presidential success and involves constituents coming to view the president as an embodiment of their institution—"the institutional logo" (McLaughlin and Reisman 1983, 185). To understand legitimacy in the academic presidency, I have applied theory from the social sciences and, in particular, from the higher education literature. Max Weber, John French, and Bertram Raven, and, more recently, James Fisher and James Koch, define legitimacy as one type of power. Edwin Hollander's work on leader legitimacy, and Mark Suchman's on legitimacy in organizations, provide alternative frameworks useful for analyzing legitimacy in the academic presidency. Drawing on these perspectives, I propose a construct of five factors that influence presidential legitimacy: individual, institutional, environmental, technical, and moral. Every presidency reflects a different constellation and interaction of these factors, some acting as impediments and others as facilitators. I also propose six threats to legitimacy (lack of cultural fit, management incompetence, misconduct, erosion of social capital, inattentiveness, and grandiosity) and strategies for gaining and maintaining legitimacy. Within the context of this discussion, I conclude with the story of my personal quest for legitimacy as president of Rollins College.

Part III, Assuring the Legitimacy of Change, focuses on stage two of a presidential cycle. It begins with a discussion of the impetus for leading change and the complex, ambiguous climate for decision making in higher education. For a theoretical perspective on the factors associated with the president's role in creating legitimate change, I draw on many sources, including the following:

On change: Peter Eckel et al.; Connie Gersick, Dan Ciampa, and Michael Watkins; Michael Cohen and James March; James Gleick; George Keller; Adrianna Kezar; Jack Schuster; and Martin Trow

On presidential leadership: Robert Birnbaum; James McGregor Burns; Bernard Bass; Estela Bensimon; Mary Ann Sagaria and Linda Johnsrud; and Fisher

On social capital: Pierre Bourdieu; James Coleman; Robert Putnam; Francis Fukuyama; Jeffrey Pfeffer; Warren Bennis and Burt Nanus

On fund-raising: Bruce Cook; Robert Payton; Kathleen Kelly; Paul Shervish and John Havens; Harland Bloland and Rita Bornstein

In this section, I propose a construct of four factors necessary to implement and institutionalize change that is accepted as legitimate: presidential leadership, governance, social capital, and fund-raising. Although the institutional context for change is ambiguous and unpredictable, measurable improvements in academic quality, institutional reputation, facilities, and financial health are generally accepted indices of presidential success. I examine the concepts of transformational and transactional leadership for their ability to facilitate change in varying institutional contexts and, finding them both limiting, propose "transformative leadership," a contextual approach to leadership.

I also discuss the relationships of trust with stakeholders and the social capital that are vital to developing a consensus for change. And, because most change depends on new resources, I propose fund-raising as a significant element of presidential and institutional success for both public and private institutions. Fund-raising provides the leverage for change and is most effective when integrated seamlessly with the academic and financial elements of administration. Today, both public and private institution presidents depend on philanthropy to promote change. Although presidents are typically recruited on the basis of their academic experience, their legitimacy depends on success in securing resources to strengthen or transform an institution.

In this section, I also explore four threats to change (precipitous presidential departure, illegitimate process, insufficient funding, homeostasis), and I propose strategies for successful change. I conclude with the story of my own challenges in seeking change legitimacy in my quest to strengthen and reposition Rollins.

Part IV, Legitimacy in the Presidential Succession Process, reviews the issues arising in the third stage of a presidential cycle. After achieving legitimacy and creating change, some presidents reinvent themselves and their institutions for another cycle or more, some take other positions, and some retire. Unfortunately, some long-term presidents fall prey to one or more threats to their legitimacy, resulting in a bad ending to what may otherwise have been a good tenure. In all cases, the institution prospers if the succession process is characterized by legitimacy. To help make sense of the importance and the fragility of the presidential succession period, I have applied the concept of "rites of passage," from the anthropologists Arnold van Gennep and Victor Turner, emphasizing the stages of separation, transition, and incorporation. John Moore and Joanne Burrows as well as Diane Downey provide a process for the assimilation of new presidents, and Terrence Deal helps explore the role of ritual and culture in succession legitimacy. Much of the work on succession in the corporate sector has salience for academe.

Factors in succession legitimacy in the context of the rites of passage are separation (the decision to leave), transition (search and selection, testing and assimilation), and incorporation (passing the baton, inauguration, acceptance). Each part of the process is crucial to the legitimacy of a successor president. The period of testing a new president undergoes is characterized by constituent suspicion and hostility, exacerbated by the typical lack of an assimilation plan to guide the transition process. The handoff from president to president should be smooth, as in a relay race, but should take into account the needs of each party. It is the board's responsibility to work with the incoming president on assimilation planning and with the departing president on the creation of a legitimate, meaningful, and nonintrusive "postpresidency." For the departing president, an important aspect of a graceful departure is satisfaction with his or her legacy and its preservation.

This section also examines three threats to succession legitimacy—Pandora's box, intrusive predecessor, and inattentive governing board—and suggests strategies for enhancing legitimacy for the incoming and outgoing presidents, as well as the institution. Both presidents have responsibilities to the process, the institution, and one another. The exiting president can be a facilitator or an obstacle as the new president seeks to establish his or her own legitimacy; the new president can assist or undermine the predecessor's quest for a legitimate postpresidential role. Part IV concludes with my own exploration of the timing, grace, and legitimacy of exiting the presidency.

Since three parts of this book are augmented by the story of my personal quest for legitimacy, the reader may question the trustworthiness of autobiography. I have struggled against two tendencies—to overflagellate and to overcongratulate myself. Carolyn Heilbrun points out that well into the twentieth century, "it continued to be impossible for women to admit into their autobiographical narratives the claim of achievement, the admission of ambition, the recognition that accomplishment was neither luck nor the result of the efforts or generosity of others" (1988, 24). Empowered by this idea, I admit ambition and claim achievement, but I also attempt a clear-eyed appraisal of my mistakes and failures. Despite the challenges of self-reporting, I hope there is something to be learned from a personal as well as a theoretical perspective on legitimacy in the academic presidency.

RESEARCH

This study of legitimacy in the academic presidency incorporates related scholarship from a variety of disciplines, including higher education, organizational behavior, management, psychology, and social psychology. I also draw on the descriptive material generated by presidents (sitting and retired) in publications and informal discussions, and thirteen formal interviews that I conducted between January 2002 and April 2003 with current and former presidents from a variety of institutions. (See Appendix A for an interview schedule.) The interviewees were not selected randomly, but are people I know and respect. I believe that these prior relationships resulted in responses that are especially open and frank. The interviews were extremely valuable as I developed my ideas, and the book contains many powerful direct quotes.

The interviewees and their affiliations when interviewed are as follows: Robert Atwell, president emeritus, American Council on Education; Myles Brand, president, Indiana University; David W. Breneman, dean, Curry School of Education, University of Virginia; Elizabeth Coleman, president, Bennington College; Edward T. Foote II, president emeritus and chancellor, University of Miami; James O. Freedman, president emeritus, Dartmouth College; Walter Massey, president, Morehouse College; Carolynn Reid-Wallace, president, Fisk University; Susan Resnick Pierce, president, University of Puget Sound; Jake B. Schrum Jr., president, Southwestern University; Steven Trachtenberg, president, The George Washington University; David L. Warren, president, National Association of Independent Colleges and Universities; and Samuel R. Williamson, president emeritus, Sewanee. I used these interviews to develop and test the concepts that inform the manuscript. Comments such as David Warren's "You've hit a main vein here" (Interview 2002) gave me the encouragement to think of this work as worth doing.

I secured a broader and more representative range of insights by developing and mailing a survey to 377 randomly selected presidents, about 38 percent of the total population, in four Carnegie Classifications: Doctoral/

Research—Extensive; Doctoral/Research—Intensive; Master's I; Bacca-laureate—Liberal Arts. The survey instrument went through numerous iterations based on feedback from presidents and researchers. The survey contained fifteen structured (multiple choice) questions with additional space for comments. There were also three open-ended questions. (See Appendix B.) I mailed the instrument on October 30, 2002, and received responses from 182 presidents, 48 percent of those surveyed.

I also took advantage of a variety of opportunities to secure feedback from scholars and practitioners. I presented a paper at the 2002 annual meeting of the Association for the Study of Higher Education (ASHE), and made invited presentations at The Educational Leadership Seminar, Charlottesville, 2002; the Southern University Conference (SUC), Santa Fe, 2002; the Association of Governing Boards of Universities and Colleges (AGB), Boston, 2002; the Council of Independent Colleges (CIC), Naples, 2003; and the Council for Advancement and Support of Education (CASE), Miami, 2003. In addition, I initiated numerous informal conversations with presidents at those meetings, as well as the 2002 annual meetings of the American Council on Education, the Associated Colleges of the South, and the Annapolis Group. Finally, I have sought to bring to life the ideas in the book by incorporating examples from actual presidential experiences since the late 1980s, without specific attribution in order to spare individuals and institutions from embarrassment. My personal story is drawn from a journal and files I kept throughout my presidency, beginning with the search process.

ACKNOWLEDGMENTS

Many colleagues were helpful to me in the development of this work. James J. Murray III, then vice president of the American Council on Education (ACE), with encouragement from James L. Fisher, president emeritus, Towson University and the Council for Advancement and Support of Education (CASE), was enthusiastic about this project from the beginning. Wendy Bresler, ACE director of publications, and Susan Slesinger, executive editor, ACE/Praeger Series on Higher Education, have been astute advisors and critics and have offered encouragement and support.

I am grateful to Robert Birnbaum, Judith Glazer-Raymo, James L. Fisher, James L. Bess, Roger N. Casey, Margaret A. McLaren, James W. Small, and M. Anne Szostak for providing helpful suggestions and references at various stages of the work. Adrianna Kezar's critique of the paper I presented at the 2002 conference of the Association for the Study of Higher Education (ASHE) was especially insightful. Jon W. Fuller, senior fellow, and colleagues at the National Association of Independent Colleges and Universities (NAICU), and James C. Eck, assistant provost for Institutional Research at Rollins College, provided valuable advice regarding the survey instrument and process. Jim Eck also assisted with the interpretation and display of the data. Carol Dacre and Connie Chambers managed the mechanics of formatting and mailing the survey, and later entering and manipulating the responses. Carol also assisted with numerous library acquisitions and kept my work life organized. The incredible Rollins College librarians were unfailingly able to produce the materials

I needed. Lorrie Kyle, executive assistant to the president, was an invaluable editor, information sleuth, and data checker, as well as a faithful source of support. I am especially grateful for the generosity of my interviewees, survey respondents, and the many presidents and scholars who spoke with me informally as my thinking developed.

I am indebted to Rollins College trustee Charles E. Rice, who encouraged me to consider the Rollins presidency and provided advice and encouragement throughout my tenure. My family has also been a great source of encouragement. My husband, the higher education scholar Harland G. Bloland, participated in innumerable discussions about the ideas in this book, and made many useful suggestions about theories and sources. He also read and commented on numerous drafts. My daughter, Rachel Setear, generously transcribed my journals, and my son, Mark, was a cheerleader for the project from the beginning. They both read and made valuable comments on portions of the manuscript.

PART I

New Roles for the New Millennium

This book proposes and investigates three phases of a presidential cycle: gaining legitimacy, achieving legitimate change, and assuring a legitimate succession process. Presidential legitimacy can best be understood within the context of the demands and challenges of the position, and, to be understood, the position must be located within the context of higher education and the larger society. This part of the book is intended to clarify the nature of the academy and the academic presidency at the beginning of the twenty-first century and to provide an underpinning for the subsequent discussions of presidential legitimacy.

CHAPTER 1

The Academic Presidency
under Siege

The academic presidency in America has always carried with it great prestige and distinction, but the position has evolved through various stages as higher education responded to social needs. In the Colonial colleges, the clergyman president served as moral leader, teacher, administrator, and fund-raiser. After the Civil War, presidential entrepreneurs built the research universities, but over time the role of the president diminished as the American Association of University Professors (AAUP) organized and faculty gained greater authority. During the period of unprecedented growth following World War II, presidents became more like political leaders, depending on persuasion and coalition building rather than the authority of the office to get things done (Kerr 1991, 218–20).

By the dawn of the twenty-first century, the academic presidency was more complex than ever before. Presidents were operating with less authority and autonomy than the giants of an earlier era and enjoying less public trust and respect (Bornstein 1995, 59–60). Some say that, because of its increasing complexity, the academic presidency is unmanageable, an "untenable position . . . mutating beyond the ability of anyone to do the job" (Pusser 2000, 13–14). A commission established by the Association of Governing Boards to examine and strengthen leadership in higher education describes the president as "juggler-in-chief, expected to meet an endless stream of individual needs and special demands within and outside the institution" (*Renewing the Academic Presidency* 1996, 9–10).

It is little wonder that many presidencies are, to paraphrase Hobbes, nasty, brutish, and short.

As the complexity and challenge of the academic presidency have grown, its duration has shortened. At the same time that constituents have expanded their expectations for a president, they have also reduced their tolerance for error. As a consequence of the attenuated commitment of boards to their leaders, the career-long presidential commitment to institutions characteristic of the early history of higher education has also evaporated. Today's relationships between institutions and their presidents are more notable for their tenuous loyalty. Presidents easily move on to "better" institutions or higher paying jobs, and boards terminate their presidents for spurious reasons. If trustees assessed ahead of time the psychic, planning, fund-raising, reputation, and financial costs of frequent searches and leadership changes, they might work harder to make their presidents successful. By the end of the twentieth century, the attenuation of loyalty and of presidential longevity, coupled with other trends in higher education, made legitimacy a significant problem for presidents and for the academy itself.

In the decade of the 1990s, higher education was vigorously attacked by academics, journalists, and legislators on the basis of some well-publicized abuses and misconduct, including rule violations in big-time athletics, misuse of government-sponsored university research dollars, and high levels of student loan defaults. Added to these issues was the widespread perception that political correctness was permeating the academy, tuition was being increased faster than the rate of inflation, there was an overemphasis on research at the expense of teaching, undergraduate education was being neglected, most scholarly research was useless, and presidents had little influence in their institutions or in the public arena. Dinesh D'Souza criticized the apparent failure of presidents to speak out on intellectual debates swirling around the academy: "Many university presidents are not intellectual leaders but bureaucrats and managers; their interest therefore is not in meeting the activist argument but in deflecting it, by making the appropriate adjustments in the interest of stability. When a debate over the canon erupts, university heads typically take refuge in silence or incomprehensibility" (1991, 246). Robert Rosenzweig (1998, 110), former president of the Association of American Universities, commented: "It would be hard to find a chief executive officer who, judged in conventional political terms, is weaker than a university president."

These attacks undermined the legitimacy of higher education and its leaders. The spate of books critical of higher education published in this period have titles designed to foment public concern. They include *Impostors in the Temple: American Intellectuals Are Destroying Our Universities and Cheating Our Students of Their Future*, Martin Anderson; *The Closing of the American Mind: How Higher Education Has Failed Democracy and Impoverished the Souls of Today's Students*, Allan Bloom; *Illiberal Education: The Politics of Race and Sex on Campus*, Dinesh D'Souza; *Tenured Radicals: How Politics Has Corrupted Our Higher Education*, Roger Kimball; and *Profscam: Professors and the Demise of Higher Education*, Charles J. Sykes. In a countersalvo, Lawrence W. Levine (1996, 4) called the charges against higher education and the tone used in these works "relentlessly apocalyptic."

In addition to the criticism by intellectuals, the media popularized disenchantment with the direction and values of higher education, and federal- and state-elected officials developed legislation to prescribe higher education requirements and outcomes. Self-appointed watchdog groups organized and became vocal, including the National Academy of Scholars and the American Council of Trustees and Alumni, "a conservative non-profit group devoted to curbing liberal tendencies in academia" founded in 1995 by Lynne V. Cheney and others (Eakin 2001, A15). Even higher education insiders were critical. Arthur Levine, president of Teacher's College, suggests in a 1997 opinion piece (*Chronicle* Archive) that higher education was "doing a miserable job" of responding to government expectations that we demonstrate accountability for efficient and effective delivery of education along with a demonstration of cost containment.

Also during this period, presidents were excoriated for failing to use their bully pulpits to weigh in on important public issues. Without understanding how much American higher education and the presidency had changed, invidious comparisons were made with the giants who led our institutions early in the last century. According to a reporter for the *New York Times*, "A generation ago . . . college and university presidents cut striking figures on the public stage. . . . They called for the reform of American education, proposed safeguards for democracy, sought to defuse the cold war, [and] urged moral standards for scientific research" (Honan 1994, E5). However, a 1994 survey I conducted reveals that contemporary college and university presidents do not speak out because they have "little time to devote to reading, thinking, or writing, and because they are concerned about offending their constituencies and jeopardizing the neutrality of their institutions" (Bornstein 1995, 61). In discussing the president's role as public intellectual, I note that the college presidency "is circumscribed by the pressures of multiple, fractious constituencies. When presidents do speak out, their voices often are lost in the cacophony

of opinions, informed and uninformed, that swirl around public issues."
Nonetheless, I conclude (1995, 62), "The call to the presidency carries
with it the responsibilities of civic leadership, and the bully pulpit provided by the position requires that presidents rise to those responsibilities."

Presidential legitimacy based on the role of public intellectual has been
supplanted by legitimacy generated by competent management of internal
affairs, leadership in community and economic development issues, and
resource acquisition. Robert Birnbaum suggests that the stature and influence of presidents is closely tied to the stature and influence of higher
education, diminished by a growing corporatization. Since higher education is driven by mission and not by profit, its attraction to corporate practices diminishes its distinctiveness and legitimacy (Birnbaum 2002, 34).
As the mission of the academy has changed, so has the basis of its legitimacy. The "Ivory Tower" ideal, with a focus on pure research and elite
education, conferred great legitimacy on higher education. Today, the
insulated Ivory Tower has had to become an interactive "Town Hall"
where legitimacy stems from the application of professional expertise to
community and state problems.

In addition to fending off attacks on the value of higher education and
responding to new demands, college and university presidents are expected
to guide and strengthen their institutions through largely unpredictable
economic, social, and political changes and events. Presidential legitimacy
depends, in part, on the ability to manage an institution through environmental vicissitudes. For example, the post–World War II period was
a "Golden Age" for higher education, based on soaring enrollments and
generous federal funding. This period was followed by an "Era of Uncertainty" in the mid-1970s and the 1980s, when the legitimacy of academe
diminished as a result of a sharp decline in enrollment and federal financial support (Cook 1997, 54). Although the health of higher education
institutions and the work of college presidents have always been affected
by economic cycles and demographic changes, the decade of the 1990s
was particularly challenging. The decade began with an economic slump,
but concluded with a strong economy and skyrocketing stock market. And
then, at the opening of the new millennium, presidents had to deal with
the impact of terrorism and another economic decline. It was a time of
testing.

CHAPTER 2

The Decade of the 1990s—
A Time of Testing

The 1990s opened as "The Age of Scarcity," and with predictions that the decade would be the worst era for higher education since the Great Depression. It was "not the most opportune moment to be an American college president" (Elfin 1992). In the early 1990s, costs were escalating, there was a steep decline in the number of students going to college, the federal government and the states were cutting back on support, and there was intense competition for students and philanthropy. This combination of constraints meant that college and university presidents had to increase tuition significantly each year to generate revenue and, at the same time, increase financial aid awards to attract students; they sought new sources of revenue and worried about balancing their budgets. To cut expenditures, they deferred maintenance, increased workloads, limited benefits, and downsized staff and faculty. Surveys conducted by the American Council on Education during the first three years of the decade found that such measures were widespread. The majority of administrators surveyed cited inadequate financial support as among their most serious challenges. They reported slashing budgets, downsizing, and eliminating programs. Most were concerned about "rising operating costs coupled with diminishing revenues" (Leatherman 1993, A16). A 1992 publication of the Association of Governing Boards, *Trustees & Troubled Times in Higher Education* (vii, 8), predicted, "The new depression in higher education will not end with the current recession. Higher education will be forced to dance to the economic music of the times. . . . The situation will get worse before it gets better."

Headlines from that period tell the story: "Budget Crisis Forces California Colleges to Bar the Doors," *New York Times*, July 19, 1992; "Harvard U. Reports $42-Million Deficit, Its First Since 1974," *Chronicle of Higher Education*, February 26, 1992; "Stanford Plans to Raise Tuition, Cut Faculty and Classes," *Los Angeles Times*, January 30, 1992; "Facing a Deficit, Skidmore to Cut 26 Positions by 1997," *Daily Gazette*, January 30, 1992; "Yale Panel Proposes Deep Reductions in Faculty and Departments," *New York Times*, January 17, 1992; "Time to Prune the Ivy," *Business Week*, May 24, 1993; "Universities Scrambling as Investment Incomes Are Declining Sharply," *New York Times*, October 20, 1993; "Board, Faculty Meetings Discuss Budgetary Problems," *The Elm*, Washington College, March 5, 1993; and "Bennington Cuts Tuition, Reduces Staff and Eliminates Tenure," *New York Times*, June 23, 1994.

Academic presidents, facing the unprecedented challenges of the 1990s, encouraged by boards to become more businesslike, and required by accrediting and government agencies to assess progress toward institutional goals, responded to these criticisms, challenges, and trends by making significant changes in operations. Despite rising costs, institutions began to exercise better control over expenditures and tuition, clean up their athletic programs, focus on undergraduate education, and assess student learning. Administrators established rigorous student loan procedures, developed new revenue sources (e.g., commercial projects and alternative investments), outsourced key operations, and augmented the academic workforce with visitors and adjuncts. By the end of the decade, higher education had undergone significant change. Some of these changes delegitimated the sector; some changes strengthened its legitimacy.

Fortunately, by mid-decade economic conditions changed dramatically, resulting in an extraordinary opportunity for growth and rebuilding. Indeed, the late 1990s unexpectedly became another "Golden Age" for higher education. By September 23, 2000, the *New York Times* was reporting, "The 1980s and early 1990s were a tough time to be a college president. Recent years, however, have been almost ideal. The stock market has soared, generating huge gifts and rising endowments" (Arenson 2000). During this period, as state governments experienced surpluses, the state investment in higher education was generous, particularly in public universities and colleges. As the economy brightened, it was accompanied by a surge in the college-going population, partly as the result of immigration. There were more immigrants to the United States in the 1990s than in any other decade. Richard Riley, former U.S. secretary of education, summed up the latter half of the decade this way: "U.S. college enrollments have risen to record levels, federal student aid has reached unprecedented heights, and college graduates have enjoyed exceptional employment opportunities" (Riley 2001, 7). Suddenly, there was a bounty of students, philanthropy, and endowment income, but because this extraordinary turnaround was not anticipated, many institutions were not prepared to take full advantage of the new climate. Those institutions positioned for aggressive fund-raising and student recruiting were able to realize ambitious strategic goals.

The lean years of the early part of the decade underscored the importance of philanthropy to educational survival; the "golden" years made fund-raising pivotal to educational quality. Between 1990 and 2000, philanthropy to higher education doubled, and the attitude of presidents to the "dirty work" of fund-raising changed as they began to enjoy securing gifts unprecedented in size and purpose. Although most of the multi-million dollar gifts went to private higher education, public institutions, faced with unpredictable state funding, established sophisticated development offices and mounted large successful campaigns. The closing decade of the twentieth century set a high water mark for huge gifts and mega campaigns, with twenty-seven gifts of $100 million or more reported and twenty-two campaigns of $1 billion announced or completed (Lively 2000, A41). The centrality of fund-raising in both lean and flush economic times transformed this tattered sister of academe into a heavily courted princess. A fund-raising campaign is often the centerpiece of a president's legacy, converting an institution's academic dreams into tangible realities. What changed in the 1990s was not so much the importance of fund-raising, but the respect and legitimacy accorded to this activity that increasingly holds a comfortable seat at the academic table.

In the late 1990s, aggressive and prepared presidents became "institution builders." Institution building was made possible by the healthy economy, the booming stock market, and the surge in college attendance. With full enrollments, unprecedented endowment returns, and a philanthropic climate characterized by mega gifts and mega campaigns, presidents began to rebuild their institutions after years of budget cutting, downsizing, and deferring maintenance.

CHAPTER 3

Millennial Requirements for Leadership Legitimacy

The decade of the 1990s created the conditions for the academic presidency in the twenty-first century. The early 1990s presented presidents with the challenges of a weak economy, unstable funding patterns, changing student demographics and markets, and assaults on the legitimacy of the higher education enterprise. These challenges required presidents to focus on external and nonacademic issues, and increasingly to function as entrepreneurs, managers, fund-raisers, economic development partners, lobbyists, and public figures. University and college boards sought these skills either by appointing candidates with these experiences and qualities or expecting that incumbents would gain the appropriate expertise. The unanticipated surge in students, endowments, and philanthropy in the latter half of the 1990s transformed higher education. Because of the possibilities for growth created by the affluence of the period, presidents who took advantage of these opportunities to strengthen their universities and colleges will be remembered as institution builders. Recognizing the need for better integration of the disparate parts of their work lives, presidents gave external relations, best known as institutional advancement, a place at the academic table. This approach to a seamless and integrated administrative structure reflected the growing reality that the president's work life—academic, managerial, financial, external—had become integrated rather than discrete and disconnected.

By the turn of the millennium, the cyclical nature of the economy was once again evident as the world faced another business recession. The catastrophic attacks on the World Trade Center and the Pentagon on

September 11, 2001, and subsequent events, caused a further decline in consumer confidence and a weakening of the economy. Today's academic presidents must have the flexibility and skill to lead in times of affluence, in times of adversity, and in unimaginable circumstances. Presidents recall vividly where they were during the September 11 attacks, and how they responded to the crisis. They were called upon to minister to the needs and fears of students, faculty, and staff, and to reassure the community through strong and compassionate leadership. As Americans learned to live with war and terrorism, markets worsened, an epidemic of corporate fraud was exposed, government revenues contracted, and philanthropy declined. The uncertain impact of this constellation of events on higher education enrollments and budgets made planning difficult.

These events were particularly hard on the colleges and universities that had grown too fast and too fat in the late 1990s and those heavily dependent on revenue from endowment for operations. Public universities struggled to manage with undependable and diminishing revenue from states. Both private and public institutions, facing significant budget deficits, responded by cutting costs and seeking new revenue. Many downsized, reduced programs, and deferred capital projects. They increased spending from endowment, raised tuition, escalated fund-raising, and initiated economic development projects. Newspaper headlines from the early 2000s are eerily reminiscent of the early 1990s. Articles from *The Chronicle of Higher Education* in 2002 include "Oberlin Faces Steep Budget Cuts" (April 26, A33); "Harvard's Kennedy School, Facing a Deficit, Cuts Positions and Programs" (June 21, A29); "Economic Forecast for Private Universities Turns Less Sunny, Moody's Says" (July 1); "The Fall of the Flagships" (July 5); "Budget Cuts Force Community Colleges to Consider Turning Away Students" (July 26, A25); "Fallout from Wall Street Hits Colleges Hard" (August 9, A27); "Public-College Tuition Jumps at Highest Rate in 10 Years" (November 1, A35); "State Spending on Colleges Increases at Lowest Rate in a Decade" (December 13). A piece in the *Wall Street Journal* was titled, "Colleges Feel Pinch as Endowments Shrink" (July 19, 2002, B1), and the *New York Times* reported, "Boom's End Is Felt Even at Wealthy Colleges" (November 5, A1). David Breneman (2002, 7, 9) suggests that the recession of the early 2000s should be viewed as more serious than the recessions of previous decades, because this one challenged higher education's commitment to affordability and access for low-income students. Breneman catalogs the changes made in response to financial pressures that threaten the integrity of the higher education enterprise, and he urges presidents to argue for the reform of state finances and tax policy.

At the dawn of the new millennium, several major social changes forced themselves into the collective academic consciousness and began to have a significant impact on colleges and universities. These trends included the ubiquity and necessity of technology, globalism, and corporatization, along with widespread challenges to affirmative action. In response to these trends, by the end of the 1990s most higher education institutions had invested heavily in technology and were dealing with its unanticipated consequences, such as conflict over the control and ownership of intellectual property, soaring plagiarism, and system safety and privacy. Another trend was the effort of boards to make higher education more efficient and effective by adopting business methods. Academic presidents accepted this mandate, in part to make their institutions more isomorphic with the larger society. As a result, colleges and universities became increasingly corporatized through the importation of business techniques, privatization of functions, development of profit-making subsidiaries, and dependence on a disposable, inexpensive, and temporary faculty labor force. Later, in the wake of a rash of costly and unethical practices that tarnished the corporate sector in the early 2000s, higher education's ties to business and implementation of business practices were called into question. Also, the higher education marketplace became far more competitive as off-site, for-profit, and distance education alternatives expanded and posed challenges to enrollments, federal and state financial aid, transfer of credits, and regional accreditation. The national accreditation structure itself underwent a major reorganization to assure the viability and credibility of the process (Bloland 2001) but came under attack again as the twenty-first century unfolded, with some critics arguing that federal financial aid should not be dependent on regional accreditation.

Another trend that demanded a response was globalism. Institutions increased their commitment to the internationalization of curricular and cocurricular offerings and promoted international study, travel, and work. This global imperative suffered a setback after September 11, as terrorists increasingly targeted Americans abroad. At the same time, diversity within our own higher education institutions was threatened by court limitations and government prohibitions on affirmative action. Presidents, believing in the educational value of a diverse community, developed legal and social alternatives to affirmative action in an attempt to provide a student body and culture that reflected the multiculturalism of America. Efforts were also made to diversify the staff, and more minorities and women were included in applicant pools for faculty and administrative positions. This trend also increased the appointment of women and minority candidates to the presidency.

The last decade of the twentieth century was a period that called upon presidents to be academic leaders, public intellectuals, civic leaders, economic development cheerleaders, lobbyists, financial managers, and fund-raisers. The impeccable religious or academic background required for legitimacy in earlier periods was no longer sufficient, and trustees turned increasingly to nontraditional candidates (fund-raisers, business executives, law and business school deans, politicians) to lead their institutions. This may also reflect what James Bess and Paul Goldman (2001, 420) describe as an increasingly managerial culture in higher education, "one in which economic efficiency and bottom line results dominate both policy and practice, often overriding most concerns for social goals, quality of teaching and research, and internal human relations." This represents, they say, "the gradual yielding of leadership responsibility from the faculty to a managerial class whose mandate is external and whose orientation is bureaucratic" (443). While Bess and Goldman correctly characterize the growing "managerial culture" of academic institutions, they do not leave conceptual space for overlapping cultures. Academe seems increasingly to be characterized by multiple cultures, including the traditional faculty-driven, high-involvement approach to academic decision making.

Nontraditional presidents may bring experience and talent especially applicable to the external roles they must assume, but they must still overcome significant legitimacy challenges. Although a number of these presidents do not succeed, they provide useful alternative models of leadership. As the academic presidency continues to evolve, we may be experiencing a sea change in the nature of the position and the most suitable qualifications for candidates. "There's an emerging view that the president is more like a corporate CEO, and directed to external duties, and the provost is the chief operating officer and the internally focused academic leader," says R. William Funk, senior search consultant (Basinger 2002, A33).

The bifurcation of the presidency, while reflecting new realities, constitutes the kind of value shift toward a "managerial culture" that Bess and Goldman identify, a shift that may diminish both the presidency and higher education. Presidents who do not have their hands on the day-to-day academic issues in their institutions are impoverished in two ways: their ability to play a part in the academic life of the college or university and their comfort in interpreting pedagogical and research developments for external constituents. In fact, they lose academic credibility with both external and internal constituents. The legitimacy of the presidency has traditionally depended on both academic credibility and fund-raising ability. While many large universities have already adapted to having their presidents serve as remote figureheads, largely devoted to external affairs, small colleges still expect and enable their presidents to be involved in all areas of the institution. To preserve and enhance this traditional notion of the presidency, we need to experiment with new administrative configurations.

This review of the challenges to legitimacy faced by the academy and the academic presidency at the turn of the century serves as the setting for consideration of the individual president's quest for legitimacy. Legitimacy in today's academic presidency takes time to achieve, and requires diligence to maintain. It can be lost easily, and it is frequently irretrievable. And, no matter how hard a president works at achieving legitimacy, not all situations can be legitimated. The challenges of the academic presidency in the new millennium reinforce its unique nature—at once a calling, a chief executive role, and a tough job. A successful president in this era is viewed as legitimate, can influence legitimate and significant change, and can exit the position with dignity and legitimacy. The president is considered the embodiment of the institution she or he serves. Because of this symbolic and highly visible role, an institution's legitimacy, in its community and in higher education, is affected by the legitimacy of its president. The failure of a president is a failure for the institution.

PART II

Achieving Presidential Legitimacy

CHAPTER 4

The Presidency: Calling, Corporate Executive Role, Job

The presidency is not a typical profession for which an aspirant can prepare through specific education and training. Unlike lawyers, doctors, military professionals, and the clergy, presidents hold the prestige and status of their position only as long as they inhabit the office. Joseph Kauffman reminds us that the presidency is a "temporary role" for which one applies but to which one is "called" (1983, 7). A sense of being "called" to the position is akin to a belief that the presidency is a spiritual vocation, and dates back to the Colonial period when virtually all college presidents were church pastors and had a religious "calling." Jill Ker Conway, president emeritus of Smith College, tells of her search of medieval thought to find an understanding of the concept of spiritual vocation. She comments on being "entranced by the twelfth-century idea that each human being was specifically imbued with a unique pattern of talents, gifts which could only find fulfillment in one foreordained calling" (1994, 60).

In addition to the qualities of pastoral leadership, the presidency today requires the attributes of a corporate executive officer. John Silber notes that

> university presidents, at least in our time, live about as far from the ivory tower as one can imagine. . . . They raise funds to balance budgets that may exceed half a billion dollars, negotiate with unions, cope with the individualisms of the professoriate and the irrepressible ingenuity of students. Quite apart from their educational responsibilities, the presidents of large universities are the chief executive

officers of hotels and restaurants; they arrange the financing and supervise the construction of multimillion-dollar projects; they deal with thousands of federal and state regulations; they operate police departments large enough to meet the needs of small cities. (Silber 1989, xii–xiii)

On the other hand, Gerhard Casper, former president of Stanford University, finds a real distinction between the corporate and the academic presidency. "[T]here is no job in corporate America that is more challenging. You are learning daily. You are never prepared for the problems thrown at you, for the questions you have to respond to, for the puzzles you have to solve" (Muller 2000, 288).

The presidency is also a job, aptly described by President Bill Clinton as "showing up every day and pushing the rock up the hill. . . . If you're willing to win in inches as well as feet, a phenomenal amount of positive things can happen. . . . If you love your country [college] and have something you want to do and you put together a good team, and you're willing to be relentless and exhaust yourself in the effort, the results will come" (Klein 2002, 208). The successful academic presidency is also characterized by good administrations, relentless efforts, and small victories that add up to large changes.

In addition to accepting the broad responsibilities of leadership and the day-to-day challenges of a tough job, academic presidents are expected to subordinate their personal lives and views to the mission of the institution. Constituents are more likely to endow presidents with legitimacy if they believe that they are answering a calling and giving primacy to human values over market concerns. However, stakeholders must also perceive the president as an effective leader who is a good fit with the institutional culture. Edwin Hollander and James Julian (1978, 118–19) suggest that legitimacy is a two-step process. First, the authority of the leader is accepted; and, second, constituents are willing to be responsive to the leader's influence. Both "competence and conformity to group norms" are important in gaining and maintaining legitimacy, but competence alone is not sufficient. A leader must demonstrate "sincere interest" in the group to be accepted (148).

Success in a presidency is hard to measure, and different constituents may have different expectations and standards by which they hold the president accountable. The governing board expects a president to improve the institution's reputation, raise money, maintain the campus and facilities, balance the budget, and prevent crises. For the faculty, presidential success is measured by improvements in student selectivity, compensation, workload, and rankings. Faculties want presidents to protect their prerogatives and enable them to fulfill their contractual and educational obligations. Presidents resistant to these indices of success will either learn to embrace them or give up the position. To strengthen or reposition an institution and to secure the necessary resources for the enterprise, a president needs to gain the support and involvement of significant stakeholders. Fundamental to securing that support is achieving legitimacy as president and holding office long enough to develop relationships of trust with key internal and external constituents.

Warren Bennis and Burt Nanus (1985, 153) believe that trust is the "emotional glue that binds followers and leaders together." They assert that a measure of leadership legitimacy is "the accumulation of trust [that] cannot be mandated or purchased; it must be earned." Thus, we can infer that as new presidents gain legitimacy through acceptance and influence, they develop relationships that serve as the basis for "social capital," the shared networks, norms, relationships, and trust that facilitate coordination and cooperation for mutual benefit (Putnam 1993, 1; Fukuyama 1995, 26–27; Pfeffer 1997, 99). This "continuous series of exchanges" (Bourdieu 1986, 250) builds "capital resources" (Coleman 1988, S102). With legitimacy, presidents can draw on this social capital to promote change.

CHAPTER 5

Theories of Legitimacy

Legitimacy is fundamental to a president's ability to influence constituents, generate needed resources, and effect institutional change. When a new president is announced at the conclusion of a search process viewed as legitimate, an institution's constituents grant the designee immediate, albeit temporary, legitimacy. People's expectations are high because the arrival of the new president "symbolizes institutional change and improvement" and represents "a new beginning" (Birnbaum 1992, 161–62). As soon as the new president begins to act, however, her or his initial legitimacy is threatened as a period of scrutiny and testing begins. "People's early assessments of the new leader can determine whether he builds (or loses) credibility" (Ciampa and Watkins 1999, 95).

Long-term legitimacy takes time to achieve, requires maintenance, and, if lost, is challenging to regain. Higher education history is littered with presidential failures resulting from a loss of legitimacy. These failures are costly both to the individuals and the institutions involved. "All too often, the high hopes with which the presidential tenure begins soon turn to disappointment when the new leader proves to have human limitations" (McLaughlin 1996b, 16). The incumbent with impeccable academic credentials may run afoul of the culture. The president with a fund-raising background may not be bringing in new resources quickly enough. The financial genius may not have stanched the red ink flowing from the budget. Expectations are dimmed and early legitimacy eroded. Before investing in the president, stakeholders want to know that she or he is a "keeper," not a "transient."

Legitimacy is the sine qua non of a successful presidency, but theorists differ about the source, locus, and exercise of legitimacy. Legitimacy is viewed by some as a top-down exercise of power, conferred mainly by the governing board and the position itself. Others see legitimacy as a bottom-up process, something to be earned from the constituents being served and led. In fact, legitimate presidents acknowledge the importance of both sources of support. Without acceptance by stakeholders as institutional personification and leader, a president will not have the influence to advance an ambitious agenda. This is because trustees, faculty, and alumni believe that they are responsible for preserving an institution's traditions and values and for protecting their college or university from inappropriate administrative action. As a result, these stakeholders accord legitimacy to those presidents who are perceived to understand and reflect the institutional culture and to strengthen the institution within that context.

Much of the work on leader legitimacy stems from the study of power, described by Peter Northouse (2001, 6) as the capacity to influence followers. Max Weber considers the exercise of power legitimate when it conforms to the values of the community. He defines authority as power viewed as legitimate. Weber identifies three types of authority derived from different kinds of legitimation: traditional authority, based on custom; bureaucratic authority, based on accepted rules; and charismatic authority, influenced by the leader's personality (Weber in Etzioni 1964, 51–52). Power in the academy is distributed differently from the centralized power of the CEO in a typical business corporation, and the president's ability to act with authority and use the power that resides in the office depends much more on the attainment of legitimacy with stakeholders. Michael Cohen and James March believe that the academy's "egalitarian norms" cause the president to be "resented because he is more powerful than he should be [and] . . . scorned and frustrated because he is weaker than he is believed capable of being." Presidents tend to overestimate their power in their early years and make many errors attempting to do things they cannot. As they reduce their estimate of their power over time, they become more timid (1974, 117–20).

James Fisher and James Koch define legitimacy as the power inherent in the presidential position and believe that only the governing board can grant presidential legitimacy. Constituent groups will accept the power arising from the position, as is the case with other roles such as judge, general, doctor, and priest; however, it is up to the incumbent to use that authority (1996, xii, 31–35). They assert that presidential power is significantly diluted when trustees grant board representation and direct access to faculties and students (331–32). Fisher (1984, 34–35, 51) views presidential legitimacy as a necessary precondition for effectiveness and longevity, and says that once constituents accept a leader as legitimate they are open to expert and charismatic leadership. He makes the following distinction: "Demonstrated expertise tends to legitimize leaders" and charismatic leadership yields a "high degree of influence and control over the behavior of a group" (42). Fisher's work is derived from John French and Bertram Raven's five types of leader power: reward (gaining compliance through favors, recognition or rewards), coercion (the use of threats or punishments), legitimate (perceived right to prescribe behavior), referent (follower's identification with leader), and expert (perception of special knowledge or expertise). Fisher and Koch equate referent with charismatic power, which, they say, is not of divine inspiration, "a special gift, grace, or talent that some have and most have not, but rather a quality of trust and confidence that almost anyone can honestly cultivate" (French and Raven 1959, 83–84; Fisher and Koch 1996, 19–54).

The French and Raven view of legitimacy as the ability of a leader to influence a follower regardless of the leader's performance was tested in a research study against an alternate view promulgated by Hollander and Julian (1978). The study verifies the latter perspective: that a leader's legitimacy is based on competence, ability, and commitment to group goals. Followers do not accept a leader's behavior based on the legitimacy and power inherent in the position but actually demand a higher level of performance from leaders they consider legitimate (Rasinski et al. 1985, 386–90). Hollander (1987, 13) also asserts that "because of its collegial nature, college and university leadership is clearly based more on mutual dependency than on power." This perspective corroborates the Weberian view of power as authority viewed as legitimate when it is derived from an institution's values.

Seen in this light, the initial legitimacy derived from the board and the office is not sufficient over the long term. Based on credibility, trust, and relationships, the new leader must convert "positional" authority to "actualized" authority (Downey et al. 2001, 202). As noted by President Emeritus of the University of Miami Thaddeus "Tad" Foote: "You may be able to affect some things with the raw power of the office, but only with legitimacy would a president be able to bring the full powers of his or her leadership to bear on the kinds of issues we deal with" (Foote Interview 2002). Key constituents accord legitimacy to a president they perceive as a good cultural fit and an effective leader. James Freedman, president emeritus of Dartmouth, says a new president gains legitimacy by being perceived as "deeply committed to the institution, speaks of it as 'we' rather than 'they,' gives the feeling of, 1) 'I'm competent,' and 2) 'I really care about this place'" (Interview 2002). Estela Bensimon finds that as "new leaders attempt to shape the meaning of the situation, they, too, are being shaped by the faculty's interpretations of their actions." They are compared with their predecessors and judged on whether they are seen as "taking the role" of the faculty. Presidents who take the role of the faculty "seem to induce commitment and support" and are forgiven for their weaknesses and mistakes. These presidents are "also able to gain approval and support for proposed changes" and are seen as "effective leaders" (Bensimon 1991, 639–52).

Once presidential legitimacy is attained, it must be maintained through behavior that continues to be viewed as competent and consistent with the culture. Differing perspectives on the sources of leader legitimacy may influence preferences for leadership style. Those who view presidential legitimacy as emanating from the board and inherent in the office seek strong, transformational, visionary, charismatic leadership. Those who believe that legitimacy derives from interactions with stakeholders seek effective, collaborative, transactional leadership. I would argue that to gain legitimacy, a president must demonstrate a leadership style that comports with the culture of the institution. In most academic settings, a president's authority is limited in scope by shared governance, and, unless an institution is in trouble, charismatic, transformational leaders may be ineffective, even "dysfunctional" in a system that militates against assertive leadership (Bensimon et al. 1989, 3). Such leaders, in fact, create more problems than they solve (Birnbaum 1992, 31–34).

At the same time, a president considered legitimate can maximize the domain of authority available to the office. In fact, faculties may cede some of their authority to administrators they trust. The literature suggests that once constituents confer legitimacy, they trust the leader to act in their best interests and they are open to the leader's influence. There are various views about the latitude accorded trusted leaders. Bennis and Nanus say leaders must act predictably and reliably (1985, 44–45). William Gamson suggests that leaders must have considerable freedom, a "blank check," to make decisions without the prior consent of constituents (1968, 43). And, according to Hollander, leaders have latitude to initiate innovation if they are perceived as highly competent and committed to the culture and group norms. "Early conformity," he says, "may permit tolerance of later nonconformity, in the form of innovation" (1987, 91–92), or, put another way, "deviations from normative expectancies" (Hollander and Julian 1978, 118).

In a comprehensive review of the literature on legitimacy in organizations, Suchman identifies three types of legitimacy that are helpful in this investigation into the factors in and threats to presidential legitimacy. Suchman's categories are (1) pragmatic legitimacy—stakeholders expect something of value from the organization in return for their support; (2) moral legitimacy—the organization acts in ways consistent with collective values; and (3) cognitive legitimacy—the organization acts in predictable, taken-for-granted ways (1995, 571–84). These categories can be applied to academic presidents, as follows. Faculties expect the president to represent their interests in return for supporting administrative initiatives, a form of pragmatic legitimacy. Successful presidents act in morally legitimate ways when they identify and exemplify institutional values in their discourse, behavior, and decision making. Cognitive legitimacy is inherent in the office of president, provided that the incumbent acts within a range of expectations for the position.

Suchman reviews management strategies for gaining, maintaining, and repairing legitimacy, the most "daunting" of which is gaining legitimacy. Once a leader has won acceptance, legitimacy is far easier to maintain. Repairing resembles gaining legitimacy but tends to be reactive rather than proactive (1995, 596–99). Appointment to a college or university presidency confers an immediate legitimacy if the search and transition processes are well handled. That legitimacy is fragile, however, as constituents observe the incumbent carefully for missteps. Over time, successful presidents gain legitimacy, but legitimacy may wax and wane with changing circumstances. This makes it imperative for presidents to work at maintaining their legitimacy. However, the unpredictability and ambiguity inherent in higher education institutions may capsize even the most diligent quest for legitimacy.

CHAPTER 6

Factors in Presidential Legitimacy

rawing on the literature on legitimacy, my interviews with presidents, and responses to my survey on presidential legitimacy, I have created an analytical construct of five multilayered factors that influence presidential legitimacy. Every presidency reflects a different constellation of these factors, and each factor may, at different times, serve as an impediment to or facilitator of the quest for legitimacy. The degree of presidential legitimacy may wax and wane, and the interaction among factors in legitimacy influences perceptions of a president's cultural fit and management expertise. The five factors in legitimacy are as follows:

1. Individual—the incumbent's personal background (career path and identity characteristics, such as race, religion, and gender)
2. Institutional—the internal structural and cultural context (presidential selection and transition processes, governance, traditions and norms)
3. Environmental—external context (economy, tax laws, funding, enrollment patterns, community issues)
4. Technical—perceived effectiveness (vision, strategic planning, management, budgeting, fund-raising, lobbying, academic and civic leadership)
5. Moral—ethical decision making, selfless devotion, and service to the mission and values of the institution

INDIVIDUAL LEGITIMACY

This factor involves a president's background, career, and identity characteristics, and how they mesh with the institution's needs. According to

Robert Birnbaum and Paul Umbach, "Presidential candidates may find their opportunities limited by the educational and career choices they make." In their view, the "royal road" to the presidency, the traditional academic route, confers the greatest legitimacy. Those with impeccable credentials are selected to preside over the most prestigious institutions. "Stewards," nonfaculty administrators who "have made a career commitment to higher education," accept positions in less prestigious colleges and universities (2001, 203–17).

Those coming to a presidency through the traditional academic route and careers at prestigious institutions reflect a high degree of personal legitimacy. According to the survey of college presidents conducted in 2001 by the American Council on Education, 28 percent previously served as provost or chief academic officer, up from 23 percent in 1986. The survey also revealed that nearly 15 percent of presidents came from positions outside academe, up from 10 percent in 1986 (Corrigan 2002, 2).

Many academic administrators have little or no experience in external relations and may be unused to public speaking, lobbying, and fundraising. They may have no experience in economic development or civic issues, and be uncomfortable interacting with trustees, alumni, business leaders, and government officials. Despite the advantages of the royal road, presidents quickly understand the importance of external relations to attaining legitimacy. And, as boards acknowledge the need to generate additional resources, they often select presidents from backgrounds in external affairs.

A 1991 survey by the Council for Advancement and Support of Education (CASE) found that more than sixty college presidents had a background in advancement, up from twenty-five in 1982 (McMillen 1991, A35–A36). A few years later, CASE reported that 167 sitting or prior presidents had come from advancement (Murphy 1997, 157–70). In her 1991 article, "More Colleges Tap Fund Raisers for Presidencies," Liz McMillen quotes advancement presidents on the value of a background in external affairs. Jake Schrum, then president of Texas Wesleyan University, points out that fund-raisers bring to the college presidency experience in institutional planning, priority setting, and fund-raising (McMillen 1991, A35–A36). Ultimately, a president will not gain legitimacy on fund-raising prowess alone, but must demonstrate an orientation to the academic enterprise—to faculty work and values, curriculum development, student life—and to financial management, as well as external relations.

Trustees have also turned to law and business school deans, corporate executives, and politicians for presidencies, believing that their experience enables them to secure resources and make the hard decisions and cutbacks necessitated by recurring economic downturns and student shortfalls. Results of such appointments are mixed. Corporate executives and politicians generally find the politics and slow pace of academic decision making very frustrating. Barry Munitz, who came to the presidency of California State University with experience in both academe and business, calls the college presidency "one of the last bastions of amateurism" and in need of corporate values (Munitz 1998). To be accepted, nontraditional presidents must demonstrate management expertise, sensitivity to the culture, and strong academic values. Those who do not feel confident or comfortable in the presidency are, sooner or later, terminated or exit on their own, returning to what they know best. Still others succeed by delegating academic leadership to a vice president or dean.

David Greenberg considers the trend toward nontraditional presidents to be leading to a retreat of the life of the mind as it succumbs to the onslaughts of capitalism. He notes that the many presidents tapped from the corporate sector march to an entirely different drum from academia, and he pillories search committees for hiring presidents from the political world (1998, 1, 18–21).

- One prominent political figure was named to the presidency of a big city university based on the expectation that his national visibility and fund-raising prowess would benefit the institution. He had no graduate degrees but had had a successful career in business and politics. His background, experience, and early decisions led the faculty to conclude that he was hired to raise money but did not understand their culture.

The appointment of politicians, corporate executives, and military heroes is not a new phenomenon in higher education. One long-term nontraditional president was James McNaughton Hester, who served between 1962 and 1975 as president of New York University (NYU). Hester, in an unpublished memoir, writes of the "audaciousness" of his appointment as an administrator at Long Island University (LIU) with "little relevant experience" (Princeton and Oxford degrees, Marine Corps and Japanese occupation, and three years in advertising research). He had neither taught nor published but spent three years at LIU and a year as dean of Arts and Science at NYU before being appointed president at the age of thirty-seven. University administration, he says, "drew on all of my principal drives: the need to serve others, be a leader, promote intellectual values, and believe that I was making a contribution to the progress of America." Hester credits "the role of fate or luck in shaping a career" (1996, 1, 9, 13–14, 122).

There is no formula for predicting whether nontraditional presidents will succeed or fail, but they may have greater problems in achieving legitimacy. Women and minorities have special problems in gaining legitimacy based on stereotyped notions about their competence and cultural fit. Mitchell Karp (personal correspondence 2001), a diversity consultant, describes the dynamic as follows. Assuming that 0 is the level playing field, people enter leadership or management positions as +1 (white males), where competency is assumed until proven otherwise, or as –1 (women and people of color), where incompetency is assumed until proven otherwise. Those who enjoy the +1 status tend to believe they are starting from a level playing field and not enjoying a special advantage. They view –1 appointees as "affirmative action" hires.

Hollander notes that although the evidence shows no difference in the effectiveness of women and men leaders, gender stereotyping means, "women begin with an initial hurdle to attaining legitimacy" (Hollander 1992, 72). When women are underrepresented in positions of leadership, they often face resistance, lowered status, and questions about their competence (Yoder et al. 1998, 209–10). In a study of women managers Carol Rusaw (1996, 19) found that those who established "credibility" exhibited three key behavioral patterns: a track record of success, technical competence, and a service ethic.

Between 1986 and 2001, the proportion of women in college and university presidencies doubled from 9.5 to 21 percent, and presidents from ethnic or racial minorities grew from 8 to 13 percent (Corrigan 2002, 2). In the 1980s, says Judith McLaughlin, chair of the Harvard Seminar for New Presidents, "it was not . . . uncommon for the chairman of a search committee to say to me privately when talking about a finalists pool: 'I don't know whether we're ready for a woman.' . . . I don't hear that anymore at all, not in the last five to 10 years" (Clayton 2000, 14). Even into the late 1990s, however, women presidents and executive recruiters were reporting that boards were uncomfortable with women presidents. Women presidents recommend investing a great deal of time with board members to develop the relationships from which trust and support can grow (Brown et al. 2001, 7). By 2002, there were women presidents at a number of America's largest and best-known institutions—Brown, Duke, Miami, Michigan, Pennsylvania, and Princeton—as well as at many selective liberal arts colleges.

Many women and minorities, because of personal and institutional constraints, follow nontraditional career paths, making their candidacies appear less legitimate than those coming from the mainstream. Presidents from underrepresented groups, often "the first" president from a particular category, are subject to continuing scrutiny arising from white male normed expectations. Such biases act as impediments to achieving legitimacy. Women report two important problems: (1) faculty nearing retirement long for the "good old days" and (2) women leaders may face sabotage from within, sometimes "from surprising sources" (Brown et al. 2001, 6–7).

An individual's particular background and identity characteristics are most significant in the search process and early stage of a presidency. Stakeholders are especially wary of those who do not appear to be a good fit with their institutional culture and traditions. However, as a president settles into an institution and begins to be perceived as legitimate and successful, these characteristics fade in importance. Over time, constituents confer legitimacy to presidents based on their actual behavior, leadership, and influence rather than their curriculum vitae, ethnicity, or gender. However, even as they become accepted, those coming to the presidency from other than the royal road often fall victim to the "imposter syndrome," the sense of not being as qualified or capable as others see you and worrying about being unmasked as a fake (Clance 1985; Topping and Kimmel 1985). During a telephone conversation (January 2002), James Fisher commented, "All presidents feel like imposters."

As presidents demonstrate their fit with the culture and their ability to lead and manage in a variety of environmental circumstances, they may also seek to increase their legitimacy, and that of their institution, through civic involvement, public speaking, scholarship, editorial writing, and board memberships. College presidents can strengthen their institutions not solely through the generation of new resources, but also through enhanced visibility and reputation. High-prestige institutions confer automatic visibility on their presidents, whether or not they are active on the national scene. On the other hand, external activity can help presidents burnish the reputations of less-prestigious colleges and universities. The role of public intellectual, judiciously handled, can enhance legitimacy for the president and visibility for the institution.

A president's prestige value depends on the type of leader an institution requires and the ability of the president to meet those needs. Public or private, large or small, denominational or nondenominational, northern or southern, urban or rural, each institution requires a different type of leadership at different periods in its history. Above all, key stakeholders must come to accept the president as effective and comfortable with their culture—the foundations for legitimacy.

INSTITUTIONAL LEGITIMACY

The institution contributes to a president's legitimacy through its practices, structures, and habits. Most significant among these influences are the search and transition processes, governance, and cultural norms and traditions. The academic presidency confers on incumbents a high degree of dignity, authority, and legitimacy. This "taken-for-granted" legitimacy of the office itself is rooted in deeply embedded social traditions (Suchman 1995, 583). Flawed search and transition processes, however, can seriously damage the initial mantle of legitimacy provided by the office. David Warren, president of the National Association of Independent Colleges and Universities (NAICU) and former president of Ohio Wesleyan University, puts it bluntly, "A fouled search makes legitimacy nearly an impossible task. If it is perceived that you are a shoved-down candidate, if it is perceived that you were brought in in violation of past practice and accepted search protocol, you are in such a deep hole that it is almost impossible to climb out" (Warren Interview 2002).

James Freedman, with two presidencies behind him (University of Iowa and Dartmouth College), says that two things confer legitimacy before a president arrives on campus. The first is the strength of the board's endorsement: "Is this someone the board really and truly wanted? Is the board thrilled to have gotten this person? Was their choice unanimous?" The second legitimating factor is whether the person's "standing" reflects what the institution values most: scholar, effective administrator, fundraiser, or someone with significant experience (Interview 2002). The search process can be an impediment to the legitimacy of a new president who was not the first choice of the board chair.

A presidential search is a long and arduous process. Once it is concluded and an appointment made, trustees are ready to return to their other obligations. Rather than developing a comprehensive succession process designed to generate support for the new president, the board generally leaves the appointee to fend for him- or herself (Marchese 2001, 34–35; Moore and Burrows 2001, 48–50). Jake Schrum, president of Southwestern University, believes that boards could ease the transition by establishing a small committee with the sole assignment to handle "the care and feeding of the president" (Schrum Interview 2002). A new president faces intense scrutiny during the first days and months of a presidency. Constituents watch closely to see if the new president understands them and their institution. They watch for mistakes. This testing period is analogous to the initial one-hundred-day period for U.S. presidents, which, according to political scientist Fred Greenstein, "has come to be taken as a yardstick of how well a new president has adapted to his responsibilities" (2000, 179).

Freedman believes that two things are of great importance during this early period: competence and commitment. It matters a lot to faculty, he says, whether new presidents come across as deeply committed to the institution, willing to submerge their own professional identity into their aspirations for the institution (Interview 2002). This view is supported by research: "[I]f new administrators demonstrate a full awareness of and sensitivity to the sacred local values, they can gradually win the trust and confidence of long time members" (Whetten and Cameron 1991, 466).

The status conferred by the search, the appointee's bona fides, and the office itself are affected by institutional governance practices. The legitimacy acquired by virtue of assuming the office may be vitiated by a campus culture in which the authority of the president is undermined by board and faculty governance structures and relationships. Limits may be placed on the president's ability to lead on "virtually every front, from the initial appointment process, to board policies and practices, to institutional governance, to presidential evaluation" (Fisher and Koch 1996, 13). Faculties accuse today's presidents of being too powerful; governing boards, legislators, and journalists find presidents too weak. The latter attribute the weak presidency to various causes: the inclusion of faculty and students on governing boards; the growing activism and intrusiveness of governing boards, especially in the public sector; and the cumbersome nature of shared governance.

The 1996 report of the Association of Governing Boards, titled *Renewing the Academic Presidency* (xi), calls for stronger leadership, consideration of nontraditional candidates for president, and resistance to "academia's insatiable appetite for . . . excessive consultation." The presidency is compromised when faculty can bring issues and grievances directly to the board and when confidential political alliances exist among senior administrators, faculty, alumni, and trustees. Faculty governance committees also undermine the president when they act under a presumption of final authority rather than as advisory bodies on administrative and institutional policy issues. Gerhard Casper, president of Stanford University for eight years, calls higher education governance "structured anarchy" and contrasts the academic president to the CEO who "in any for-profit enterprise has policymaking and executive powers. An American university president has little of either because universities are governed from the bottom up. . . . In the modern university the president is an authority with little authority who, however, is held accountable for virtually all activities in and of the institution" (Muller 2000, 276).

On the other hand, legitimacy can be enhanced in a campus culture that accepts presidential leadership within the shared governance framework. Faculties construct their image of new presidents by observing whether their actions are consistent with faculty "values, beliefs, and patterns of thinking" (Bensimon 1991, 638, 641). Communication, consultation, and collaboration are vital to faculty. When a president is responsive to the faculty culture and takes shared governance seriously, the faculty is more likely to reciprocate by supporting presidential initiatives. Edwin Hollander and James Julian (1978, 117–19) demonstrate that leader legitimacy is a two-way process involving an exchange of rewards with followers. In addition to acceptance of the leader in the role of authority, legitimacy depends on "the willingness to respond affirmatively to [the leader's] assertions of influence over time." Thus, although the board first confers legitimacy with the appointment of a president, other constituents, especially faculty and alumni, must come to accept the influence of the president.

Legitimacy ebbs and flows differently among various constituencies, and there may be different degrees of legitimacy granted the president by various groups within constituencies. For example, a president might lose credibility and influence with an academic department after reversing a tenure recommendation or with a fraternity being sanctioned for rule infractions. At large universities, students, and even faculty members, are relatively isolated from their presidents. Legitimacy, at this distance, is often granted to the office of president, not to the person in the office. Alumni tend to grant legitimacy to leaders seen as devoted to their institutional culture and traditions while building their pride in its growing reputation. Presidents can survive with legitimacy granted by some but not all constituents. The legitimacy granted by the faculty is most fragile; that granted by the board, most essential.

- One well-known long-term president of a small Southern liberal arts college, although censured several times by the faculty, continued to be enthusiastically supported and rewarded by the board.
- At a prestigious university in the mid-1990s, a letter from senior professors calling for the president's resignation was met with a unanimous resolution of support by the board.

The reverse situation is less likely to occur since presidents serve at the pleasure of their boards and cannot long survive the loss of trustee confidence and support. Once this occurs, even vigorous faculty and student protests do not generally influence the board's opinion.

ENVIRONMENTAL LEGITIMACY

The vicissitudes of the economy, tax policy, sponsored research, philanthropy, college attendance, town-gown relations, and other external pressures, such as government funding, regulation, and legislation, make this area the wild card of presidential legitimacy. To avoid being "swamped by outside events" (Cohen and March 1974, 2), during lean times a president must assure that the institution continues to function with as little disruption as possible while preparing for the inevitable upturn in events. In good times, a president's success is measured by the ability to generate resources and enhance quality; in bad times, success rests on the ability to deploy scarce resources judiciously to maintain quality. The unpredictability of the environment also influences the success and legitimacy of U.S. presidents. Greenstein points out that some U.S. presidents "take office riding tailwinds . . . [some] battle headwinds." Three months into his presidency, Harry Truman had the good fortune of presiding over the end of the war in the Pacific. Gerald Ford took office after a failed presidency and pardoned Nixon to free the country of preoccupation with the Watergate debacle, an action that caused "a body blow to his presidency" (Greenstein 2000, 116–20).

The unpredictability of the environment tests the management competence of a president. One college president reported in my survey on legitimacy that the "economy TANKED when I showed up," serving as an impediment to gaining legitimacy. Although it is fair to say that presidents have no control over such events and trends, they are not powerless to protect their institutions from environmental effects. A proactive perspective is vital to avoiding disastrous consequences arising from poor planning. Good management is the key to building an institution in good times and protecting it during lean times. To begin with, presidents can assure that relevant external and internal patterns are monitored along with critical indices of institutional health. The challenge during flush times is to control growth in programs, facilities, and staff. Without such discipline the inevitable downturn in the economy and decline in student enrollment may require downsizing, program elimination, and deferred maintenance, actions that faculty and staff interpret as insensitive, incompetent, and destructive of the culture. Because a president is held responsible for protecting the institution, its people, and its culture, the result tends to be a loss of legitimacy.

Another negative impact on presidential authority and legitimacy arises from the growing number of requirements and constraints on institutions imposed by external bodies. These involve federal, state, community, accreditation, corporate, and foundation mandates and expectations, as well as alumni and donor influence. Institutional leaders are also called upon to assist their communities in solving economic, social, and educational problems. Those colleges and universities located in depressed neighborhoods with underprivileged populations have a special challenge. Institutions such as Trinity University in Hartford, Columbia University in Harlem, and Yale University in New Haven are viewed as having a special obligation to ameliorate the problems of their communities. On a broader scale, Myles Brand (2002, 28), who served as president of two public universities, asserts that since a college or university does not pay taxes on its property or mission-related auxiliary enterprises, the institution has a reciprocal obligation to "assist in enhancing the quality of life and economic prosperity of its local community, its state, and beyond." Brand points out that funding for education is good if the state's economy is healthy and diminished when the economy falters.

These demands on the university have transformed the insulated ivory tower to an open and involved town hall. No longer solely focused on seeking knowledge for its own sake, the university serves society by applying its knowledge to the solution of social problems. Even as college and university faculty and staff do their best to discover, create, and transmit knowledge and culture, they also become drawn into social issues and apply their expertise to real problems. This involvement promotes the legitimacy of higher education and its leaders in the wider society.

TECHNICAL LEGITIMACY

A major facilitator of legitimacy is the perception that the president is a visionary leader and competent manager, willing to use the authority of the office to provide effective leadership in academic, financial, and external affairs. A president who engages the institution's constituents in these processes is also building the relationships of trust and mutual influence that will ultimately provide the social capital necessary for change. Campus constituents want their leaders to make the institution work for them in a dependable and timely way. This reflects the leadership challenge of not neglecting the trees while focusing on the forest; in other words, keep the underbrush cleared.

Following a search process perceived as thorough and fair, the new appointee arrives with initial legitimacy, and then "there is the inevitable setting in of reality. No president walks on water and no institution is without challenges, so that presumption [of legitimacy] may be tested in the early period . . . and that's a different kind of legitimacy that may or may not arise." A president must "earn his spurs and therefore the right to be respected because, in a sense, until legitimacy forms around the presidency it's not as easy to get things done as after it's formed" (Foote Interview 2002). William Cooper, in the early years of his presidency at the University of Richmond, commented in a letter to the *Chronicle of Higher Education* (2002, B16), "Even for an accomplished academic administrator, the first year of a presidency is fraught with special challenges—there is so much to learn and assess, especially in the area of personnel, and so little time to learn and assess it adequately while a flood of decisions awaits."

In the quest for legitimacy, most new presidents feel under pressure from their constituencies to articulate a vision for the institution. Presidents responding to my survey on presidential legitimacy overwhelmingly consider presidential vision a necessary element of successful change. But vision is a double-edged sword. Robert Hahn refers to vision as "one of the shibboleths deflecting us from serious thinking about leadership." What we long for, he says, is someone who will see "with x-ray vision, the long-hidden archetypal mission of the institution; will see the future; will tell us how to get there" (Hahn 1995, 18). The expectation that a new leader will deliver an uplifting vision derives from the corporate sector, where visionary CEOs are legendary. However, accepting a leader's vision in a corporate setting is "a profoundly different dynamic from doing so in the context of shared decision making in a decentralized, values-driven" institution (Eckel et al. 1999, 7). Ann Die, president of Hendrix College, writes, "The president who presents a carved-in-stone vision on the first day of office had better have done a great deal of homework, be a perfect culture fit, or like living on the edge. Many presidents get off on the wrong foot—and will continue on the wrong foot—because their articulated vision cannot be embraced by most of their stakeholders (1999, 35). Peter Flawn, president emeritus of the University of Texas at Austin, minces no words: any grand design promulgated by a new leader will be "challenged, disputed, and resisted" by the faculty (1990, 188).

An alternative visioning concept is that of "robust design," described by Adrianna Kezar and Peter Eckel (2002, 441) as a clear view of the future tied to goals and objectives for implementation, but flexible enough to respond to emerging opportunities. Kathryn Mohrman (2002), in the last months of her nine-year presidency at Colorado College, wrote, "I've always been suspicious of the 'vision thing,' [and] believe that strategic directions for an institution . . . are collaboratively developed within the community, not presented from on high." She goes on to say that she learned "that a president needs to create a sense of excitement and shared purpose—if not a vision, at least a well-articulated direction for the future. If I were starting over, I would spend more time on that articulation, in one-on-one conversations as well as major public occasions."

As Mohrman suggests, although more time consuming, a communal visioning and planning process has more credibility. Rather than issuing an oracular pronouncement, new presidents can collaborate with members of the campus community to develop an institutional vision. The vision must be uplifting and resonate with the institution's history, traditions, and values. Even a communally developed vision statement will have its naysayers. The unique characteristics of the academy inhibit community-wide agreement on institutional vision, mission, and goals. Participation in decision making is undependable, there is an absence of information, goals are vague, and professors value their autonomy (Cohen and March 1974, 2–3, 206–7).

The vision statement is best understood as a management tool. It makes academic institutions isomorphic with the corporate world, greatly legitimating their work. As in the corporate world: "Key constituencies must come to believe that the new leader can lead the company to a desirable future before giving him their loyalty" (Ciampa and Watkins 1999, 95). But, beyond providing a general sense of direction for the institution, the usefulness of an institutional vision has been questioned. Richard Chait says that "the value of vision has been oversold, and the likelihood of success has been overstated" (1993, B1–B2). Perhaps we should look to the president as storyteller rather than visionary. A good story, oft repeated, can motivate a campus as it weaves together the institution's history and values with the potentialities of its future (Birnbaum 2002).

What happens when a new president arrives to find a recently developed vision statement and strategic plan, derived through an institution-wide, comprehensive process? This situation can have both a salutary and a negative impact on the new presidency. The new arrival learns a great deal about an institution from a fresh planning document, especially one that is the result of wide deliberation, input, and acceptance. On the other hand, the new president will not gain legitimacy without making his or her mark on the vision and plan through a process of review and deliberation.

New presidents are also welcomed with expectations for change. Different constituencies have different changes in mind (e.g., inefficient processes, facilities needs, administrative reorganization, program addition or elimination, and personnel changes). Despite the pressure to demonstrate management expertise and decisiveness, major systemic changes should be avoided until the president has time to study the situation. An exception to this caution is a crisis or urgent situation requiring immediate action. In such a case, and with the board's backing, the new president can risk alienating some constituents by acting quickly while still in the honeymoon period. The costs and benefits of such moves should be carefully considered before acting.

More important to stakeholders than institutional visioning, planning, and change is the hope for improved operations. Virtually every organization is prisoner to "the way we do things here." Often, it takes new leadership to ask, "Why are we doing things this way?" Many new presidents are unprepared for the role of chief executive, with its broad spectrum of responsibilities that include parking, facilities, athletics, human resources, litigation, food plans, financial aid, budgeting, investments, commercial development, fund-raising, lobbying, and management of a complex organization. Effective management can enhance presidential legitimacy; management errors are viewed as an assault on the culture.

According to Bensimon et al. (1989, 75), "To the extent that failure of a college can be attributed to a failure of leadership, it is usually not the result of a lack of charisma but the lack of basic organizational competence." A Rollins College trustee commented to me that the analysis of presidential legitimacy in this book is "too complicated." He said, "You know a good president by the way she handles the job. Legitimacy is not an issue." New presidents realize that their first acts may have "a profound effect on their terms of office and strive to develop an image of skill and decisiveness" (Birnbaum 1992, 85). Susan Resneck Pierce recalls that as a new president at the University of Puget Sound, "I listened . . . and then tried, in those areas where administrative decision making could work, to move as rapidly as I could to address some of those concerns. I think that one gains legitimacy by following through quickly on matters of importance." She was an experienced administrator but a new president. "I came in and behaved, whether I knew what I was doing or not, as if I did. I can remember taking deep breaths before I walked into a room, having a moment of absolute calm and saying, 'be presidential' (whatever that meant), and sort of getting myself into a mind-set for a role" (Pierce Interview 2002).

New presidents may begin thoughtfully, by articulating a statement of institutional direction, initiating strategic planning, and introducing an agenda for change. However, crisis situations arise and must be resolved quickly. "Legitimacy will rise or fall" based on the president's actions (Warren Interview 2002). Poorly thought out, precipitate management decisions and actions often lead to a reduction in the influence, authority, and legitimacy of a president.

MORAL LEGITIMACY

We expect that a president responding to a spiritual calling will exemplify the highest standards of ethical behavior in all aspects of life and work, be a role model to constituents, and serve as a good steward of the college or university. "Stewardship" refers to the president's responsibility as "the guardian of the integrity" of the institution (Kauffman 1989, 34). Put another way, the president is the ethical standard bearer for constituents.

A myriad of decisions with ethical ramifications come to the president's desk. A wise president first considers whether to delegate the issue to a staff person or governance committee, and, if not, consults those with expertise before making a decision. The proper choice depends on the following question: If a similar situation arises in the future, will this decision serve as a good model? Flawn warns against ad hoc decisions. He says, "The *ad hoc* decision is one that may satisfactorily resolve a problem of the moment but sets a precedent that may hang you down the road. . . . Decisions that rest on principle will stand against charges that they were made arbitrarily, whimsically, or capriciously" (1990, 11).

John Casteen, president of the University of Virginia, notes: "What makes us something more than knee-jerk organization women and men are the critical and moral faculties that we apply in the exercise of our duties" (Casteen 2002, 25). Presidents regularly face complicated moral dilemmas and competing values. Every decision is part of a road map for future action and must therefore be taken seriously. At the request of an on-line journal, I wrote twelve diary entries on ethical issues I have confronted. I selected the following from many possible examples: a request to admit a student in return for a gift; the demand of parents for tough rules and sanctions, except when their own children get into trouble; providing benefits to domestic partners; the offer of a large gift for a program inconsistent with the college's curriculum; the alleged promise of a coach regarding a student's aid and playing position; encouraging students to become civically engaged while withholding my own involvement in issues that might compromise the college's neutrality; adding a rose garden to honor a woman who had left the college millions of dollars even though students and faculty thought it a frivolous investment; accusations that the college's commercial investments violated its academic values; objection to odious posters versus the protection of free speech; reviewing the college's management practices in the light of reports of poor institutional controls at another institution; an alumni attack on the administration for making what seemed to be a good management decision to outsource the college's radio station; trying to convince a parent that his son deserved a failing grade for plagiarism (Bornstein 2001).

On the personal side of the ethical front, power and status offer temptations and opportunities for self-aggrandizement. A number of presidents have been terminated, and some imprisoned, for serious misconduct. Such actions as the misappropriation of funds, sexual misconduct, fraud, and other examples of nefarious behavior undermine the moral dimension of presidential leadership. Fortunately, leaders with a flawed moral compass are extremely rare.

Beyond serving as personal exemplars of good behavior, presidents are also called upon by Harold Shapiro, Princeton University president, "to engage higher education's moral issues." Shapiro contrasts the nineteenth-century president's responsibility for imparting specific moral beliefs with the contemporary president's concern about the ambiguities of moral leadership. He suggests that the responsibilities of the presidency be re-examined and observes, "The more pluralistic and complex the university, the tougher and the more important this task of moral leadership" (Shapiro 1998, 94–96).

Although presidents may eschew moral absolutes, they can model and expect behaviors consistent with the values and customs of the academy and the society. As citizens, however, presidents do not practice the civic engagement they preach. Before making public statements, particularly on controversial subjects, presidents have to consider the consequences for their institutions and the impact on their varied internal and external publics, for when a president speaks, the institution is presumed to speak (Bornstein 1995). For many, the dissonance between personal belief and public restraint creates serious inner conflict. Gerhard Casper acknowledges that the power of the bully pulpit is considerable and unique to academe (Muller 2000, 276). However, Hanna H. Gray, president emeritus of the University of Chicago, writes: "The president has the obligation of spokesmanship and action on behalf of academic purposes. That being the case, the president cannot become an advocate for other causes that are not germane to that mission, cannot presume to speak for the institution on matters that fall outside its own special functions and competence. To do so would imperil both institutional autonomy and individual freedom within the academy" (Gray 1998, 107–8).

The selfless leader is expected to exemplify the values of the institution and also to serve as the chief executive of a business, although success in higher education is not measured by profits or stock prices. To many presidents and faculties, the corporate CEO model is unwelcome and inappropriate. The challenge for academic presidents lies in integrating the spiritual calling with good management practice and the quotidian challenges of the job. To be successful, presidents must demonstrate business acumen without sacrificing academic values—to incorporate useful business practices where appropriate, while giving primacy to the less efficient but more democratic functioning of academic life. Above all, a president must come to be accepted as the legitimate embodiment of the institution.

PRESIDENTIAL LEGITIMACY RATING

Most of the presidents who responded to my survey do not recognize legitimacy as an issue. They may be unfamiliar with the concept, unaware of problems with their constituencies, or simply take legitimacy for granted. Presidents indicated that one or more of the legitimacy factors impeded their legitimacy just 11 percent of the time. Within this 11 percent, presidents most often selected the environment, faculty governance, and their predecessor(s) as impediments. Presidents with nontraditional backgrounds did not find this to be an impediment to legitimacy, perhaps responding to the changing demands of the position. Eighty-six percent of the respondents said that success in fund-raising facilitated their legitimacy. Three out of four presidents indicated that they had attained legitimacy within three years; however, 14 percent of presidents indicate that they are still working on legitimacy (including some who said they had it). Legitimacy, it appears, does not become an issue until it is lost.

Table 6.1, Presidential Legitimacy Rating, which follows, is a simplified representation of the presidential legitimacy construct, and demonstrates the way in which each of the five factors can affect the degree of legitimacy available to a president. Importantly, presidents can have low legitimacy in some areas, yet high legitimacy in others, and the factors in legitimacy interact with and influence each other. The degree of legitimacy a president has on one or all factors may wax and wane through the course of a presidency. Attention to these factors can help presidents gain and maintain legitimacy, although some factors (e.g., institutional and environmental) are less subject to influence than others. Nothing can

Table 6.1
Presidential Legitimacy Rating

Factors in Legitimacy	Degree of Legitimacy	
	Low	High
Individual Legitimacy	Nontraditional Career Path (Politician, Business Exec, Fund-raiser, Law Dean)	Traditional Career Path (Academic Vice President)
Institutional Legitimacy	Nonrepresentative Search Process Governance Practices Undermine President Faculty & Trustees Resist President's Influence	Representative Search Process Effective Shared Governance Faculty & Trustees Open to President's Influence
Environmental Legitimacy	Weak Economy Poor Enrollment Diminished Funding Political Pressure	Strong Economy Good Enrollment Increased Funding Independence
Technical Legitimacy	Poor Management Vision without Consultation Action without Information	Good Management Inclusive Visioning & Planning Process
Moral Legitimacy	Self-serving Decisions Poor Judgment & Behavior	Ethical Decisions Good Judgment Model Behavior

alter an individual's background and career path, but when an institution needs a leadership change, a nontraditional candidate may be desirable and legitimate. Most responsive to a president's efforts at securing legitimacy are the technical and moral factors, although it must be remembered that the best intentions can be thwarted by uncontrollable and unpredictable circumstances.

CHAPTER 7

Threats to Presidential Legitimacy

To become accepted as the "logo" or embodiment of an institution, presidents must acquire legitimacy in the eyes of key constituents. Most presidents take office following a legitimate search and transition process. They have been chosen for relevant bona fides and apparent institutional fit. Some new presidents enter forcefully with an appealing charisma and vision; others focus on making good management decisions and getting to know the culture. Nonetheless, no president is immune from losing legitimacy. This can occur early or late in a president's tenure, and generally terminates the presidency. Sometimes the loss of legitimacy is rapid; more often it happens gradually.

A president may lose legitimacy with one constituency, yet retain a high level of credibility and support from others. When a board is enthusiastic about the president, discontent among the faculty, alumni, or students, even over long periods of time, tends to be discounted. Boards have continued their support of presidents who have mental breakdowns, publish inflammatory material, or violate faculty cultural norms. On the other hand, boards have fired presidents who lost the support of the faculty. On occasion, faculty support for a president has increased as the board's has decreased. This kind of profound dissonance among an institution's key stakeholders eventually resolves itself in the termination of the president. Often, presidents are unprepared for such an outcome. After a period of recovery, unless terminated for misconduct, many go on to other presidencies where they find success in more congenial environments. This is less true for women, who have been drawn to struggling institutions. If their presidencies go sour, they tend not to go on to another.

Examples abound of unpleasant and involuntary departures that reflect the way in which legitimacy based on a new president's background and the authority of the office is eroded by the interplay of individual, institutional, environmental, technical, and moral factors. A failed presidency is a failure for the institution, distracting the community from its academic purposes. Unfortunately, there are numerous examples, widely reported in the media, of presidents in trouble or ousted for misconduct, lack of cultural fit, poor management, or some combination of these. However, each situation is different and subject to a varying combination of delegitimating elements, generally unpredictable in advance but seemingly inevitable in hindsight.

Awareness of the threats to legitimacy should serve as red flags to presidents as they consider appropriate decisions and actions throughout their tenure. While all presidents are vulnerable to all threats to legitimacy, new presidents are especially at risk for lack of cultural fit and poor management. Long-term presidents tend to lose legitimacy in four ways: misconduct, erosion of social capital, inattentiveness, or grandiosity.

The examples provided for each threat to legitimacy are taken from media reports, but, in most cases, presented without attribution in order to protect the people and institutions involved. Many of the situations described are multidimensional and transcend several categories. The examples demonstrate the ways in which sources of legitimacy can interact and impact the presidency. For example, environmental conditions can result in management decisions made without sufficient consultation, leading to a perception that the president does not understand the culture. Birnbaum notes, "The most common cause of a failed presidency is taking precipitate action without faculty consultation, usually early in the presidential career. It almost always involves the president engaging in a task-oriented, rational managerial act that appears insensitive to the human aspects of organization and misreads faculty culture" (Birnbaum 1992, 95). Although presidents can control and manage many aspects of the role, their acceptance by constituents and success also depend on a measure of luck since they have little direct influence on the unpredictable external environment and the ambiguous institutional environment. Indeed, a number of presidents who responded to the legitimacy survey indicated that luck plays a part in a president's success.

LACK OF CULTURAL FIT

A key element in the quest for legitimacy is the ability to work within the institutional culture. The most lethal mistake a president can make in seeking legitimacy is failure to understand and enact the institutional culture. A new president must quickly learn the importance of what David Dill calls the "nurturance of myth, the identification of unifying symbols, the ritual observance of symbols, the canonization of exemplars"—all part of the management of meaning. "Shared beliefs and traditions," he observes, give rise to "professional loyalty, commitment, and identity" (1991, 191). Presidents perceived as the most influential "are those who fit well into the socially constructed story of the institution" (Levin 1998, 420). Those who do not fit into the culture have been characterized as "alien tissue" which is rejected, like an unsuccessful "graft" (McLaughlin 1996a, 9–10). The search for cultural adaptation and acceptance is a mutual process between the new president and the institution's constituents. Most presidents work hard to learn and adapt to their new culture. Some, generally to their peril, turn their backs on the institution's history and traditions as they seek to make change. And, on occasion, despite a president's best efforts, significant groups of faculty, alumni, or trustees will not accept the new leader as their own.

The problem of cultural fit may be due, in part, to the tendency in academe to seek new presidents from positions in other institutions. Internal candidates are considered to have too much baggage, but external candidates with some prior association with the searching institution may have an advantage because they know the specific institutional culture but have broadened their perspectives on higher education by working elsewhere. On the other hand, institutions may look beyond familiarity with the culture for a leader with fresh ideas and perspectives. Cohen and March (1974, 22) report: "The American college president is distinctively a local," because presidential career paths have "a strong tendency to circle back" to institutions with which presidents have prior connections. This "circling back" was true for Walter Massey when he became president of Morehouse College, his alma mater. Despite his apparent ideal cultural fit as an African-American male graduate with a stellar academic background, Massey had legitimacy problems because his professional experience was at research universities and the federal government, and always in the North. He was not a natural fit for a Southern, historically black liberal arts college. Further, he inherited a culture of what was described to him as "presidentialism," very formal, with no tradition of faculty governance, where the president was clearly in charge. He estimates that it took two to three years and his handling of a serious budget problem before he was truly accepted. "It takes a long time," he says, "before you really feel comfortable" (Massey Interview 2003).

In the corporate world, there is considerable emphasis on CEO succession planning by "growing the talent you need from within." This is important because "66 percent of senior managers hired from the outside usually fail within the first 18 months" (Caudron 1999). Downey et al. (2001, 3) report that "there is only a 50 percent chance that when someone takes a new job at a new company, he will remain with the company for more than two years." Additionally, the Corporate Leadership Council found in a survey that "an average of 50 percent of newly hired executives left voluntarily or involuntarily in three years or less" (Sweeney 1999, 15). The high rate of attrition is attributed, in part, to difficulties "negotiating cultural differences" (Downey et al. 2001, 16).

The growing number of external affairs professionals tapped for presidencies have cultural difficulties of a different sort. They know the academy, but they may not be comfortable with the academic culture. Michael Adams, commenting on this issue, points out that the fund-raiser "who doesn't grasp the academic enterprise" is in trouble (McMillen 1991, A35–A36). Additionally, a problem of fit often arises for presidents selected from outside of academe entirely (e.g., business leaders, politicians), a growing trend according to the 2001 ACE survey (Corrigan 2002, 2). Theodore J. Marchese, a search consultant, points out that nontraditional presidents often have a "steep learning curve about academic values" and can do "brilliantly" with board and external responsibilities, but "can easily be undone by the on-campus part of the job, by gaffes and goofs from a misreading of culture" (Basinger 2002, A33).

Neither the academic nor the corporate sector adequately attends to the integration of new leaders. Downey et al. propose a structured assimilation process as a key factor in executive retention (2001, 7). When embarking on a search, college and university trustees should place as much emphasis on cultural fit and management expertise as on charisma and vision, and, when the selection is made, they should work with their institution to design an assimilation plan for the new president.

Here are some examples of situations where cultural fit was an issue.

- The president of Converse College resigned in 1993 after a difficult four years. The first woman president of this women's college, she was very well qualified academically, but apparently offended older alumnae because she tried to create a more diverse climate and because of her hairstyle, clothing, and marital arrangement (her husband lived near another South Carolina college where he taught). One alumna reportedly commented that the president "is short, with short gray hair that is not in the least bit attractive, and wears godawful clothes" in contrast to previous presidents who were "dignified, wonderful men [with] high morals and wonderful backgrounds" (Leatherman 1992, A17). In a 1993 presentation at a professional meeting, the former president sums up her experience: "At its core, the clash occurred because I was the first female to hold this position. In the reality which enmeshed me, and which enmeshes all of us to a greater or a lesser extent, women are defined more by how they look, the men to whom they are married . . . than by what they can do. Being president did not matter. Having a long history of academic success was irrelevant. . . . There was no way for trustees, faculty, staff, or alumnae to have another sense of how a different new president . . . might look and act" (Hall 1993, 19).

- The president of a denominational university resigned after repeated clashes with constituents over the school's religious identity, and a perceived top-down, noncollaborative, corporate management style. She was accused of violating the institution's culture and traditions.

- In a well-publicized example of management initiatives in conflict with cultural norms, the president of the University of Chicago responded to serious enrollment and budget pressures with management decisions to increase undergraduate enrollment, revise the core curriculum, and enhance athletic and cocurricular opportunities. Prominent faculty and alumni protested what they interpreted as a gross violation of precious traditions that give the university its character, and the president stepped down in 1999 after six years. As perceived by some faculty, he did what needed to be done but "the practice was bungled." Although he was described as having "a tin ear for Chicago's soundtrack," it is worth noting that since he resigned "all his priorities are firmly in place" (Kirp 2001, 42, 44). Sometimes, the main contribution of a president is to serve as a sacrificial lamb for change.

A number of embattled, and ultimately terminated, women presidents in traditionally male cultures have found a strong, aggressive management style an impediment to perceived cultural fit. It is difficult to assess the degree to which these failures can be attributed to management incompetence, cultural mismatch, or gender stereotyping.

- A New England university fired its female president for being a poor decision maker and for ignoring the faculty's ideas.

- The president of a women's college in the South was terminated for a management style perceived as authoritarian and noncollaborative.

Presidents' initiatives to change their living or working patterns can cause a firestorm of protest over a perceived failure to understand the culture.

- When the new president of a New England university decided not to live in the official residence on campus, constituents were outraged that he would not wish to live close to students. Many felt he should be required to do so. The symbolism of the move was seen as negative, despite the fact that the trend among presidents has been to live off campus.

- Another president initiated his own departure from an Ivy League institution after just two years, citing a lack of cultural fit. Both that president and the institution would have been better served if that conclusion had been reached during the search process.

A final thought on culture. When presidents make tough decisions (such as downsizing, compensation freezes, cutbacks, and program retrenchment) in response to financial pressures, they are often accused of a lack of consultation and cultural understanding. Stanley Fish characterizes faculty as wanting to be downtrodden and oppressed, because, "in the psychic economy of the academy, oppression is the sign of virtue. . . . The sense of superiority so characteristic of the academic mentality requires for its maintenance continued evidence of the world's disdain, evidence that takes the form of poor working conditions" (1994, 276). It is worth considering whether an administrative policy seen as inimical to the interests of the faculty is ascribed to lack of cultural fit, whereas a policy beneficial to faculty may not be criticized for lack of consultation. The conflation of poor management and cultural fit is further discussed under the next threat to legitimacy.

MANAGEMENT INCOMPETENCE

Not all presidents come to their positions with wide-ranging management expertise and an understanding of the importance of culture. First-time presidents tend to "rush off in search of problems to solve," to fix things, and to "take charge and act boldly" (Bensimon 1989, 6–7). As a result, there are often missteps in management that can seriously undermine a president's legitimacy. Presidents report that their biggest mistakes were made during their earliest years in office (usually in the first three years) (Neumann 1990, 387, 396). Mistakes can be those of omission or commission, process or substantive, and provide opportunities for learning for presidents who survive (390). The recognition that certain actions were errors reflects presidential learning (400). There are numerous examples of early presidential missteps.

- Shortly after assuming his presidency, the head of an urban commuter campus in a large state system jumped, without preparation, into a debate on a major, divisive campus issue. He also made some poor choices for top administrative staff, took control of departmental budgets, and revised long-standing ceremonial functions. These early actions created significant legitimacy problems and within three years he was out.

- One president, five years into the job at a northeastern women's college, made the mistake of publicly warning the campus community of potential financial difficulties and suggesting consideration of co-education. Thought to have caused a decline in applications as well as violating a precious historical commitment to single-sex education, despite some important successes, the president was asked to leave.

- A distinguished academic in his first presidency resigned under pressure from a prestigious college in the early 1990s after a tumultuous year on the job. He was criticized for a management style and downsizing process that were seen as inhumane and a violation of the college's historic family-oriented culture.

Well-known presidential missteps have involved spending too much on home or office renovations, receiving excessive compensation, failing to deal with allegations of administrator or faculty misconduct, making unpopular staff changes or arbitrary program cutbacks, and a host of other actions.

MISCONDUCT

Inappropriate, unethical, or illegal behavior is completely indefensible in leaders at any type of institution—government, business, religious, or nonprofit. However, college and university presidents have a greater moral responsibility because they serve as role models for students and citizens. Despite this call to service and leadership, there are lapses that diminish the moral authority of the academy. Brand says that presidents should ask themselves, three times a day, whether their actions will pass the "front page" test. If their actions would not look good on the front page of the local paper, they are "skating on dangerously thin ice" (Brand Interview 2002).

- In a widely covered debacle, the well-known, once powerful, thirteen-year president of the University of South Carolina stepped down in 1990 after criticism for his "lavish" lifestyle, spending practices, and mismanagement (Smothers 1990, 16). In 1995, already on probation for the misuse of university funds and tax evasion, he was indicted on eight counts of bankruptcy fraud. A local prosecutor reportedly said, "He was the best snake-oil salesman that ever came to town" (Johnson 1995, 8A).

- In one of the most publicized cases of misconduct, the board of Adelphi University allowed the president, who was later terminated, to live "a

luxurious life on Adelphi's tab while the campus was suffering from declining enrollments, reductions in course offerings, and major administrative turnover." As a result, the New York State Board of Regents
took the unprecedented step of ousting all but one of the trustees, including Peter Diamandopoulos, the president, for "neglect of duty"
(Leatherman 1997, Archive).

- In another high-profile case, the well-qualified, much-admired president
  of a public university resigned after two successful years following media reports that he had used escort services while traveling on university business.

- The president of a northeastern state university committed a felony by
  impersonating a police office and pulling over a speeding car.

Each of these behaviors delegitimates not only the president, but also
the president's institution and the entire higher education enterprise.
There is no justification for behavior that undermines the social values
of academia.

EROSION OF SOCIAL CAPITAL

According to Pierre Bourdieu, "The reproduction of social capital pre-
supposes an unceasing effort of sociability, a continuous series of exchanges
in which recognition is endlessly affirmed and reaffirmed" (1986, 250).
Presidents who forget or forgo the obligation to build and reaffirm the
exchanges basic to social capital are in danger of losing legitimacy. Sooner
or later, every president makes unpopular decisions that may fray the
institution's social capital, however the judicious leader is attentive to
making the necessary repairs. Dissatisfaction with a president's actions
accumulates in the institutional memory. Even after a good run, there may
come a tipping point when such an accumulation spills over and jeopar-
dizes the presidency. In cases where on-campus constituents simply tolerate a president's behavior for years because of strong trustee support, an
action perceived as egregious and illegitimate may completely wipe out
any remaining capital.

Bourdieu says that social capital provides members with a "creden-
tial" entitling them to reciprocal social obligations similar to the practice of "credit" in economic capital (1986, 243, 248–49). James Coleman
describes the "capital resources" that can be developed through social
relations. If one person does something for another and trusts the other
to reciprocate in the future, this obligation is conceived as a "credit slip"
that can be called in at a later date (1988, S102). However, these credits
may erode over time. Robert Atwell, president emeritus of the American

Council on Education, describes the resources provided by social capital as "poker chips." "You start out a presidency by accumulating a stack of poker chips and you spend the rest of the presidency spending them down. There comes a point at which you don't accumulate any more very easily" (Atwell Interview 2002). Samuel Williamson, president emeritus of Sewanee, says he is of the "six silver bullet school of executive power." A president has six silver bullets that are not replenished. A bullet is used when a president puts his or her "prestige and future on the line for an issue." They should not be used up gratuitously, for "when they are gone they are gone" (Williamson 2001; Williamson Interview 2002).

Overwhelmingly, respondents to my survey on legitimacy said that the loss of faculty or board support is a major reason that presidents lose their jobs. According to Brand, "friends come and go but enemies accumulate" (Brand Interview 2002). And, Breneman reports, "more presidencies go awry when, for whatever reason, the president loses the trust of the faculty. If you ever lose it, you just can't regain it, and without it you are dead. . . . Trust is the highest value you can bring to a presidency or sustain in it" (Breneman Interview 2002). My own view is that although social capital may erode with time, presidents should act as though it is not finite, but replenishable. Capital resources, social as well as financial, can be deposited as well as withdrawn. Relationships should not be neglected and trust not taken for granted, for when a president's credit with constituents is gone, so is legitimacy.

Often, the erosion of social capital is exacerbated by negative personal characteristics, real or perceived.

- In one case, faculty of a public university in the South criticized their long-term president's speech patterns, commenting on grammatical agreement errors and mispronunciations.
- After nearly twenty-five years in the position, the president of a private southern university received a letter from faculty asking him to step aside because he lacked "academic vision."
- Two other presidents, one at a small college and one at a public university, had each served more than ten years before losing the confidence and support of their faculties in the 1990s. In the first case, the faculty voted no confidence in the president's leadership; in the second situation, following a no-confidence vote, constituents sent a letter criticizing the president's personal style, and suggested that the concept of shared governance had been violated. Despite their time in office, both presidents were terminated based on accusations of managerial incompetence and a lack of cultural fit.

Although media reports should be accepted cautiously, we read of presidents described as "iron-fisted" with a "militaristic management style," accused of ignoring faculty ideas, governing "with Thatcherite imperiousness," "a crude misfit" with a "brusque manner," having "a quick temper, a heavy-handed managerial style, and a devastating lack of political skills," "authoritarian and non-communicative . . . inaccessible," putting corporate above academic values, and running the institution "in the spirit of a diploma mill, the academic equivalent of a fast-food outlet."

Higher education is replete with stories about presidents exhibiting inappropriate emotional behaviors, which erodes the social capital that has been built up over time. In these cases, as in many others, the president's personal style is entangled with perceptions of effective leadership and cultural fit. Greenstein (2000, 5–6) identifies this characteristic as "emotional intelligence," the ability to manage one's emotions for constructive purposes, one of six qualities that he relates to the job performance of U.S. presidents. According to Daniel Goleman, emotional intelligence includes the ability to control impulsiveness, persist in the face of frustrations, regulate one's moods, and empathize with others (1995, 34). A number of academic presidents have lost their positions after an outburst of intemperate language.

- One president publicly berated his faculty.
- Another remarked that African American students lack the genetic heredity to do well on admissions tests.
- A West Coast university president made negative comments about some state legislators and a regent.

In a college presidency, constituents may accept behavioral volatility for a while, but it clearly acts as a threat to legitimacy and leads to the erosion of social capital. David Warren labels this the "rub-you-raw" personality; one that over time makes enemies and leads people to say, "You just don't seem right for the place" (Warren Interview 2002).

INATTENTIVENESS

Cohen and March (1974, 4) call the attention that leaders "can devote to the various things demanding their attention" "a scarce resource." Elsewhere (Cohen and March 1976, 52–53), they say that there are routine rules for the allocation of attention. People, including executives, allocate their time to fulfill their obligations. "Organizational actors allocate attention in large part according to standard operating procedures associated with concepts of duty, role, and obligation." Further, they suggest that "[d]eviation from [routines] by one person produces a chain of difficulties for other persons." Distraction from presidential duties can have devastating effects on an institution: decisions unmade, finances mismanaged, administrators unsupervised, students and faculty ignored. In cases like this, faculties and boards tend to fill the attention vacuum in order to keep the institution on its course.

Because presidential attention is a finite resource, when presidents become heavily involved in civic, economic development, policy, professional, or personal issues, their institutional availability is diminished. Why do long-term presidents become inattentive to the problems and decisions their office requires? Respondents to my survey on legitimacy provided the following reasons: loss of enthusiasm, too much external activity, burnout, alienation, too invested in other projects. Inattentive presidents may experience a sense of boredom with the repetitiveness and predictability of the problems and issues of college life. Brand says "boredom is no excuse. . . . If the job isn't exciting, maybe you should do something else—take another presidency or go back to teaching" (Brand Interview 2002). When a president becomes complacent, bored, or distracted by professional or family concerns, the loss of focus on management can result in inadvertent misconduct by administrators, trustees, faculty, or staff.

- When significant financial mismanagement came to light at a young, underendowed college, the well-known and much-admired twenty-three-year president had to resign. This was not a case involving the misuse of funds for personal gain, but was reflective of a disengaged president who had made some poor staffing decisions and then turned affairs over to his administrators. Neither the president nor the board seemed to know that a significant portion of the college's small endowment had been used for capital expenses. The board, because of its complete confidence in the president, had also become inattentive to the fiscal affairs of the institution. In this situation, a long-term president took his hand off the tiller, resulting in an ignominious conclusion to an extraordinarily successful career.

- In another instance, the president of a state university inherited a badly managed institution, but did not focus her efforts on managing the institution. She made some poor administrative appointments and then compounded the problem by delegating to them the management of internal operations while she concentrated on external affairs. Over time, the president's inattentiveness and disconnection from the process exacerbated the institution's problems. She was later relieved of her duties.

- At a small liberal arts college, the president was forced out after almost twenty years when the faculty presented a petition to the board urging his removal. While the faculty had a great deal of affection for the president, they knew that he was not aware of national trends in higher education, new business methods, and professional fund-raising techniques. As a result, he was not helping the college or its people adapt to the changing environment. Faculty and staff were undercompensated, the endowment was not growing, and business was conducted like a "mom and pop" shop. The institution was stagnating.

- In contrast, Robert McCabe, the long-time president of Miami-Dade Community College, periodically renewed himself and the institution by launching new initiatives. He was knowledgeable about important trends because of his active participation in national organizations, conferences, and programs.

GRANDIOSITY

Greenstein (2000, 21–22) uses the term "grandiosity" to describe U.S. presidents whose past successes lead them to act without consultation. Franklin D. Roosevelt's early triumphs and persuasive rhetoric led him to initiate several bold moves without first discussing them with Congress or his aides. Thus, his proposals for increasing the size of the Supreme Court and his interactions with Stalin were dismal failures. Greenstein writes of the perils of grandiosity, "The boldness and aplomb that Roosevelt's aides found awesome could be a prescription for ill-conceived ventures." Others have labeled such leadership behavior "the dark side of charisma," causing people "to become intoxicated by the devotion and adulation of followers" (Hogan et al. 1990, 352; Yukl 1989, 227). The concept of grandiosity can be applied to college as well as U.S. presidents who, after considerable success, begin to rely on their own interpretations and judgments, and are "less likely to solicit counsel, and therefore less likely to be seen as amenable to constituent influence" (Birnbaum 1992, 99). Put another way, these leaders have a flair for the dramatic and tend to launch bold ventures without consultation (Kets de Vries in Bass 1990, 158).

- One charismatic president was able in her first nine years to inspire faculty, trustees, and foundation officials to participate with her in creating an exciting new curriculum. She was also prominent and influential on the national higher education scene. Fueled by a passion for social justice, she made financial commitments and personnel decisions in support of a community redevelopment project without the degree of consultation and collaboration expected by the faculty. Her own perception of matters differed, but, whatever the reality, her legitimacy had eroded and her resignation was inevitable. Presidents who act to transform their institutions based on their own vision without involving the campus community invite disaster.

- The president of a midwestern university, formerly a dean there, was forced to resign after seventeen months. During his brief tenure, the president, hired by the board as a change agent, reorganized the institution according to his own bold vision. He was criticized for failing to consult or communicate with his constituents, and consequently lost the "trust" of the community.

- Adelphi University president Diamondopoulos was credited with "bold and visionary leadership" and a plan to transform a commuter campus into a prestigious liberal arts institution but lost his position because of excessive personal financial benefits and a breakdown "of the principles of governance" (Leatherman 1997, Archive). He acted with the support of the board but without the involvement of the faculty.

- Another visionary president worked closely with the board to transform the quality and reputation of a regional liberal arts college despite continuing faculty enmity and repeated no-confidence votes.

A number of presidents have gotten into trouble through what is often referred to as an "edifice complex" or a drive toward "empire building" that stems from a vision for expansion and growth out of proportion with the other needs of the institution. To be successful, a plan for significant enhancement of a campus needs to grow organically from the institution's communal culture, history, and ambitions; it requires the involvement of affected constituents, as well as the president's leadership.

Pierce warns that presidents lose their jobs because "they confuse themselves with their role and get too self-important" (Pierce Interview 2002). Legitimacy survey respondents used these terms to characterize presidential self-importance: arrogance, ego, hubris, imperial, failure to listen, aloof and distant, out of touch with constituents. These qualities were said to cost presidents their jobs. Breneman calls grandiosity "a banana peel; you begin to believe your own press clippings" (Breneman Interview 2002). Brand suggests that the best antidote against developing ego problems is to make sure that you do not surround yourself with "yes" people. He says, "Seek out criticism and those who disagree with you" (Brand Interview 2002).

Although grandiosity is most associated with presidents toward the end of a long tenure, it can also arise in a new president with prior presidential experience. Such cases may be even more difficult.

For example, during the first years of the twenty-first century, a new president came into a major university with significant prior presidential experience and an impressive overall resume. This president understood the issues, had a vision for the university, and made some bold moves without much consultation. Although the president's actions may prove to have been appropriate, the failure to consult broadly with faculty and trustees caused a negative buzz. The president was technically competent but not yet accepted into the culture.

In sum, there are five significant threats to presidential legitimacy—two most often associated with the early years, three with the later years. In the earliest period of a college presidency, when the effort is focused on gaining legitimacy, a lack of cultural fit quickly tends to become apparent. Management mistakes, often due to inexperience or a desire to demonstrate decisiveness, are common. In a long-term presidency, although legitimacy may have been attained and then maintained over time, a successful and charismatic leader may abuse the office, lose social capital, become inattentive, or develop a grandiose perspective. Respondents to the survey on legitimacy provided two additional threats to legitimacy that cost presidents their jobs. These are problems in athletics and bad luck. Luck is an environmental factor outside a president's control, but big-time athletics presents a minefield of decisions which can threaten presidential survival. In response to ongoing pressure from boosters for athletic victories, presidents, tacitly or overtly, may violate ethical practice by condoning fraud and National Collegiate Athletics Association (NCAA) rule violations, such as the admission of athletes with unacceptable grades, the alteration of grades to preserve eligibility, and financial contributions to athletes by boosters. Such practices may also occur through a president's inattentiveness to the athletic program or through a grandiose sense of imperviousness to accepted standards.

CHAPTER 8

Strategies for Gaining and Maintaining Legitimacy

Mark Suchman cautions that managers "rarely can afford to treat legitimation as a completed task." Managers, he says, "must guard against becoming so enamored with their own legitimating myths that they lose sight of external developments that might bring those myths into question" (1995, 594). To promote institutional improvement and change, a president must develop relationships of trust with key constituents and become accepted as the embodiment of the institution. Although constituents confer legitimacy, presidents can influence the process. Suchman (587) considers legitimacy building a "proactive enterprise" of three types. These are becoming an "insider" by conforming to the dictates of the preexisting culture, recruiting a credible group that will support some new initiatives, or creating new groups and new legitimating beliefs. He states (585–86), "Managerial initiatives can make a substantial difference in the extent to which organizational activities are perceived as desirable, proper, and appropriate within any given cultural context." To be successful, Suchman suggests, such initiatives require extensive communication of all types to all constituencies.

Once again, cultural fit and management expertise are identified as the core elements of legitimacy. Before making changes in the culture, presidents must achieve long-term legitimacy by becoming "insiders" and embracing the institutional culture they inherit. To make change, secure resources, and strengthen their institutions, presidents need to "recruit" or "create" groups willing to support new directions. An important caveat in this process is that the irrationality and capriciousness of the academic world tend to undermine rational approaches to attaining and maintaining legitimacy. Chapter 11 of this book reviews the unpredictable higher-education context that challenges a president's ability to implement a change agenda. With this context in mind, a president's approach to seeking legitimacy and change must be flexible and adaptive.

Applying Suchman's legitimacy-building activities to the five factors in presidential legitimacy proposed in this book suggests the following strategies a college president can employ to overcome impediments in the quest to gain and maintain legitimacy and to begin a process of change. Constituents, especially trustees, faculty, and alumni, who wish to support the development of presidential legitimacy can also be helpful in promoting these strategies.

ENHANCING INDIVIDUAL LEGITIMACY

Newly selected presidents should participate in designing the process by which the trustees introduce them to their constituents and the community. Despite perceived delegitimating factors of background or identity, new presidents must act with confidence, make judicious decisions, learn the culture, and become insiders. Presidents should take the time to get to know the institution's history and important stories and to become the chief celebrants in their institutions' rituals. Features of a president's background and identity characteristics that create some discomfort for constituents can be overcome through performance, fit, and the passage of time.

ENHANCING INSTITUTIONAL LEGITIMACY

A new president should work with the predecessor president on a productive and legitimating process of transition for both. The new president must focus on developing relationships with key constituents, identifying those internally who may be open to change and those externally who may be sources of financial support. Presidents should choose a limited number of initiatives to promote and gather support from key constituents in advance of any announcement. Before making complex decisions, presidents should gather input from all appropriate constituents, communicating through formal governance bodies, as well as through informal conversations. Controversial decisions and changes should be explained in the context of institutional history, mission, and vision. Presidents need to understand when to exercise the authority of their office and when to work collaboratively.

ENHANCING ENVIRONMENTAL LEGITIMACY

Since this is the area over which presidents have little control, they should conduct institutional affairs with the sure knowledge that external events tend to be cyclical. The key to success in both good and bad times is planning, preparation, and execution. A collaborative and ongoing process of environmental scanning, strategic planning, assessment, program improvement, and budget discipline can help to mitigate the unpleasant effects of environmental change. Honest and thoughtful leadership, collaboration with the board and the faculty, and the effective management of environmental challenges will greatly enhance presidential legitimacy.

Actions taken in good economic times can help to protect the institution in tough times. These include aggressive fund-raising, appropriate investment strategies, reduction in the endowment spending rate, increased tuition (along with financial aid), and development of additional sources of revenue. When facing challenging circumstances, an institution may have to reverse some of these actions, reduce benefits, and increase the temporary workforce of faculty visitors and adjuncts. The latter trend is not optimal for providing the highest-quality education or building a top-flight faculty; however, it is a way of protecting the institution from the embedded costs of a heavily tenured faculty during hard times. Presidents can protect their legitimacy in this process by making the budget as transparent as possible and involving other stakeholders in decision making.

ENHANCING TECHNICAL LEGITIMACY

Successful change is rooted in an institution's history and culture, and as presidents contemplate change initiatives, they must create and articulate an inspiring vision along with stories that, while celebrating the institution's past, help people imagine its future. To be seen as competent leaders and managers, presidents must demonstrate a willingness to communicate, collaborate, and consult with all constituents, and value the shared governance system for its democratic distribution of decision making among expert groups. At the same time, the community will be grateful for procedural administrative changes that make life better for employees and students. In higher education, management expertise should extend to all aspects of institutional functioning—academic, financial, and advancement. Presidents are well served by becoming comfortable and involved with all areas, and, while delegating responsibility, not becoming inattentive to any of them. The educational mission of the institution is paramount and thrives on prudent financial management. In addition, since fund-raising is a major lever for change, a president's legacy is often measured by new facilities, increases in funding and endowment, new programs, and improvements in the quality of the students and faculty.

ENHANCING MORAL LEGITIMACY

The exercise of ethical leadership is a vital element in gaining legitimacy. A president's every decision and act is scrutinized for its moral wellspring, so thoughtless, ill-considered behaviors can be destructive. Presidents earn moral legitimacy by serving as role models for their constituents and by engaging the college community in the ethical dimensions of academic, financial, and advancement decision making. Presidential decision making benefits from consultation with colleagues, has ramifications for all subsequent actions, and should stand as a template for future action. Presidents can also undertake a judicious involvement in social issues that affect their institutions.

CAVEATS FOR PRESIDENTS

The strategies for presidential legitimacy are summarized in the following caveats: (1) resist pressure to undertake major systemic changes without thorough review and constituent involvement unless the institution is in a crisis situation; (2) make all possible procedural changes to facilitate the work of the institution; (3) respect the mechanisms of board and faculty governance; (4) consult, collaborate, and communicate; (5) absorb the culture and listen to opinion leaders; (6) stay attuned to trends in higher education and society; (7) develop a vision consistent with the culture and aspirations of constituents; (8) when the groundwork has been laid, act; (9) make principled decisions and expect the same of others; and (10) maintain a scholarly life and participate in the public discourse on educational issues.

The achievement and maintenance of legitimacy can be enhanced by awareness of the factors, threats, and strategies involved. Presidents who have failed to achieve or have lost legitimacy in one institution can sometimes rehabilitate themselves in another. Legitimacy is critical because it provides the acceptance and influence necessary for the success of a president's change agenda.

CHAPTER 9

A Fund-raiser's Quest for Legitimacy

AN "INTERRUPTED AND DISCONTINUOUS" LIFE

I review here my own experience in seeking and acquiring legitimacy as president in order to test the assumptions I have made regarding the factors in and threats to legitimacy. I was a first-time president, but had the advantage of a wide range of experience in educational leadership. I made my share of missteps and, with experience and insight, might have done many things differently, but, from the beginning, I enjoyed and was greatly challenged by the position. I was a nontraditional candidate for a presidency and do not propose to generalize from my experience. Each president brings to the position a unique set of experiences and characteristics, and each institutional context is unique. I present my story to illustrate the factors in gaining and maintaining legitimacy. Here is the first part.

I certainly had not traveled the "royal road" to the presidency. My parents were from immigrant families and without much formal education. My father had dropped out of high school to work in his parents' grocery store so that his three younger brothers could attend college. One of them later helped him open his own small business, and he earned his high school equivalency degree and took years of night classes to graduate from college. Although my mother never attended college, she educated herself by reading good literature. I absorbed the belief that education is the key to a successful life and a good society. Despite this understanding, like many women of my generation, I dropped out of college, got married, and had a family. Like others, I later returned to school at night; after completing two degrees, I became a high school English teacher and administrator. Perhaps because my professional career began later in life than most, I eagerly accepted the challenges and opportunities offered by a series of mentors who saw potential in me. My enthusiasm for educational innovation was formed in the early 1970s, the heyday of experimentation, during my years at North Miami Beach Senior High School, a brand-new facility that we were able to configure to accommodate a radically new approach to education. Although I was new to teaching and administration, the principal enlisted me to help plan and later to help lead the school. This educational experiment served as the basis for my Ph.D. dissertation.

My experiences continued to mirror those of women who came of age in the 1950s and 1960s. Many educated women were place bound and could not move to take appropriate positions, so they developed fulfilling but nontraditional career paths. After completing the Ph.D. at the University of Miami in 1975, I was greatly disappointed to learn that the institution preferred not to hire its graduates into the professoriate. I was place bound because of my family so I remained at the university in other positions, first working with its race desegregation assistance center, and then securing federal funding to direct a center providing schools in the southeast United States with education, training, and assistance in promoting sex equity and compliance with Title IX. I also secured federal funding to direct one of five national sex-equity demonstration projects, working with colleagues to develop innovative approaches to equity in staffing, in the classroom, and in athletics. I had to overcome my reticence and learn to speak convincingly to small and large audiences throughout the South about educational equity. Many remained unconvinced or hostile. Along the way, I learned the extraordinary difficulty of creating and institutionalizing systemic change and the importance of strong relationships to organizational improvement and innovation.

Several years later, worried about the unreliability of soft money, I sought, and was offered, a position in a field about which I knew nothing—development—having been advised that it was just opening up to women. I was concerned about moving to a marginal part of the academy (I had never known it existed), and that concern was exacerbated when, as I consulted with a wide network of colleagues, a foundation official remarked, "It's all right, if you don't mind being a supplicant." I accepted a position as director of Foundation and Corporate Relations, and with it a reduction in status and compensation. Making this move was a professional gamble, and I could not have predicted that five years later, after a series of increasingly challenging positions, I would become vice president. I had never contemplated a presidency until a faculty member from one of Florida's universities nominated me for one. The possibility, although remote, intrigued me.

How did such a nontraditional background prepare me for a college presidency? In her book *Composing a Life*, Mary Catherine Bateson examines her life and the lives of four other successful women, and she sees the "creative potential" and adaptability that can arise from "interrupted and discontinuous" lives (1990, 15). Because fluidity and discontinuity are central to our lives today, Bateson considers the model of improvisation as more creative and appropriate than the male model of "single-track ambition" (15). She suggests that women's traditional adaptations are a positive resource not available to most men (14–15). These ideas have helped me understand how my own complicated life and the circuitous paths I traveled prepared me for a college presidency. Indeed, the varied professional and personal experiences in my background provided me with skills and strengths that were useful later in my quest for presidential legitimacy.

AN UNLIKELY CANDIDATE

The groundwork for the choice of a nontraditional president at Rollins was laid when the trustees and the prior president diversified the board in the 1980s. Most significant to my selection, however, was being nominated by a member of the presidential search committee who knew me well from my previous position. Having a supporter in the search process helps a candidate overcome anomalies of background and experience. Without such support, a nontraditional candidate often will not move to the interview stage. However, once in the search process I had to make my own case for the position. The search committee comprised trustees, alumni, students, and faculty (the latter had been elected). The search firm played a supporting rather than a primary role, working to build the capacity of the institution to define its needs and find a new president. I had little interaction with the firm's representative, although it seemed clear that I was not the candidate he thought would (or should) be selected.

In addition to reviewing the material sent to me by the search committee, I conducted research about Rollins in the University of Miami library, reviewing several years' worth of articles from the local newspaper, faculty publications, and books on the history of Winter Park. I also consulted with experts at the University about areas such as admissions and the business school. This preparation allowed me to come to the interviews thoroughly immersed in the college's history and current concerns and to communicate my vision for a more distinctive institution. I inquired about the college's prospects, the commitment of the faculty, and the support of the board of trustees. The advice I received from professional colleagues about job interviewing proved very helpful, and the frequent, friendly feedback I received from the chair of the committee kept me involved throughout a lengthy process. In the spring of 1990, the board elected me unanimously and presented me to the community without reservation and with great enthusiasm. This lent prestige and legitimacy to my appointment as thirteenth president of Rollins. Nonetheless, as the first woman, Jew, and fund-raiser to be called to the presidency at this liberal arts college founded by the Congregational Church, I had formidable legitimacy problems to overcome. As I noted in my journal (April 1, 1990), "It is hard to believe that I have overcome the negatives of being divorced, a woman, a Jew, and a development officer, with an education Ph.D. and degrees from Florida schools; and also amazing to believe that a very good liberal arts college . . . would have made me its president and at a perfect time in my life."

Although my predecessor had worked without a contract, I was familiar with stories of failed presidencies and felt a special vulnerability. Also, the college had a long-standing practice of not awarding tenure to administrators, so I would be in a challenging position without a safety net. I wondered in my June 21, 1990, journal entry, "how long will I last as president? . . . I don't think that I will be thrown out on my ear, but I'm going to guess at this point that I won't have a presidency that lasts beyond five years, maybe seven. I need to begin now to plan for the future beyond that." As a result, I asked for a formal agreement spelling out the terms of my employment and of termination. The Rollins College attorney had never prepared a president's employment contract and sought assistance. At that time, there was little written material and few experts on the subject, so I engaged a lawyer who had negotiated coaches' contracts. He worked with me privately because I did not want to appear too aggressive.

BIG SHOES

When I was elected to the presidency in 1990, both the institutional tradition and the governance culture conferred dignity and authority on the office. There were four living, previous Rollins presidents when I was elected. Each of these men was important to me. Each of them had stories, traditions, and history to share, which I incorporated into my own Rollins narrative. Also, where they had circles of influence, their strong support of my leadership was helpful in establishing my legitimacy. My immediate predecessor was concluding his twelfth year as president of Rollins and his twentieth year as a college president. He was ready to retire from the position, and he went to great lengths to make me feel welcome and comfortable. Still, I was intimidated by the numerous comments about "big shoes to fill."

My predecessor stayed at the college in various capacities throughout my presidency, and although he was always supportive, at first I felt that his presence delayed my achievement of legitimacy. Over the years, he served in many roles, among them, teacher, coordinator of the freshman program, member of the prelaw committee, adviser to the honor society, member of the student scholarship committee, and coordinator of Habitat for Humanity. He appeared at campus events, hosted alumni parties, and led historical tours of the campus for alumni. In time, I recognized that my predecessor was a champion of mine and that he reassured some uncertain elements among our constituents about my leadership and cultural fit. I was also uncomfortable initially with the former president's close relationship with a trustee, who stayed at his home during every board meeting. At first, I thought this entirely inappropriate and a threat to my presidency, but it faded in importance as the trustee proved supportive and loyal to me.

Despite an equable transition, my atypical background and experience made legitimacy a challenge. Although my academic credentials included the Ph.D., college teaching, and a considerable publication record, I was coming not from an academic position but a development vice presidency. My background did not confer traditional legitimacy, but it was appropriate to the needs of the institution. Mention of the $517.5 million we had raised in the just-completed University of Miami fund-raising campaign caused a frisson of excitement at Rollins, where the most recent campaign had raised just $43 million and the endowment was a meager $38 million. The president of the Rollins Faculty Senate was quoted by a reporter as saying, "This college absolutely had to have a fund-raising president" (Mercer 1995, 35–36). In this circumstance, a fund-raising background provided a measure of legitimacy. Additionally, as an experienced administrator with a track record in management, I had considerable technical legitimacy. Almost halfway through my first year as president (February 11, 1991), I noted in my journal that, lacking the traditional lineage and academic background, I would have to find acceptance as a different kind of president. "What makes me comfortable on a day-to-day basis is my supreme confidence as an administrator, my understanding of how to get things done, how to make decisions, how to mobilize people and resources."

The board and the faculty made an unorthodox choice, but it was clear that they saw in my background and experience the fund-raiser they needed with sufficiently respectable academic bona fides. I learned later that I was following a long line of Rollins presidents who also came through nonacademic, non-"royal," career paths. My immediate predecessor had been a student affairs dean before becoming a college president. Previous Rollins presidents had come from the positions of admissions director, studio art professor, corporate executive, newspaper editor, and minister. In fact, a 1929 promotional brochure made a virtue of President Hamilton Holt's "Unacademic Leadership," referring to "a man who understands business methods . . . who has been a national and international figure in great movements . . . [who] brought to this College a fresh viewpoint and a willingness to discard or cut through traditional academic routine" (*Rollins College Adventure* 10–11).

While most people voiced enthusiasm about my appointment, I had detractors from the start. Just after my election, a prominent administrator was heard to say despairingly, "Rollins is not ready for a Jewish woman president." (It also seemed to me that some Jewish trustees and alumni were uncomfortable about having a Jewish president—a failure would make them look bad.) Within several months, before getting to know me well, another administrator commented to his staff that Rollins no longer had any leadership, still another suggested that I lacked vision, and one mocked me as "Born Queen." Some students called me the "Queen of Mean." A young alumna wrote a nasty, four-page letter in which she called me a "heartless bureaucrat" (July 1994).

Although I continued to receive a great deal of encouragement and support, there was a steady stream of gossip, rumor, and innuendo criticizing my actions and suggesting that I was about to be fired. I noted in my journal that this rumor was "almost an annual event." Among the swirl of comments were the following. The alumni and community could not relate to a Jewish woman president, and I would never be able to raise money from them. I lacked the warmth and attention to students that characterized my predecessor. I had a corporate management style and was destroying the college's traditional family atmosphere. And, of course, morale was at an all-time low. I was grateful for the words of Flawn, president emeritus of the University of Texas at Austin, who points out, "faculty morale is always 'at an all-time low'" (1990, 9). Because morale was also putatively low among administrators, I relished and used this quote from George C. Marshall, Harry Truman's secretary of state: "[E]nlisted men may be entitled to morale problems, but officers are not. I expect all officers in this department to take care of their own morale. No one is taking care of my morale" (McCullough 1992, 560).

In those early years, I, fortunately, did not know the full extent of the discontent being expressed. And, despite the negativity that I did know about, I had no alternative other than to focus on the demands and possibilities of the presidency. Complete acceptance and legitimacy were still illusive, and on May 30, 1994, I made this entry in my journal: "How is it that even after such a successful year, with much success and not even a spring crisis, I learn that a rumor is circulating among colleagues across the country that I am out as president, having received a vote of no confidence from my board?"

THE TESTS OF LEADERSHIP

In June 1990, just before I began my official duties as president, I attended the Harvard Seminar for New Presidents. I found it very helpful and I noted in my journal (June 21), "The central learning of the experience had to do with the importance of culture and of moving into an institution very mindful of the power of that culture and the costs of disturbing it." This was a lesson to which I was faithful. Unfortunately, while dealing with concerns about my background and cultural fit, I was also faced with the serious economic challenges of the early 1990s.

At Rollins, we had two years of budget shortfalls and, although they were very small, we decided to reorganize the staff and lay off twenty staff members. In a letter to faculty and staff, I explained, "The staffing cuts we made were painful for all of us to accept, but were necessary since, in order to attract students, we had limited the tuition increase to the lowest percentage in a decade and raised the financial aid budget to an all-time high" (June 9, 1993). Similar actions were being taken in institutions around the country, but, as elsewhere, they caused a firestorm among Rollins staff and faculty. A faculty committee reported staff to be "very demoralized and alienated. They feel that the current top administration is not committed to Rollins College as a community in which they are included and respected" (Letter May 20, 1993). Looking back, I could have engaged the faculty more collaboratively in decisions regarding budget priorities. This is a classic case of environmental forces necessitating management decisions that are perceived by faculty and staff as inimical to the culture. Some presidential colleagues who took similar action did not survive. Unfortunately, several of my classmates at the Harvard Seminar were among them.

During these early years, budgetary concerns impelled us to initiate a number of other unpopular actions. We outsourced the bookstore, reassigned the affirmative action function to a human resources staff person, and sought to reduce the tuition-remission benefit. The tuition-remission proposal caused one faculty member to write, "I am angry and disheartened, because I believe the document is inhumane and punitive . . . [and] indicates that we no longer value each other's contribution to the community . . . [and] demonstrates that this community no longer shares common values" (Memo September 8, 1992). In this case, although we worked with a faculty committee on the plan, no committee member defended the changes when the matter was presented to the full faculty. This issue threatened to escalate into a crisis, so we withdrew the proposal. This was another case in which environmental, managerial, and cultural factors interacted to delegitimate the presidency.

In addition to these challenges, several major decisions I made added to the hostility in the system. The first had to do with the assignment of a major bequest to the general fund instead of to an academic department. This controversial move was made at the suggestion of family members during settlement of a lawsuit, but was seen by the department's faculty and many community members as a misapplication of the funds. In addition, acting on the strong advice of staff and faculty, I reassigned one senior administrator and terminated another. One of these situations became a crusade for a local newspaper columnist, who printed an angry letter from an alumnus and asked in a headline, "Who, If Anyone, Minds the Store at Rollins?" (Guest 1991, C-4). Fortunately, I was able to repair my relationship with the alumnus, who later became a volunteer leader of the alumni association and a great supporter of mine.

Because both administrators had lost the confidence of their colleagues, faculty, and staff, our ability to make progress was stalled. I took the inevitable and necessary actions, but handled the situations badly, in one case severing a personal and professional relationship in a legalistic instead of a humane fashion. One alumni trustee, agitated by his private discussions with students, staff, and faculty, copied me on a letter he wrote to the board chair: "Rollins College does not need, nor can it afford another controversy. . . . We in the alumni association are having our loyalty to Rollins greatly tested while continually being asked to provide more financial support" (Letter March 25, 1993). I was learning that alumni are especially sensitive to the possibility that a president's actions will violate the values of the institution they love and take their time in accepting and granting legitimacy to a new president. And, as I later noted in my journal (July 14, 1991), trustees want to know the president "has the place under control. When it gets out of control, I think the trustees get nervous."

The early years of my presidency demonstrated the lessons of legitimacy. Environmental conditions required difficult management decisions regarding personnel and budget that, even when we consulted with faculty and staff, were considered an affront to the culture. As a faculty member of the search committee that brought me to Rollins said during one of the feedback sessions I convened periodically, "It is important to recognize the symbolic value of decisions, especially regarding personnel, affirmative action, and the bookstore." And another remarked, "This is a different style administration from the last; it takes getting used to" (Meeting Notes May 13, 1993). I do not wish to paint an entirely negative picture, because during this period I also received many signs of acceptance, such as this comment in an alumna's letter: "[I]t is your own life that is a model for me. You are the first woman president of Rollins College and as such an example for us all to follow" (September 12, 1993).

Three years into my presidency, a faculty member wrote me about a rumor "that the President and the VP & Treasurer each received $10,000 bonuses from the Trustees for balancing the budget. In this time of sacrifice & retrenchment, say it isn't so!!" It wasn't. Six months later, a dean wrote a memorandum to the provost stating, "the morale of faculty and staff is as low as I can remember in my nine years of employment here." However, the nadir of my presidency occurred when the trustees received an anonymous letter that said, "Shame on you! Rollins College is being destroyed by [the chief financial officer] and Rita Bornstein and the Board of Trustees appears oblivious to the problem. . . . There seems to be near universal dislike and distrust of Rita and [chief financial officer] among all segments of the campus, including students, faculty, and staff." The letter goes on to accuse us of being aloof, abrasive, mendacious, incompetent, and untruthful. Key trustees forwarded the letter to me and said it should be ignored. It later became clear that much of the hostility expressed was directed to the CFO, although I was clearly targeted as well. While I found it difficult to ignore the letter and the sentiment it conveyed, once again I felt I had to continue leading the college without exhibiting any diminution of confidence.

At first I was criticized for a corporate management style. Although I did not realize it at the time, my image as a corporate CEO was exacerbated by the "dress for success" look that I, like other professional women, adopted in the early 1990s (pin-stripe suits with white shirts and dark ties). Rollins public relations materials and publications reinforced this image by portraying me almost exclusively in "grip and grin" photographs with donors. Since I had worked hard from the moment I took office to be more than a manager and fund-raiser, this did not reflect the reality of my presidency. I participated in every aspect of campus life: faculty governance and social activities, pancake flips for students during finals, student retreats, and countless campus cultural performances and sports events. I accepted invitations that brought me closer to students, including a challenge to put on a harness and climb a tree. As I gained confidence in my own sense of the presidency, I insisted that portrayals of me represent a range of activities and include students, faculty, staff, and alumni.

I gained legitimacy slowly, and it was not until my fourth year as president that I felt I had gained acceptance and influence and was comfortable in the presidency. Most people viewed me as a good leader, competent manager, and caring colleague. As president, I learned that it was my responsibility to help people deal with loss and grief during times of crisis. Rollins experienced some tragic student and faculty deaths over the years, and in each painful situation I responded openly, both emotionally and intellectually, as I convened the campus community to grieve and to heal. The college chaplain commented, "You are at your best when we are at our worst." Although Fisher (1984) believes that a president should be friendly, but distant, and Ciampa and Watkins (1999, 101) assert that accessibility "should go hand in hand with maintaining some psychological distance from employees," I learned that, to gain acceptance and legitimacy as president, people had to know me as a person.

ACCEPTANCE

My greatest concern when I assumed the presidency was that I would be viewed mainly as a fund-raiser and not as "our president." I was reminded by a faculty member who had been on the search committee that "when we asked you in the search process if you saw yourself as a fund-raiser you said, 'That's fine, if I am also seen as an academic'" (Notes May 13, 1993). I did find that my background as a fund-raiser was an initial impediment to my being seen as an intellectual leader. When I first took office, some faculty treated me like a development officer, asking for help in securing funds for their projects. Later, faculty suggested that I was not raising money fast enough. In 1995, when asked by a reporter whether I was an intellectual leader, a faculty member said that the president is "intellectually minded, [but] she hasn't yet provided intellectual leadership"—apparently, according to the reporter, because I had not promoted curricular changes. Another commented that the academic vice president "advances much of the college's academic agenda" because the president lacks the "academic resources" (Mercer 1995, A36). Since I had made it a point to be actively involved in academic matters as well as external relations, I was disturbed by those comments.

My intellectual life was important to me and I harvested precious time on weekends and holidays to continue my scholarship. This enabled me to publish and speak regularly on issues related to higher education, civic engagement, the presidency, fund-raising, and governance. Throughout, I promoted intellectual and issue-oriented discussions among constituents in a variety of settings. While this satisfied my own enjoyment of stimulating conversation, it also promoted a spirit of community. One of my most satisfying initiatives was the national conference I mounted in February 1997 that engaged well-known scholars and fifty college presidents in a three-day conversation on pragmatic liberal education. The College Board, a cosponsor of the colloquy, subsequently published a book with a series of essays that grew out of the presentations. I wrote the Afterword, based on Rollins's own history with John Dewey and experiential education (Orrill 1997), a legacy that gave the college its orientation to innovation.

From the inception of my presidency, I was invited to serve on boards of higher education associations (e.g., American Council of Education, National Association of Independent Colleges and Universities), corporations (Tupperware, NationsBank, Barnett Banks), and local nonprofits. I was fortunate in my timing because women were being sought for board service. I was selective about such invitations and limited the extramural activities I undertook, but these boards gave me an opportunity to be involved in higher education and business issues on the national, state, and local levels. I believe that my publications, presentations, and board memberships enhanced my legitimacy and the institution's reputation.

I was interested and involved in all aspects of institutional life, and I needed the faculty and others to recognize the breadth of my interest and involvement. Over time, attitudes in the Rollins community changed, and I became accepted as the president and as an intellectual leader. I also had to learn not to be self-conscious about my background in fund-raising, and to see success in fund-raising as vital to success in institutional improvement and repositioning. A resolution passed by the Arts and Sciences faculty in 2001, congratulating me for my "pivotal role in the capital campaign" just ending, also commented on "her love of Rollins and her dedication to making it as remarkable intellectually as it is architecturally." This delighted me, as did the expression of thanks for "continued wise stewardship of the college" (Resolution). At about the same time (October 10, 2001), I received an affirming letter from a faculty member referring to "Rita's Rollins renaissance," which had produced a transformation of the campus and "the academics we now take pride in."

The transformation of Rollins was the result of a clearly marked direction and a steady hand on the tiller steering toward continuous improvement in quality, reputation, and financial health. It took years for me to understand the extent to which a legitimated president's views and values permeate the institution. In a private conversation in August 2001, our master-planning architect commented that the Rollins people with whom he was working adhered to the highest standards of quality because they knew my expectations were high. A professor noted my "refusal to accept anything but the best" (Letter October 10, 2001). A high point for me came when the professor who questioned my intellectual leadership in the 1995 *Chronicle* article said to a reporter, "I'm taking back that comment. . . . I think it's fair to say that Rita has proven to be a strong intellectual person herself" (Powers 2000, B4).

As I review my early years, I am reminded how the struggle for legitimacy, coupled with the challenges of a depressed economy, budget deficits, and downsizing, made the presidency feel vulnerable. On my daily walk, I contemplated the worst and made contingency plans. My experiences underscored the report by Clark Kerr and Marian Gade that presidents have a nearly universal sense of being under constant observation, a concern about possible exit, "a sense of loneliness, [and a] sense of being driven" (1986, 28). Despite the continuing pressures, like many of my colleagues I loved the position and approached its challenges with confidence and enthusiasm. Although my nontraditional background made legitimacy difficult in the beginning, my varied experiences, leadership and management skills, and comfort with external relations proved to be immense advantages. In time, my background and expertise began to legitimate my presidency.

From the start, I recognized my responsibilities as moral leader and sought to establish an example of integrity. I set high standards for myself and for others, tried to learn from mistakes, and invited feedback, although I cannot pretend that I was not stung by criticism and buoyed by praise. I had strong feelings about issues, but tried not to act precipitously, knowing that I made better decisions after consultation with colleagues. I also sought to make decisions that would serve as models for future practice. The challenges of the presidency called on everything I knew and believed and had experienced. The job was never easy, but it was exhilarating. I noted in my journal: "The interesting thing about this job . . . is the huge diversity of activities in the course of a day and a week and a month; the array of constituencies, issues, problems that challenge the very fiber of one's being, call upon every experience and every ounce of intelligence and sensitivity that one has accumulated" (January 1991).

Throughout my presidency, I sought to ground decisions and actions in the culture, history, and traditions of the college. My sense of vulnerability diminished as I discovered that the key to a president's staying power is the perception of success among key constituents, especially faculty, alumni, and trustees. As the college improved in quality, reputation, and financial health, I found that my presidency gained legitimacy. I also developed an extensive network of relationships as I became embedded in the culture. An important milestone for me occurred when a special alumna and trustee began calling me "prexy," the term of respect and endearment used for Hamilton Holt, the college's legendary eighth president. In the first years of my presidency, three of the five factors in legitimacy—individual background, institutional culture, and the environment—worked against me, while technical expertise and moral leadership were advantages. Although it took years, I developed legitimacy as president, gained acceptance and influence, and built significant social capital. The ground was laid to reposition the college for the future.

PART III

Assuring the Legitimacy of Change

CHAPTER 10

The Impetus for Change:
Crisis, Niche, Quality

Presidents seek to establish their legacy by significantly transforming or strengthening their institutions. There is tremendous pressure on new presidents to enunciate a grand vision and initiate change immediately, which should be resisted. The most successful processes of visioning and change occur collaboratively with faculty and trustees, but presidents feel they "have three or six or nine months to make significant changes on campus before the faculty begin to refer to the former regime as *la belle époque*" (Plante with Caret 1990, 1). During the honeymoon period, a president's latitude for change is somewhat more elastic and constituents more forgiving than they are later on. This provides opportunities to make necessary, though controversial, changes. Missteps in this early period may be forgiven; on the other hand, they may be seen as violations of cultural traditions and relationships. A miscalculation in taking such an action can easily diminish a president's legitimacy.

The surest spur to transformational change is a crisis, but under normal circumstances presidents focus on steady improvements in quality and reputation. A new president wisely acknowledges and seeks to build on the accomplishments of previous eras. The needs of the institution at that moment in its history should determine whether radical or incremental change is appropriate and legitimate. The president who forwards an agenda inconsistent with an institution's needs and readiness for change is courting trouble.

Radical change, a shift in institutional mission or niche, may be necessary or desirable in response to new opportunities and significant changes in the environment. A president can use environmental pressures to legitimate the strategic repositioning or remaking of an institution. Radical change might involve a move from one to another Carnegie classification, athletic conference, or division of the NCAA. It can mean an institutional restructuring, downsizing, or upsizing. It might involve a major increase or reduction in the size of the student body or the faculty. Presidents who aspire to move their institutions higher in the media-ranked hierarchy within a Carnegie classification or to the next category may convert strong departments to schools, add graduate programs, and move to another athletic status. Colleges may be renamed universities. The pursuit of prestige through a gradual increase in status is often referred to as "mission creep," but institutional repositioning may not be achievable, or, if successful, may fail to provide the hoped-for impact on quality, reputation, and financial support. While some institutions establish themselves successfully in a new niche, others experience budget deficits and no improvement in quality, visibility, reputation, student numbers, or fund-raising. "Mission contraction" is a repositioning mechanism that occurs far less frequently because it requires the elimination of programs and a reduction in scope. The most successful of such changes are generally made more palatable through a narrative celebrating the institution's return to its core mission.

Most higher education institutions are less in need of radical change than enhanced quality and reputation. Incremental change is appropriate at stable and successful institutions that exist in comfortable niches. Incremental change generally focuses on the quality, size, and diversity of the student body, standards for faculty evaluation and compensation, improvements to physical plant, endowment management, fund-raising, and budgeting. Incremental change is most appropriate for an institution not in crisis, but, over time, incremental changes can transform an institution. Either type of institutional improvement, gradual or swift, burnishes a president's legitimacy and legacy. Successful leaders gain credibility by seizing opportunities for change when they present themselves (Ciampa and Watkins 1999, 117).

The process for making transformational (deep and pervasive) change requires time, attention, and money, and all are everywhere in short supply. If change is adopted through a legitimate process, an important indicator of its durability will be "the extent to which it becomes reflected in the budget" (Eckel et al. 1999, 45–48). The American Council on Education (ACE) Project on Leadership and Institutional Transformation, a multiyear, multisector project involving twenty-six institutions and funded by the W.K. Kellogg Foundation, provides instructive background and advice that presidents can use to help legitimate institutional change. To institutionalize a change effort, the researchers emphasize the importance of altering the underlying assumptions or deep structure of the culture. They point out that change efforts not accompanied by changes in underlying assumptions may have little lasting impact on the organization (Eckel et al. 1999, 24).

In addition to transformational change, this report (Eckel et al. 1999, 14–16) also identifies three other types of institutional change as measured by depth and pervasiveness. "Adjustments" are minor changes in a particular area. "Isolated change" is deep but not pervasive. "Far-reaching change" is pervasive but does not affect the organization very deeply. Although administratively appointed ad hoc groups may develop change initiatives, the formal campus governance processes must be followed in order to garner legitimacy (19). Successful institutional change also requires agreement and acceptance from a critical mass of campus constituents. Often a major change can be legitimated first by a small group in an experimental project. This report reminds us that the process for change is as important as the vision, and that most institutions are "change-averse, with loosely-coupled units and diffused decision-making processes." Also, those whose status depends on the current equilibrium may prove resistant to change (19, 3–4). The ACE report on institutional transformation reminds us of the difficulty of changing the basic assumptions of constituents and the importance of assuring a legitimate process for change. These challenges are reason enough for presidents to take their time in assessing the needs and potential for change in their institutions. In healthy institutions, transformational change efforts are not only unnecessary, they may also be dysfunctional. In her extensive review of the literature on change, Kezar (2001, 113) points out that generalizations about change are risky because of the complexity of the dynamics of change in higher education institutions.

Before initiating or supporting a major change effort, experienced and legitimated presidents conduct an informal cost-benefit analysis: What is to be gained? What are the likely costs to the institution for implementing this change? Will it erode the social capital I have worked hard to build? How vital is this change? Is the timing right? Can I lay the groundwork for community support? Is the administration united on the need for this change? Will the faculty be supportive? Have the trustees been adequately informed and involved? Will they stand firm in the event of some negative reaction? A collegial process of consideration can yield unexpectedly helpful insights for presidents. The uniqueness of the academy is that while its liberalism promotes social criticism and discovery, its conservatism makes it resistant to ephemeral fads and markets. It is easy for others to propose changes, but the president pays the price if the process does not go well. In fact, it is in times of change that the president most needs the support of the trustees. A board should expect a thorough educational and consultative process before it accepts responsibility for establishing policy and endorsing major changes, but once having done so, trustees need to defend the effort even in the face of opposition.

The need for change may be apparent to administrators; the challenge is to make change appear necessary and desirable to constituents, who may see themselves as protectors of the status quo. As Brand writes, "It is the president's (or chancellor's) role to understand the need for innovation and lead the institution toward meeting the challenges of change, while simultaneously working to sustain the fundamental values of the academy" (Brand 2002, 27). Using both the institution's formal and informal mechanisms, a president can influence the vision, strategic goals, and change efforts through processes the community will accept as legitimate. To be effective, says Birnbaum (1992, 10), leaders must "align their strategies with their institution's culture rather than compete with it."

When change efforts violate cultural norms, they generally fail. Even when successful, change initiatives are modified and shaped by the culture (Kezar and Eckel 2002, 456, 438). A smart leader will couch the rationale for a significant change in the language and symbols embedded in the institution's history. Overblown rhetoric envisioning unrealistic goals is misleading and creates a negative backlash if innovative efforts fail. In evaluating a failed educational innovation of major proportions that was driven by the leader's grand vision, I noted: "Visionary rhetoric should be avoided—it is hard to live up to." On the other hand, procedural matters of importance should be handled efficiently and thus eliminated as an impediment to innovation (Bornstein 1975, 336). Technical competence is vital and legitimating to the successful functioning of systems, whether at equilibrium or undergoing change.

Change is uncomfortable and may imply a criticism of past leaders, current practice, or the culture. There are common responses to new initiatives: "It isn't broke, so why fix it." "We've always done it this way." "We should not be catering to the market; we know what students need." "You don't understand our culture." "It would destroy morale." "We haven't been consulted." "We need more time to study this." Negative reaction to change efforts can poison the atmosphere for years. Many, if not most, change initiatives fail. However, presidents with legitimacy among their constituents can have a significant impact in creating an environment for change—a "culture of risk" (Kezar 2001, 121), an "innovation-friendly climate" (Tierney 2001). The potential for change in an institution—incremental or transformational—depends in large measure on the degree of trust and social capital that has been developed. New corporate leaders are advised that their initial charge from their board is not sufficient. They must "earn the right to transform the organization" (Ciampa and Watkins, 1999, 32). This is true also for academic presidents.

Presidents must persuade constituents that change is necessary. Then they need to assure an inclusive, collaborative, but time-limited, planning process for the change effort; conduct a scan of the internal and external environments; assess the institution's needs; develop a compelling narrative for change anchored in the institution's history and culture; and mobilize support for change among the institution's key stakeholders. A change effort that is accepted as necessary and legitimate stands a good chance of becoming institutionalized and establishing a new equilibrium. However, we know from experience that rational planning approaches are likely to be sabotaged by an institutional context characterized by anarchy, chaos, and stasis.

CHAPTER 11

The Context for Change

ORGANIZED ANARCHY

Presidential vision, plans, and change agendas notwithstanding, the context for administrative and faculty decision making and innovation is largely chaotic and unpredictable. The poet John Keats (1818) wrote, "there is nothing stable in the world—uproar's your only musick." Nowhere is this more applicable than in higher education. Aspirants to a college presidency who require stability, rationality, and predictability in their work lives *need not apply*. Robert Atwell, president emeritus of the American Council on Education, notes that presidents must "have a high tolerance for ambiguity. Situations are never very clearly black or white, right or wrong. They're very complicated and your ability to do anything about them is very limited, so if that drives you crazy, it *will* drive you crazy!" (1996, 7). Presidents who undertake institutional planning and change initiatives must learn to operate successfully and legitimately within this climate.

Daily activity mirrors the unpredictability of the academy as the president careens from one problem to another, often from the ridiculous to the sublime and back again. A decision about whether the garbage cans throughout the campus should be metal or stone may be followed by a debate about what students should know when they graduate. Jill Ker Conway (2001, 59) describes the complex, unpredictable, and conflicting roles a president plays throughout the course of a routine day as "the comic element" of the presidency. Stanley Fish, dean of the College of

Liberal Arts and Sciences at the University of Illinois at Chicago, extends the comic element by comparing the bizarre range of mail that "seems to have flown in from the stratosphere" to the regular activities of administrators. The pleasure in administration lies in the daily challenge arising from "problems, questions, requests, and crises you could not have anticipated no matter how long you've been in the job" (2002). Indeed, for those comfortable with chaos, complexity, and ambiguity, the academic presidency is an exciting challenge.

On the other hand, those who subscribe to a rational, linear planning orientation cannot understand the cultural resistance to change in academic policy and programs or the perennial resurfacing of problems thought to have been solved. Academic "policy," according to Cohen and March, is less the result of "systematic collective decision making," than "the accretion of hundreds of largely autonomous actions taken for different reasons, at different times, under different conditions, by different people in the college" (1974, 103–4). And every president learns that while institutional policies may be established, often after lengthy, contentious discourse, sooner or later someone will raise the issue again.

For example, at one college, after almost a year of rancorous debate with faculty, the administration promulgated a retirement plan. A year later a faculty member told the president that the "fascistic" language of the plan was disturbing to long-time faculty who had given their lives to the college. Explaining that this was a legal document, written by lawyers, did not help. The professor wanted to know what the president thought of the document, and was the president "happy to have this on our books." This issue will very likely surface periodically.

In identifying colleges and universities as prototypical "organized anarchies," Cohen and March (1974, 2–3) suggest that they have goals that are "either vague or in dispute," processes that are "familiar but not understood," and participants who "wander in and out of the organization." These qualities, they say, make higher education institutions "a problem to describe, understand, and lead." They point out that college presidents "live within a normative context that presumes purpose and within an organizational context that denies it" (197). Experienced presidents who have tried to direct change without success can identify with this analysis of leadership in higher education. Presidents also have experience with Cohen and March's five properties of decision making: low salience of most issues for most people, high inertia in the system, the use of decision processes as garbage cans for other problems, system overload, and a weak information base (206–7). The authors do identify ways in which

presidents can influence change. I have applied these properties of decision making to strategies for legitimating change in chapter 14.

Accepting that the academic climate is anarchic, tending toward maintenance of the current equilibrium, I believe that thoughtful presidential
leadership can make a difference. However, it is imperative that presidents
understand the constraints within which they operate and learn to legitimate appropriate change, transformational or incremental, by working
within that context. Organized anarchies can be managed if leaders approach them with an eye toward identifying the kind of patterns scholars
find in chaos theory.

CHAOS THEORY

A framework that helps to make sense of academic life can be adapted
from chaos theory, which finds patterns and predictability within disorder,
irregularity, and randomness. If we accept the view of academic institutions as organized anarchies, we also need a way of promoting change
within that environment. Patterns in college life, like those in nature, are
expected and recognizable. Academic patterns exist and are predictable,
but, like hurricanes, their exact timing and effect is uncertain. Thus, a
spring crisis is anticipated every year, but not the precise issue, time, or
severity. This phenomenon is surprisingly like Edward Lorenz's "Butterfly Effect" in chaos theory, technically the "sensitive dependence on initial conditions" (Gleick 1987, 23). A butterfly stirring the air today in
Beijing, China, can create a storm next month in New York. We expect
certain weather patterns at certain times of the year, but, because "small
perturbations" can result in "large consequences," even experts cannot
predict the weather precisely (8–31, 67). In similar fashion, an apparently
minor campus conflict in the fall can erupt dramatically and virulently
in the spring.

Sensitivity to the patterns and relationships that characterize academic life provides a vital tool for presidential leadership in change. It
creates the rationale for agency instead of passivity, and agency legitimates the presidency. Barbara Mossberg notes that from the president's
perspective, "Chaos theory causes a re-valuation of all those elements
in a system previously understood to be disturbing, insignificant, 'noise,'
irrelevant, or 'wrong.'" Further, she says, "the existence of simultaneously
coexisting, competing, conflicting, various points of view does not mean
that the institution is not functional or whole and cannot sustain a co-
herent self-image of its common work" (2001, 238–39). Thus, presiden-

tial leadership requires the ability to identify and understand the institutional patterns and the network of relationships that exist within the chaos of everyday academic life. Presidents seeking to promote change can then work actively within an anarchic and chaotic but predictable context to keep their constituencies focused on institution-wide issues and external challenges.

PUNCTUATED EQUILIBRIUM

The tendency to avoid systemic change is ascribed by Connie Gersick to "fears of losing control over one's situation if the equilibrium ends" (1991, 18). This is nowhere more accurate than in academe, where professionals tend to protect their prerogatives and resist change, unless confronted with a threat to their work or the viability of their institution. Gersick (11–12, 31) proposes a model for change based on Stephen Jay Gould's notion of "punctuated equilibrium" that builds on Darwin's concept of gradual evolution. The deep structure of the underlying order limits change during periods of equilibrium and "disassembles, reconfigures, and enforces wholesale transformation during revolutionary punctuations." While incremental changes do occur during the long periods of equilibrium, they do not fundamentally alter the system. And not all changes make a system better; in the paradigm of punctuated equilibrium "systems do not inevitably evolve toward improvement." The paradigm of punctuated equilibrium is applicable to higher education in that it involves relatively long periods of stability punctuated by short periods of revolutionary change. Changes in higher education are not always improvements.

In the punctuated equilibrium paradigm, systemic change is unlikely to occur unless the deep structure is interrupted by significant internal or environmental changes that threaten survival. Such a crisis provides the opportunity to alter the deep structure of the institution during the change and often requires different leadership (Gersick 1991, 19, 23). Chapter 7 of this volume reviewed the controversial changes led by the University of Chicago president in the late 1990s in response to a survival crisis. The president's leadership was necessary to revive the institution but cost him his job (Bartlett 2002). Faculties and alumni, like those at Chicago, will resist an overhaul of curriculum or graduation requirements if recommended by a dean or president but will initiate such changes themselves when confronted with financial exigency or the loss of accreditation.

Although the context for systemic change in higher education is characterized by "uproar," ambiguity, and anarchy, presidential leadership can make a difference. Planned, rational approaches to change help constituents make sense of the chaotic academic environment. And, despite the comfort of the status quo, significant environmental threats do periodically cause punctuations of change in the equilibrium of colleges and universities as they are forced to reinvent themselves.

CHAPTER 12

Factors in Achieving Legitimate Change

Based on the literature, my interviews, and my survey on legitimacy in the academic presidency, I propose a construct for successful and legitimate change that depends on four complex and interrelated factors: (1) presidential leadership, (2) governance, (3) social capital, and (4) fund-raising. Individually and through interaction, these factors facilitate or impede the legitimacy and institutionalization of change. The appropriate leadership style depends on the institutional context and the system's readiness for change. Many scholars, pundits, and presidents consider strong, visionary, "transformational" leadership the key element in successful organizations. And, indeed, strong leadership is important. However, academic institutions are collectivities of well-educated and trained experts with a tradition of participation in governance. To be successful in the academic culture, presidents will use the authority and influence of the office but also develop collegial, collaborative, "transactional" relationships with faculty through active participation in governance. Governance and strategic planning processes that involve trustees and faculty are critical to the legitimacy of change. In addition, the accretion of social capital is necessary to provide a culture of strong relationships and trust on which presidents can build as they influence their constituents toward change or improvement. Finally, resources that can be deployed at the discretion of the president are critical to the success of his or her change agenda.

Presidents can focus the attention of stakeholders on change through their discourse and their written communiqués. Importantly, they can employ a number of mechanisms outside the governance and planning systems. These include the ability to make administrative appointments, create administrative structures, control the flow of information, initiate staff-driven programs, organize groups for decision making, allocate the budget, and apply discretionary resources (Trow 1991, 360–63). The ability to establish an agenda for change and to apply "slack" resources, defined by Cohen and March (1974, 87) as "the difference between the resources of the organization and the combination of demands made on it," can provide important, and legitimate, leverage for presidential leadership. Slack can come from a variety of sources, including positive budget balances, reallocation, and reorganization; however, philanthropy provides the president with significant influence over change efforts. This analytic construct for institutional change suggests the implementation of rational strategies to enhance legitimacy. To be even moderately successful, presidents must learn to maneuver in a climate of uncertainty, ambiguity, and complacency. Following are descriptions of the four factors in change legitimacy.

PRESIDENTIAL LEADERSHIP AND CHANGE

The 1966 "Statement on Government of Colleges and Universities" (1991, 161), promulgated by the American Association of University Professors, and loosely accepted by the American Council on Education and the Association of Governing Boards of Colleges and Universities, endorses the president's authority for agenda setting and change. The document asserts that a president "has a special obligation to innovate and initiate." However, a change initiative can wreak havoc in a college or university and delegitimate the president. Although presidential leadership is an important factor in major institutional change, there is no single prescription for leadership style that is appropriate to every situation. Institutions need different kinds of leaders at different junctures and in different eras; there is no one-size-fits-all presidential model. The appropriate and legitimate leadership style is contextual and must be a good match with an institution's needs at that time in its history.

The literature on the college presidency focuses on two models of leadership—transformational and transactional—each with its partisans. James MacGregor Burns (1978, 19–20), in his magnum opus, *Leadership*, defines "transactional" leadership as "the exchange of valued things," economic or political or psychological, between leaders and followers without a call to a greater purpose. He defines "transforming" leadership as the engagement of people "in such a way that leaders and followers raise one another to higher levels of motivation and morality." Burns's notion of transforming leadership involves mutual influence between leaders and followers on behalf of social change. According to Richard Couto (1995, 103–6), Bernard Bass later redefined transforming into "transformational" leadership, a very different, top-down rather than mutual influence process, oriented to leaders interested in institutional rather than social change. From Bass's perspective, leaders create and control the conditions and followers remain subordinates.

Fisher and Koch call upon presidents to be transformational leaders, strong, visionary, charismatic, who inspire others to believe in a new vision and bold, innovative goals (1996, x–xii, 22–26). Charisma has a variety of meanings. It can be viewed theologically as "an endowment of spiritual grace from God" or secularly as "an endowment of an extremely high degree of esteem, value, popularity, and/or celebrity-status attributed by others" (Bass 1985, 39). Fisher and Koch (1996, xi) characterize transactional leadership pejoratively as reactive leadership that "responds to the consensus reflections of constituents." Others interpret transactional leadership positively as collegial and sensitive to the culture, traditions, and values of an institution, interacting with others to achieve institutional goals (Bensimon et al. 1991, 392–93). From this perspective, influence is reciprocal between the president and his or her constituents.

Taking into account the appropriateness of the transformational and transactional models of leadership to differing institutional conditions, I draw on the literature and responses to the interviews and legitimacy survey to develop the perspective that good leadership is derived from a continuum of available behaviors. I call this view "transformative" leadership.

Transformational Leadership

The transformational leader is most effective in a new organization, an institution in crisis, or one in need of significant change. The great-man theory of history, notes Burton Clark, "has a specific version in education in the frequent claim that the institution, especially the noteworthy one, is the lengthened shadow of a man. In the history of the successful college, so the interpretation goes, lurks the forceful president . . . who made it what it is today." Many of our institutions were created or re-created by such leaders. Aydelotte at Swarthmore, Hutchins at Chicago and Conant at Harvard created an institutional "saga" which survives today (Clark 1992, 238–40). When Hamilton Holt was called to Rollins in 1924, he reinvented the failing college, and in his twenty-four years as president, he gave it a national reputation for innovative, student-centered education. The college still operates in Holt's "lengthened shadow," and his influence is palpable in the physical and cultural life of the college.

Burns (1978, 244) notes, "Heroic leaders—in contrast with leaders merely enjoying popular favor—usually arise in societies undergoing profound crisis." Joe Klein, writing about President Clinton, agrees: "[G]reatness in politics is rarely self-created; it is a consequence of trouble in the world. . . . A leader without a crisis is usually consigned to the periphery of history" (2002, 210). The same has been said of academic presidents, and, indeed, the extraordinary social pressures on American higher education at several junctures in its history created the legendary presidents we all admire. I would argue that heroic presidents are not what today's higher education institutions need. What they do need are leaders smart enough to determine whether the institutions they serve require incremental or radical change and courageous enough to adjust their own style and vision accordingly.

Circumstances and crises shape a presidency. In the early 1990s, Bennington's president, Elizabeth Coleman, and her board, reacting to a drastic decline in students and straitened financial circumstances, acted boldly, if controversially, to make radical changes to the curriculum and faculty. Coleman, then six years into her presidency, worked with the board over a two-year period to redesign the educational program based on the institution's unique history and culture. With the board firmly behind her, the president installed the new program, and as part of the plan, eliminated the tenure-like system for faculty employment, terminated a third of the faculty, and abolished academic departments.

Although the institution was sued by faculty members and censured by the American Association of University Professors (AAUP), the crisis enabled the president to make radical changes not normally possible in the academic culture. Faculty accused President Coleman of destroying the college's "atmosphere," "listening only to herself, [and] operating by fiat" (Edmundson 1994, 42, 74). As the financial crisis abated, the president prevailed—with reduced legitimacy among some stakeholders and increased legitimacy with others. Credited with saving the college, she will be remembered by some for being a transformational educational innovator and by others for undermining traditional academic prerogatives and values. Importantly, before she acted, Coleman secured the board's involvement in creating the new educational program, as well as its unwavering support for the change and for her leadership. A crisis threatening the historic college's survival called for innovative action, and the president responded. The plan and practices she implemented were not developed or approved through the typical faculty governance processes. Board members believed that the "buck stopped on the boardroom table," and the decisions they made "could not be achieved consensually" (Barr and Borden 1995, 11–12). History will record the actions of the board and the president as either heroic or destructive.

There are certain conditions that call for transformational leadership. In addition to institutions in crisis, such leadership is possible mainly at small colleges, where the influence of a president may be significant, and institutions in need of upgrading (Bensimon et al. 1989, 42–43, 74; Birnbaum 1988, 205). Brand points out that transformational leadership is also important for public research universities that need to respond to changing environmental conditions by attempting new directions. Sometimes, he says, transformation is "thrust on you" by circumstances and "sometimes you choose to do it" (Brand Interview 2002). I would add two additional circumstances where transformational leadership may be desirable and legitimating: a young institution struggling to define a distinctive niche and enhance its reputation and an institution in a community with a rapidly changing population and business environment. Absent such special circumstances, a leadership style "that conforms to the group's norms while also seeking to improve them may be of greater benefit than heroic attempts at redesigning an institution" (Bensimon et al. 1989, 393). In any case, Chait (1993, B2) notes that, despite all the emphasis on vision, there are, at most, two dozen colleges out of 3,300 that have been successfully "reinvented" from a desperate state.

I interviewed Carolynn Reid-Wallace, who came to the presidency of Fisk University in 2001, with a mandate to transform the struggling, historically black institution through diversification. Despite constituent support for change, she encountered resistance and protest against a direction that threatened the "identity" of the university. She describes "having to sell ideas and having to step away from pushing some things," because she feared winning the battle and losing the war. Transformational presidents, Reid-Wallace says, "have to be prepared to sell their vision, and they have to continue to repeat and redefine it and work with small groups of people to get buy-in." Reid-Wallace refers to herself as "a transformational type," who "would not succeed at a school that did not need some form of transformation" (Interview 2003). This president's characterization of herself makes an important point. The board and faculty of an institution need to assess their current needs and select a president who brings the experience, strengths, and leadership style that can make a difference. A president who is unsuccessful at one institution may be successful at another.

Despite questions about its appropriateness for most academic institutions, the ideal of transformational leadership is a siren call for many enthusiasts. Bass (1985, 14–32) asserts that transformational leadership inspires people to transcend self-interest for the sake of the organization and produces greater results than transactional leadership. Many presidents agree. Frank Rhodes says, "A university presidency is one of the most powerful of all positions because of its persuasive influence and its long-term and wide-ranging leverage." In his view, the landscape is littered with "pallid institutions" reflecting the "listless leadership" of passive presidents, and the greatest task of a president "is to articulate the vision, champion the goals, and enunciate the objectives" of the institution (Rhodes 1998, 14). Brand believes that "change cannot take place by consensus; change has to take place by leadership" although he acknowledges the need for collegiality. "It makes no sense to run up the hill by yourself," he says; "If you don't have the troops with you, you are not going to get it done." This takes "a lot of work, a lot of leadership, a lot of use of the bully pulpit, a lot of meetings." Brand finds most presidents to be transactional rather than transformational; "they seek to be loved, not to make change" (Brand Interview 2002).

In the corporate sector, the transformational leader's vision is considered key to motivating an institution. Transformational leaders "must provide people with an image of what can be and motivate them to move ahead into the future they envision" (Tichy 1990, 122). Another management perspective is that vision is "non-specific directional guidance" that changes with changes in leadership, organizational structure, or the environment. It describes a company's conceptual orientation in general but inspiring terms (Higgins 1991, 155–56). In an ironic twist, visionary leadership came under attack in the wake of the business scandals and failures of the early 2000s. The expansionist vision of many corporate CEOs led to overextension beyond their core mission and a drive to do almost anything to generate confidence on Wall Street and elevate the share price of their company stock. Following a series of corporate scandals, bankruptcy filings, and a precipitous stock market decline, boards turned away from visionaries and saviors. Instead, they sought legitimacy by hiring CEOs with reputations for integrity and good management.

Transactional Leadership

Although heroic leaders emerge in response to crisis situations, Burns points out that when the crisis is passed, institutions and societies turn to captains who can steer the ship ably through calmer seas (Burns 1978,

243–44). In 1993, when Lou Gerstner became CEO of a troubled IBM, he said that a new vision was not what the company needed at that point. Gerstner's story is instructive. He was chosen to lead the company although he had no experience in the computer industry and thus little traditional legitimacy. The IBM board, after considerable debate, gambled that the company needed a strategist and a manager, not a visionary. To avoid a protracted internal debate about the company's vision, Gerstner said that what was needed in place of vision was to save the company economically. He focused on three goals—changing the company's economic model, its strategy, and its culture—that in hindsight can be seen as his vision. By the time of his retirement in 2002, under a leadership style characterized as "unsentimental pragmatism," IBM had, once again, become the industry leader (Lohr 2002, 1, 11).

Charismatic leaders are not selected for successful institutions because they "are inappropriate for the stability, continuity, and maintenance of the existing power structure" (Clark 1992, 241). Transactional leadership—collegial, collaborative, and participative—may be appropriate at established, successful, well-regarded institutions—institutions that need to be better at what they do, improve their quality through incremental change, and secure greater resources to support their efforts. A transactional leader may be far more effective in strengthening a good institution than a leader trying to effect an unwanted transformation. Although faculties often express a longing for a visionary leader, they tend to resist major institutional changes. Flawn (1990, 190) suggests that although faculties complain about weak leadership, they resist the strong leadership that they believe they seek. To establish a change agenda, successful presidents, he says, work through "suggestion, reason, persuasion, blandishment, coercion, intimidation, and indirection."

Harold Shapiro (1998, 95) contrasts the style of presidents of an earlier era with that of contemporary presidents. Of the former he says, "[T]hey seem to have believed that they were both called and empowered to transform an institution that needed transforming on a grand scale." By contrast, today's leaders "are often more sanguine about the fundamental soundness of the institutions over which they preside, frequently believing that more gradual and thoughtful change, rather than utter transformation, is called for." Donna Shalala (2001, 3) echoed this sentiment at her inauguration as president of the University of Miami. She said, "I did not come to Miami to reinvent this university. A healthy institution does not need to begin again. In fact, it cannot—at least not without violating its integrity." These are persuasive arguments for transactional leadership made by strong presidents who are obviously not embarrassed to be strengthening, not revolutionizing, their institutions. These experienced presidents know full well that "organizations can probably tolerate only a limited level of transformation and the constant changes of values induced by a succession of transformational leaders" (Bensimon et al. 1989, 75).

One of the most useful ideas about leadership is that presidents may use transactional means to achieve transformational ends. Chait (1993, B2) suggests that a president's vision is far more evident "through a rearview mirror" when the incumbent leaves office than it can possibly be during the search process. James Fisher, ardent advocate for transformational leadership, responds to this assertion by saying it denies "any real prospect for improvement in our colleges and universities" (Fisher 1993, Archive). However, transactional leadership can be associated with institutional improvement. Jim Collins (2001, 39), in his research-based book, *Good to Great*, describes the type of leadership necessary to transform a company to greatness as "more plow horse than show horse." Collins (22) argues that we do not need "larger-than-life saviors" with big personalities to transform companies, because corporate transformations are not characterized by a "single defining action, no grand program, no one killer innovation, no solitary lucky break, no wrenching revolution." Instead, he describes a step-by-step, decision-by-decision, cumulative process that adds up to "sustained and spectacular results" (165).

Published in the early 2000s, Collins's work is especially significant at the end of an era characterized by disenchantment with visionary corporate leaders. Those visionaries had caused havoc in the business world through their unbridled quest for expansion and their willingness to participate in unethical and illegal practices. As a result, charisma and vision took a backseat to the "plow horse." As federal regulators stepped in to establish controls, corporate boards began to recognize the value of solid, effective, ethical leaders who understand and can manage their businesses. It is apparent that transactional leadership can achieve significant, legitimate, and lasting change in corporate as well as academic settings.

Birnbaum (1988, 26, 204) believes that the glorification of transformational leadership is demeaning to the skilled and competent administrator who keeps the institution functioning in both bad and good times. Bensimon et al. (1989, 74) suggest that the transformational model makes three assumptions in conflict with norms in higher education. These assumptions are: leadership emanates from a single individual, followers are motivated by needs for organizational affiliation, and leadership depends on visible, significant change. The authors point out that in academe, contrary to these assumptions, authority is diffused, affiliation is likely to be to a department or professional association, and radical change is generally not needed or accepted.

If transformational leadership is incompatible with the accepted norms and values of the academy, then, we can infer that, from Weber's perspective (in Etzioni 1964, 51–52), this use of power is not legitimate. A president acting without authority (power viewed as legitimate) cannot initiate change successfully and will likely need to move on. This view of today's presidency reflects the reality that nonprofit higher education is no longer an entrepreneurial venture, and generally requires a different kind of leadership. "Leadership has many faces, and charisma comes in long-lasting and relatively quiet administrative containers as well as in the messianic fervor that bursts upon a scene and quickly stirs the passions of men" (Clark 1992, 244).

Feminist Perspectives on Leadership

Although theories of leadership are, for the most part, based on research conducted with and by men, the growing number of women presidents has encouraged scholarship on gender and leadership. Helen Astin and Carole Leland (1991, 8, 11) propose a nonhierarchical model of feminist leadership, with the leader "as a catalyst or facilitator" who promotes collective planning and action toward the accomplishment of the community's goals. This model comports with the transactional view of leadership. Some feminist scholars find women more open, collaborative, and communicative than men. Mary Ann Sagaria and Linda Johnsrud (in Jablonski 2000, 245) have developed a "generative leadership model" that encourages participation, creativity, empowerment, trust, and collaboration. Judith Glazer-Raymo (1999, 207) calls for adoption of "new institutional prototypes that replace hierarchical management, in-house rivalries, and ladder climbing with nonbureaucratic, responsive models."

These views posit gender-based differences in leadership style. A study of successful women managers suggests that, in certain organizational settings, so-called feminine qualities may actually be more effective. The leadership style of the women in this study is called interactive, and involves "encouraging participation, sharing power and information, enhancing other people's self-worth, and getting others excited about their work." Of particular interest is this study's conclusion that the women managers gained "credibility and legitimacy by achieving results," a finding that reinforces the importance of technical competence, identified in chapter 6, as a factor in presidential legitimacy. This study also reinforces my suggestion that the "best" leadership style depends on institutional need and context (Rosener 1990, 119–20, 125). Once again, I would argue that a repertoire of leadership behaviors is available to presidents (women or men) depending on the needs of their institutions.

There is ample research to support the view that successful leadership is less a matter of style or gender then it is a good match between the president and the university or college. Sue Freeman (2001, 33, 43) reports that although traditionally female relational and interpersonal qualities are now being emphasized for successful leadership, no difference has been found between men and women as transformational or transactional leaders. Birnbaum (1992, 44, 46), in a five-year longitudinal study of presidents, found "no apparent relationships between gender and leadership . . . and women are no less effective than men as presidents." However, in a "reinterpretation" of some of these data from a feminist perspective, Bensimon (1993, 466, 468) finds previously unnoticed gender-based differences. She assumes "gender plays a critical role in issues of power and decision making" and "translates into a different experience of leadership." Her subject, a female president, has a less "grandiose" view of leadership than the transformational and is more responsive, connected, and collaborative. Bensimon (472) reflects on whether women's leadership would be marginalized and "trivialized" because a female president's language and style "is associated with woman's role as nurturer."

While there are certainly differences in the life experiences that women and men bring to the presidency, generalizations about gender-based leadership inhibit experimentation with the full continuum of behaviors and reinforce the stereotypes that followers use to evaluate leaders. One study found that although women college presidents believed themselves to be participatory and empowering as leaders, their faculties characterized them as they describe male presidents—"hierarchical, bureaucratic, directive, and controlling." The study attributes this discrepancy to the traditional male influences, role models, and structures that provide women presidents their perceptions of good leadership and also to the conflicting expectations among both male and female faculty for leaders who are strong and those who are participatory (Jablonski 2000, 248–50).

Research lends support to both perspectives: that women's ways of leading are different from those of men and that there are no gender-based differences. I have been comfortable with the idea that there are more differences within than between the sexes, while I recognize the influence of the special circumstances of women's lives. Both men and women have a continuum of "masculine" and "feminine" behaviors available, as appropriate to the situations they encounter. Mary Patterson McPherson

(1996, 158), president emeritus of Bryn Mawr College, puts it this way: "Biologically there are only two genders, but sociologically and culturally there are many distinguishable shades of masculine and feminine intermixed in endlessly unique ways in the spectrum of individuals." In a blistering attack on a spate of books about "mean" girls, social psychologist Carol Tavris (2002, B8) writes, "[M]ales and females, being human, share in equal measure all the attributes of humanity, its graces and furies. . . . Both are equally likely to be empathic, kind, altruistic, and friendly and to be mean, hostile, aggressive, petty, conformist, and prejudiced. Both sexes can be competitive or cooperative, selfish or nurturant . . . and reveal all of those qualities on different occasions." Conway (2001, 125) applies this view to the presidency: "To me, the argument for including women was one of equity and utility, not some biologically based transformative capacity. I thought the executive role very little modified by the sex of the person who played it."

Transformative Leadership

Transformational and transactional models of leadership are typically presented as dichotomous. Burns (1978, 19–20), for example, describes transactional and transforming leadership as "fundamentally different." Fisher (1994, 61, 65) promotes transformational leadership for a strong, successful, change-oriented academic president, and considers the terms *collegial* and *transactional* coupled with the word *leadership* to be "oxymorons." The key characteristic of Fisher's transformational leader is "social distance," an idea eschewed by academic presidents who prefer to get into the trenches, "down and dirty," through ongoing interaction with constituents.

We do not, however, have to accept transformational and transactional leadership as dichotomous. Bass (1985, 22, 26) asserts that most leaders exhibit a variety of both types of leadership depending on the circumstances. He says, "while conceptually distinct, transformational and transactional leadership are likely to be displayed by the same individuals in different amounts and intensities." Construed as a single continuum of behaviors (Bass 1985, 26; Northouse 2001, 135; Hollander 1987, 7), the two models of leadership can be viewed as available to presidents at different times in the same institution or in institutions with different circumstances. A slightly different take on transactional versus transformational leadership is that good presidents synthesize the two approaches (Birnbaum 1992, 29).

The magical ideal of transformational, charismatic, visionary leadership captivates most academic presidents who feel insufficient if they do not perform that role. In the early stages of this work, I informally queried presidential colleagues on the question of leadership and found that those who consider themselves "transactional" are embarrassed to admit it. Asked to name transformational presidents, however, at most they offer only one or two. Some of those who consider themselves to have transformed their institutions presided over restructuring driven by fiscal exigency, mission creep, or environmental change. These conversational comments on leadership are echoed in the structured interviews I conducted. Pierce, who took advantage of opportunities that arose to lead significant change at the University of Puget Sound, commented, "People who are transformational look at what is, think creatively about how things might be and then go and make it happen. People who are more transactional are more willing to live within an inherited framework and make it work or keep it going" (Pierce Interview 2002). Successful presidents respond to the needs, opportunities, and potential of their institutions, whether for dramatic change or steady strengthening.

To secure additional data on leadership style, I included questions on the topic in the legitimacy survey. I asked presidents if they are transformational, which I defined as "bold, visionary, inspirational," or transactional, which I defined as "collegial, interactive, collaborative." I purposely avoided a more instrumental definition of the latter. Almost 50 percent of survey respondents consider themselves transformational, but, of these, 71 percent say most presidents are transactional. In fact, only 28 percent of the respondents consider themselves transactional. These responses by presidents led me to the conclusion that the terminology about leadership in common use is freighted with outdated conceptions. Transformational leadership gives rise to a strong, heroic, entrepreneurial image recognizable in historically prominent presidents such as Robert Hutchins and James Conant. Transactional leadership, on the other hand, conveys a negative connotation of weakness and incrementalism. A gendered view of leadership also sheds light on why presidents are not comfortable being considered transactional. Gender stereotypes connect the male model of top-down, authoritarian management with transformational leadership and the female model of inclusiveness, teamwork, and communication with transactional leadership. Many presidents who are self-deprecatory about being more transactional than transformational are doing a splendid job. They may find a legacy of transformation when they look into the rearview mirror as they prepare to move on.

Although I did not ask the question on the survey, 23 percent of the respondents indicated they consider themselves both transformational and transactional. Following is a sampling of their instructive comments. "I have never regarded the two styles as contradictory." "Good leadership is both." "Contextual/Situational." "This is not a helpful dichotomy." "Transformational sometimes; transactional often." "A little of both." "I see myself as collegial and collaborative, but have definitely set forth a vision and produced many changes." "Can't one be both?" "About equal—Transformational—This style more for what we'll do; Transactional—This style more for how we do it." "Style is transactional but my goals are transformational." "You have to have both depending on issues." "I urge you not to consider these as mutually exclusive approaches."

I propose adoption of the term "transformative" leadership, which I define as the exercise of either or both presidential authority and constituent collaboration, as appropriate to the situation. Transformative leadership is a more salutary concept than either transformational or transactional for a legitimate and successful president who is promoting a change agenda. It is also different from Burns's notion of transforming leadership, which involves large-scale social change. The use here of transformative leadership is meant to suggest a continuum of behaviors available to all presidents. The concept accepts leadership as contextual and responsive to the needs, opportunities, and challenges confronting an institution at varying points in its history. Importantly, transformative leadership need not diminish the authority or influence of the president. The balance between the president's authority and constituent influence may change as circumstances in institutions change, and presidents must be agile enough to adapt to these new challenges. Experienced presidents see this as evident.

Barry Munitz (1998), former chancellor of the California State University System, says, "[T]here is no single definition of leadership . . . there are different styles . . . different settings . . . [and] contexts. . . . Strong executives require courage, a willingness to take risks, an ability to dream about alternatives while weighing their consequences, and the capacity to engage colleagues . . . toward common goals." Steven Sample (2002, 25), president of the University of Southern California, agrees. He writes, "[L]eadership is highly situational and contingent; that is, what works for me as a leader may not work for you, and what works for me as a leader today may not work for me tomorrow." Despite a contingent view of leadership, both Munitz and Sample have made an impact on their institutions and on higher education. And so has Stephen Trachtenberg, president of The George Washington University, who acknowledged the need for situationally driven leadership in our interview. He says, "Presidents who come in intending to transform an institution can come up against a cultural situation which will push back and defeat them and injure the institution. By contrast there are institutions that seek out a president to do certain kinds of tasks and they are ready for that kind of leadership at that time. Then, when that president leaves, it is not uncommon for the pendulum to swing and for them to seek a totally different personality and skill set" (Trachtenberg Interview 2002).

To initiate and implement change successfully and legitimately, presidents must adapt their style to the imperatives of the institution's needs and culture. Transformational leadership is an alluring idea, which may be inappropriate in situations where there is a powerful culture of collaboration and consultation. Transactional leadership carries with it the liability of perceived weakness, lack of vision, and an inability to inspire. Perhaps by applying new, less freighted, nomenclature, we can legitimate a range of leadership behaviors available to presidents promoting institutional change. "Transformative" leadership is more modest than transformational and more positive than transactional. In the end, what you see in that rearview mirror is what counts.

GOVERNANCE AND CHANGE

Governance Structures

Strong presidents exercise their influence and authority to promote institutional change directly, through the administrative domain of responsibility, or indirectly, through the domains of faculty and board governance, or, most likely, all three. Unless otherwise explicitly formulated by bylaw, the three domains of decision making (trustee, administrative, and faculty) generally operate in silos rather than through a "shared" system. Kenneth Mortimer and T.R. McConnell (1991, 166, 174) draw an important distinction between the notions of shared authority and the more common practice of "separation of jurisdictions." Although the distinction between separate and shared governance responsibilities is significant, the authors maintain that trust and cooperation can enhance legitimacy in governance.

Fisher and Koch (1996, x) hold a different view. From their perspective, collegial leadership presents "insurmountable contradictions," and undermines the president's authority. The president, they say (13), is the final authority under the board in all matters and must be willing to exercise that authority. This view is echoed in the Association of Governing

Boards' (AGB) 1996 report on the academic presidency. The report calls for clarifying and simplifying faculty decision-making processes in order to enhance the president's authority. It also states, "What some academic insiders take pride in as democratic decision making is, in reality, a web of inefficiency that severely limits the ability of some colleges and universities to address the urgent issues they now face" (*Renewing the Academic Presidency* 1996, xi, 8, 19–28).

The AGB view that shared governance weakens presidential leadership and is inimical to responsiveness and adaptability is not universal. According to Martin Trow, faculty governance "is as much a source of presidential power as a limitation on it." He suggests that a strong academic senate is "an instrument for the defense of academic and scholarly standards" and that it exercises its power through "advice to and influence on the president," recognizing that when the president has little power, the faculty has little power (1991, 360). These different perspectives on whether shared governance strengthens or weakens the president emanate from top-down or bottom-up theories of the sources of power. David Hollinger (2001) suggests an inverse power relationship: faculty governance is most powerful when the administration is weak and reactive when the administration is strong.

Trow (1991, 365) argues that presidents exaggerate the importance of shared governance and underplay their own power and effectiveness. He says that successful presidents "have learned the trick of exercising authority without appearing to do so." This is, indeed, the way in which many presidents learn to operate. In crisis situations, presidents have more latitude for administrative action than usual, but even during normal times there are important ways in which presidents can directly influence their institutions. They can, for example, strengthen the quality of the faculty through rigorous hiring and evaluation processes; improve the quality, diversity, and size of the student body by shaping admission and financial aid policies; and assure the quality of facilities by investing in ongoing maintenance. A legitimate, successful president will be very influential in all realms of policy and practice.

To outsiders, the decision-making structures and procedures of higher education seem to be impediments to rather than facilitators of innovation and change. To insiders, though often cumbersome, shared governance is egalitarian and inclusive, drawing on the expertise of professors, administrators, and trustees in decision making. The important concept for trustees and administrators to understand about shared governance is that the faculty comprises well-trained professionals with the expertise and values necessary to participate in decision making, especially, though not exclusively, in regard to the educational program and faculty evaluation standards. To be accepted as legitimate, a change initiative affecting the educational program or academic standards should be validated through the formal faculty governance processes in which the president is presumably an active participant. And although participation is time consuming, the outcomes unpredictable, and the environment ambiguous, inclusiveness in decision making legitimates the president's change agenda.

William Tierney (2001) believes that genuine shared governance is necessary for sustained, successful reform. He calls shared governance the "sine qua non of a culture of respect and innovation." Where such a cultural climate exists, the governance system can facilitate necessary and legitimate changes. Eckel (2000, 33–34) reports on a study of the processes by which four research universities dealt with the hard decision of academic program discontinuance. This study found that the faculties and administrators worked together through their formal governance structures, as well as through informal gatherings and made the tough decisions to eliminate programs. In contrast to the AGB view of the faculty's need for excessive consultation and consensus, Eckel reports that the faculty at those four institutions understood their challenges, worked out an efficient process for decision making, and participated in developing effective strategies. These results contradict the accepted wisdom that faculty will not participate effectively in making tough decisions regarding financial, personnel, and program cutbacks. Hollinger (2001) asserts, "If you give the faculty something important to do, they can often do it, contrary to the slander of some career administrators that rank-and-file faculty cannot be trusted with power."

Presidents with an academic background tend to enjoy the thrust and parry of faculty governance. Despite its frustrations, they appreciate the value of the deliberative process. Conway (2001, 62) writes, "I actually enjoyed faculty politics, because I believed in the tradition of faculty self-governance, no matter how shortsighted the immediate outcomes. Over time, the traditions of scholarly discourse usually brought a sensible conclusion. And the tension between president and faculty was mostly creative." In my conversation (2002) with Christopher Nelson, president of St. Johns College in Annapolis, he noted that shared governance is "an impediment to bad change."

Although the highly discursive and consultative decision-making processes of the faculty are frustrating to many presidents and boards, higher education provides a working example of shared governance and democracy in action. Nannerl O. Koehane (1998, 15–17), president of Duke

University, compares the modern campus to a democratic political system, with extensive checks and balances governing relationships among the board, faculty, and administration. The president sets the agenda and involves the appropriate stakeholders in the processes necessary to create change. As discussed in chapter 5, faculty attribute success or failure to their presidents based, in part, on the latter "taking the faculty role" and communicating, collaborating, consulting, and acknowledging faculty governance. Presidents who can take the faculty role are also able to gain approval and support for their change initiatives and are seen as effective leaders (Bensimon 1991, 639–52). This is consistent with responses to my survey on legitimacy. Presidents overwhelmingly indicated that successful institutional change requires "consultation," "communication," "listening," "involvement," "trust," "buy-in," "collegiality," "partnerships," "constituent support," "shared vision," "shared goals," and "shared governance."

The 1966 Statement on Government of Colleges and Universities (1991, 160) attempts to clarify the respective roles of governing boards, faculties, and administrations, while acknowledging the increasing control of external bodies and the decreasing autonomy of higher education institutions. In essence, the board has policy and fiduciary responsibility for the institution, and the faculty, based on its professional expertise, has responsibility for most academic decisions. The "conduct of administration" is entrusted to the president, who runs the institution based on board policy and faculty prerogatives. Since the 1966 statement was promulgated, the encroachment of external bodies (e.g., the federal and state governments, business, alumni, and donors) on academic decision making has increased. Robert Berdahl points out that when an institution has fewer powers of self-governance, the substantive domain to be shared is diminished and must be redefined (Berdahl 1991, 217, 223). A diminished domain of decision making results in a reduction in the share of governance responsibilities allocated to trustees, administrators, and faculties.

Strategic Planning

An inclusive, collaborative, and comprehensive strategic planning process can serve as a major legitimating mechanism for change. With sufficient legitimacy and social capital, the president, working with senior faculty, can establish an ad hoc planning process; however, formal governance procedures should be followed to legitimate the process, as well as the resultant plan. In his influential 1983 book, *Academic Strategy*, George

Keller (61) assesses traditional governance as inadequate, "slowly collapsing or becoming dormant," and refers to traditional faculty senates as "ragged, poorly attended oratorical bodies." Keller's (127) special contribution is his identification of an emerging phenomenon, a new kind of "cabinet government," comprising senior faculty members and key administrators, able to provide wiser, speedier counsel in connecting academic and financial issues through long-range planning. In a follow-up study testing Keller's thesis, Jack Schuster et al. (1994, 192) propose a variant type of collaborative body, the "strategic planning council," to bridge the traditional gulf between planning and governance. The two spheres, they point out, are most often "out of sync" with each other. Planning is generally "administratively driven and externally responsive," and governance is "faculty driven and internally oriented" (193–94). The best plans, they point out, are of little use if the faculty does not consider them legitimate (7). The strategic planning council is strategic and transparent, connects with governance, and requires "astute" presidential leadership to make it successful (199–200).

The first element in strategic planning is the aspirational vision statement, anchored in the history and values of the institution and developed by the president together with the faculty and trustees. Unfortunately, vision statements tend to be generalizations about competitive institutional positioning. "We will be the best in our category." "We will move into a better category." "We will be number one in this group." "We will be the only institution in this niche." The problem with most institutional vision statements is that they reflect an aspiration to be the best, the first, or the only. Rarely are vision statements focused on achieving excellence in what the institution already does well, or becoming one of the top performers instead of number one within a peer group. This point is well made in Bloland's (1987, 6–7) stinging critique of the aggressive, military, winner-take-all approach of most strategic plans. He suggests that, instead, "universities might come to grips with their own vulnerability and seek cooperation with other institutions as they begin to see how much they need their neighbors, and they understand how little of value will remain in a game that leaves one player alone in a niche."

A vision can be articulated and forgotten, engraved on paperweights and trivialized, or enacted through institutional behavior. The president keeps the vision alive and the institution focused. A loyal and thoughtful board participates in strategic planning, policy development, and funding of initiatives, but a president must depend on the leadership of senior administrators and faculty to help translate the vision into action. The faculty generally has its own academic agenda and may be resistant to change, requiring a deft, enthusiastic, and legitimate president to use every opportunity to promote the vision and influence the institution's direction. While the strategic planning process can be orchestrated by the administration and take place outside the constraints of the governance system, the prospects for successful institutionalization rest on the legitimacy of board and faculty action in support of the proposals.

Once the community has accepted a vision for the institution, the process of establishing the mission and strategic goals for change can begin. An inclusive process involves all constituencies in a review of the institution's challenges and opportunities and a reassessment of its mission and goals. The president's challenge is to find a way to collaborate with others in the planning process, not dominating, yet influencing, the outcome. The president's imprimatur is vital because he or she will have to believe in, communicate, and raise money for the institution's strategic goals. Although vision and strategic planning are concepts adopted from the business world, they serve as useful tools for colleges and universities when undertaken seriously, implemented, and assessed. The process itself can be renewing, affirming, and community building, and it makes the institution isomorphic with the business world, thus enhancing its credibility with key external constituencies. There are also important symbolic aspects of change that should be encouraged along with rational, instrumental approaches. "Leaders need to think about how they can convene, encourage, and become active participants in rituals, social dramas, and healing dances as a means of transforming modern organizations" (Deal 1985, 324). A strategic plan should create momentum for change; it should drive institutional positioning, decision making, budgeting, and fund-raising. And, not least, the planning process should enhance presidential legitimacy by embedding the incumbent deeply into the fabric of the institution.

The environment for planning is increasingly complex and as Ronald Barnett (2001, 15) points out: "In an age of uncertainty, in which perhaps nothing can count as its 'core' business, what substance—if any—might attach to a university's 'mission'? Is the idea of mission not now simply an attempt to carve out an arena of sureness where none exists?" Barnett goes on to question whether a university can actually develop a strategy for itself given the difficulty of predicting the future in a complex, rapidly changing world. Barnett (26–27, 31) concludes, "[T]he university's self understanding has to be kept more or less permanently under review" and that managers need to present new frameworks and create forums for discussion. It falls to leadership to enable the university "to make collective *choices* over the frameworks with which it will be primarily identified, even if other contesting frames are still to be found in the practices and self-understandings of its internal networks." Thus, we need to alter our approach to planning, to accept it as an ongoing process, and to create a strategic plan that is flexible and responsive to the changing environment. The administration is best situated to maintain a process to scan the environment for changes that may be inconsistent with the institution's operating frameworks. Today's strategic plan must be constantly under review in response to changing internal and external conditions and trends.

Successful change and improvement define a president's legacy, but new initiatives generally call for new resources, without which most strategic plans are dead on arrival. The most flexible resources are those garnered in a fund-raising campaign, which often follows the planning process. Given the ambiguous and unpredictable environment for decision making and the complexities of leadership, governance, and strategic planning, a president must be able to rely on significant internal and external social capital to assure support for institutional change.

SOCIAL CAPITAL AND CHANGE

Social capital (the erosion of which was discussed in chapter 7, as a threat to presidential legitimacy) is the accretion within a community of honest and cooperative behavior, shared norms, and a "prevalence of trust" (Fukuyama 1995, 26). This is important, says Coleman, because groups with extensive trustworthiness and trust are able to accomplish much more than comparable groups without them (1988, S101). A president can draw on social capital to develop a consensus for change. In a report on change in higher education institutions, the authors found that in the absence of trust, "stakeholders will focus on preserving rights and privileges rather than taking risks to create a future with the common good in mind." Distrust, they say, makes organizations dysfunctional (Eckel et al. 1999, 9). The president's ability to initiate and implement change depends on the development of relationships of mutual influence and trust with internal and external constituents—the bedrock of social capital. Bourdieu (1986, 251) states that every group has a mechanism allowing it "to concentrate the totality of the social capital, which is the basis of the existence of the group . . . in the hands of a single agent, to mandate this plenipotentiary . . . to represent the group." From this perspective, presidents who are explicitly or tacitly granted the authority to represent or embody the group's values and goals have attained a high degree of legitimacy.

Relationships are at the heart of a successful presidency, and cannot mature in a short time; they depend on both presidential legitimacy and longevity. Good relationships are key to improvements in institutional quality, reputation, and resource development. To initiate and implement change successfully, a president who has achieved legitimacy depends on the network of relationships developed over time. Judith McLaughlin calls relationships "the coin of the realm" for college presidents (Basinger 2001, A22). Experienced presidents and trustees know that longevity makes a significant difference in the ability of a president to promote change and to generate significant external support. This was affirmed in a 1988 survey in which presidents of top-ranked colleges and universities report spending an increasing proportion of their time in external relations and note that the longer they are in office, the more time they spend with these constituencies (Dyson and Kirkman 1989). These relationships are vital to generating support for the institution. Stephen Trachtenberg puts it this way: "Gifts, though nominally to the institution, celebrate the relationship of the president and the benefactor." Further, Trachtenberg believes that longevity is "imperative" for change because it creates "the possibility of consistency of vision." Most things in universities, he says, "don't happen fast, so it calls for tremendous persistence" (Trachtenberg Interview 2002).

Every constituent group is important to an institution, but trustees, faculty, and senior administrators are the president's key constituents. A president who has secured the support of all three constituencies is considered successful and "has a claim to being a good leader" (Birnbaum 1992, 56–61). The president's spouse serves as a vital ally in developing these relationships. The spouse has a role to play with each constituency, and she or he must also come to be accepted as a good fit with the culture. Such acceptance adds to the legitimacy of the president and strengthens the institution's social capital.

For change, radical or incremental, to occur, key stakeholders must feel they have been a part of the planning process, understand how the change fits into the culture, and be supportive, if not enthusiastic. It is the president who inspires and enables key constituents to consider and embrace change. Hanna Gray, president emerita of the University of Chicago, asserts that academic leadership is about enabling individuals to "meet their own highest standards," and enabling institutions to reach their goals (Gray 1998, 114). The challenge for the president is to develop consensus around the need for change among the disparate cultures of constituent groups. This requires that the president move comfortably from one group to another, serving as interpreter, translator, and cheerleader. In the process, the president creates a narrative that evolves to reflect the interests of each group, incorporates familiar institutional symbols and heroes, and engages constituents in a common enterprise. To be credible, proposed changes must be anchored in the institution's history and traditions, and grow out of a collaborative institutional process of envisioning and planning the future.

In times of crisis, presidents and boards may feel they must act decisively and quickly, without much communication or collaboration. They worry that if they involve the faculty, necessary and immediate action will be delayed by lengthy deliberations, an attempt to preserve faculty status and prerogatives, or an effort to save traditional programs. Although unilateral administrative action may be necessary to protect an institution, it must be weighed against the inevitable loss of trust and support among faculty, students, and alumni. Such was the case at Bennington, where the president and board took action to keep the college alive but, in the process, suffered a loss of social capital, at least in the short run. Presidents successful in implementing their agendas for change are attentive to their ongoing relationships with all constituencies—trustees, faculty, administrators, students, alumni, community leaders, politicians, and donors.

Trustees: Leaders and Servants

The board's enthusiastic support is vital to the legitimacy, success, and longevity of the president. Respondents to my survey on legitimacy made it clear that board support is vital to a president's change agenda, and also that the loss of board support leads to the loss of the presidency. Kauffman points out that "it is very difficult for any constituent group to dislodge a president who has the full confidence of the governing board . . . [and] difficult to retain the support of constituencies when it becomes evident to them that the board has lost confidence in the president" (1989, 36). The board's support for change is more readily forthcoming when the president has gained legitimacy, is successful at fund-raising, meets enrollment targets, balances the budget, prevents crises, improves the quality and reputation of the institution, has the support of key constituents, and is noncontroversial. Trustees do not like controversy and may waver in their support of the president in the face of constituent discontent. They would do well to remember that controversy about a president's actions is inevitable, and they need to evaluate the source, cause, and significance of the opposition before intervening. Actions such as program elimination, downsizing, tenure denial, and budget reallocation are likely to generate negative reactions. As long as the board has been fully informed in advance about the rationale for such actions, members need to stand behind the president.

Because the board is a president's most important constituency for change, it also deserves the most attention. Shaping, educating, and collaborating with a board are key to the implementation of a president's vision. In both independent and public boards, the chair should be a staunch supporter of the president, provide helpful feedback, and be available for frequent consultation. Highly politicized state boards tend to be more responsive to gubernatorial and legislative interests than to the priorities of the president and the faculty. This undermines the president's ability to exercise strong leadership, develop a collective vision for the future, and mobilize the human and financial resources necessary for growth and change.

In an effective relationship, the president and the chair assume responsibility, with the nominating committee, for building a strong board. The ideal board is ethnically and racially diverse, comprising women and men, with a mix of corporate, alumni, philanthropic, and community leaders. It should include representatives from the range of occupations that are helpful to the institution—for example, academics, lawyers, accountants, real estate developers, bankers, investment advisors, former government officials. At the same time, boards must enforce a strict conflict of interest policy to assure that business and personal interests do not influence decision making. Attorney Martin Michaelson (2002, 37) asserts: "At the core of superior college and university governance is a vibrant collaboration between president and board." He refers to "great trusteeship" as requiring "extraordinary knowledge, insight, judgment, and commitment," and wisely notes that the success of president-board collaboration depends "on a mutual ceding of primacy." A long-time board member describes the board's responsibility as "the most exquisite exercise of cooperation and self-discipline," which requires, in part, that the board express its active interest in university affairs without micromanaging (Levao 2002, 36–37).

Board members should be informed early and thoroughly about all issues and problems. Presidents must also assure that their administrators are honest and open with the board. No board can be helpful or make good decisions if not educated, informed, and involved. Susan Resneck Pierce (Interview 2002), president of the University of Puget Sound, warns against "getting out ahead of your board and moving to initiate or deny things that are surprises. . . . Even for a good idea, not paving the way with the board (or the faculty) will create a problem. . . . If the president and the board are not seeing things in the same way, nothing is going to work." Board orientation and continuing education are vital. Board members need to be familiar with the institution's academic, athletic, and student life programs, appreciate the rationale for tenure and academic freedom, understand the financial statements, and participate in establishing investment policies. They also need to be clear about their role as advisers and policy makers, and not get involved in micromanaging the institution. Nothing undermines and delegitimates a president as much as trustee overinvolvement in the day-to-day affairs of the institution. Although some trustees express dismay over repeated requests for annual and capital support, board members have an obligation to support the institution financially as their capacity permits. The old adage "give, get, or get off" is still appropriate.

Although the president is the board's primary liaison with the faculty, often trustees, especially alumni, have their own special relationships with campus constituents. Unaware of the scope of these contacts, presidents may be blindsided by issues raised by trustees based on private conversations with students, faculty, or staff. As part of ongoing trustee orientation, the president and board chair must make it clear that all such issues are better discussed first with the president, enabling her or him to investigate the matter in advance of any discussion at the board level. While it is healthy and necessary for trustees to have opportunities to hear directly from faculty and students, such interactions must not reduce the president's authority or legitimacy. Trustees can protect themselves and strengthen their presidents by refusing to accept complaints and issues brought to them by constituents. All such matters should, as a matter of course, be referred to the president.

Most trustees recognize that no institution is better than its faculty, composed of highly trained and committed professionals who deliver the educational program. Rarely, however, do corporate trustees understand the value of tenure, which seems to many to be a boondoggle. At the same time, faculties are suspicious of the corporate mind-set of trustees and the incursion of business values into the academy. The cultures of the board and the faculty are so different as to require interpretation, and the cultural boundaries between the groups are challenging to navigate. One of the president's key roles with the board is to explain and defend faculty prerogatives, especially tenure and academic freedom. With the faculty, the president is often called upon to explain the board's interest in strategic planning, fiscal prudence, and accountability. As Koehane (1998, 14) points out, "Caught between . . . trustee authority and faculty prerogatives, presidents can sometimes feel more like the rope in a game of tug-of-war than a chief executive officer."

Despite the inevitable tensions, to be successful in promoting change and improvement, presidents need guidance and input, as well as support and independence from their boards. A president's ability to lead and inspire change is directly related to the board's willingness to empower the president to influence policy and manage the institution. Unless a board is ready to replace the president, a move costly to the institution, it needs to reign in members' tendencies to micromanage and to initiate their own ideas for change. At the same time, board expertise is vital in financial, investment, construction, and commercial matters because it rounds out the experience of the administration and its consultants. The board's endorsement and support are especially necessary in times of campus conflict, and the board's feedback from community, business, and political leaders about institutional change is invaluable. The board must grant the president independence of action, consistent with board policy, to experiment, innovate, and make decisions—even, occasionally, mistakes. When things are going well, board members should find opportunities to express their enthusiasm and encouragement to the president, who often hears nothing but criticism. Trustees are aware of the extraordinary and unremitting pressures on their presidents but may not realize how their own involvement, constancy, and support can assuage the stress and tension of the job. Positive board behaviors legitimate both the president and the institution.

Faculty: Experts and Innocents

Building relationships of trust and collaboration with the faculty is vital to moving an internal agenda for change. Although presidents must focus on building relationships with external constituents—trustees, prospects, legislators, community leaders, and corporate executives—they neglect relationship building with faculty at their peril. A faculty that does not feel a sense of community will not be supportive of change initiatives but will be more likely to sabotage them. Faculties tend to be nostalgic for some imagined Eden when there was a communal instead of a "corporate" environment. When the faculty perceives the power balance in governance to be unfairly tipped toward the administration or the board, campus community breaks down. It is arguable that the idea of community is a chimera and that faculty members preserve their identity in part by nurturing a schism between themselves and the administration. This separation of interests is at its most formal when the workforce is unionized. The gulf that exists between faculty and administrators is larger or smaller depending on the history and type of institution.

Faculty relate to administrators in three ways.

1. There are those who are always hostile and do not believe that administrators ever have their best interests at heart. Flawn warns presidents
   not to take faculty criticism personally: "It is not you as an individual
   but rather the position of president that offends them. They resent
   authority and particularly the fact that you receive a salary higher than
   theirs" (1990, 79).
2. Some faculty members are apathetic and uninvolved; they remain indifferent to the best efforts of their colleagues and their president.
3. Finally, and fortunately, there are those who are energized by visionary
   administrators and willing to work collaboratively for institutional improvement.

Presidents who have a change agenda need to involve the latter group
and to build a critical mass of support. With sufficient social capital, along
with mutually developed, legitimate decision-making mechanisms,
change, incremental or radical, has a chance of being implemented and
institutionalized. Even the most harmonious campus communities, however, may be resistant to systemic change unless the institution is facing
a threat to its stability. While administrators may scan the environment
and develop plans for curricular change responsive to student needs, faculties tend to focus on pedagogy and scholarship related to their personal
fields of interest. In the end, we need to accept faculty preoccupation with
their students and their professional work as a good thing. Universities
and colleges are strengthened and students well prepared more through
the commitment and contributions of individual professors than through
overarching educational schema that may be devised by administrators.

Presidents often complain about the resistance of faculties to change.
Experts in their disciplines, faculty members tend to be innocents regarding trends in higher education. Fisher and Koch write, "The innate academic conservatism of tenured, senior faculty at American institutions of
higher education reflects many things, including their own significant
managerial role and their insulation from the forces of the marketplace"
(1996, 155). Faculties tend not to follow trends in education, curriculum,
student attitudes, or faculty work. They value their traditional culture,
resist "newfangled" ideas, and distrust administration reports about financial or environmental challenges. When administrators propose changes
to the curriculum, based on changing student interests and preferences,
the faculty's sense of expertise and control is compromised. Trachtenberg
says, "What faculties want from their presidents is more facilities and resources, not innovation. . . . If I were to propose new curricular innova-

tions, I would be seen as meddling in faculty affairs and behaving inappropriately" (Trachtenberg Interview 2002). Despite the turf issues and the tendency to parochialism and insularity of faculty, Fisher and Koch (1996, 155) admit, "little of consequence can happen on a campus without at least their implicit agreement." They suggest that the president use the power of the office and communicate an exciting vision, a sense of mission, and incentives to increase faculty openness to change.

Presidents of emerging institutions or those in crisis have a great deal of latitude to lead academic innovation, and those who have gained considerable legitimacy may be able to lead the faculty in strengthening evaluation criteria, making curricular revisions, and shaping admissions criteria. However, despite the concept of the "academic" presidency, faculty governance mitigates against presidential leadership in relation to educational programs. Daniel Perlman (1989, 4) reports on the common experience of presidents who, as candidates, are quizzed about their views on academic matters, but whose involvement, as incumbents, is resisted. In practice, curriculum and student life issues are generally delegated to faculty and deans since external relations require the president's personal attention as the sole embodiment and personification of the institution. There are exceptions to this, but they are rare.

Even for presidents with a traditional academic pedigree, relations with the faculty are a challenge. This vital constituency, says David Warren, "is the source of greatest angst for the president . . . especially on issues of budget, tenure, and the curriculum. . . . The president must be politically adroit, using the process that faculty honors" (Warren Interview 2002). The president's main influence is through persuasion and reward, using the leverage available through budgeting, fund-raising, and slack resources. A president may also influence the process indirectly through academic administrators and faculty leaders, who can orchestrate the political effort necessary to develop a consensus for change. Christopher Nelson points out that some presidents act "invisibly" and "behind the scenes" in order to effect changes in curriculum, evaluation, or other areas of faculty governance without appearing authoritarian. This approach is validated by the ACE Project on Leadership and Institutional Transformation. A project report indicates that presidents in the participating institutions "had to balance both visible and invisible work in the change process." Publicly, the president must champion the change agenda and focus the institution on the effort. At the same time, the president has to delegate the work, as well as the credit for success, to others. And, importantly, the report urges governing boards to "value a president who is a collaborative leader" (Hill et al. 2001, 8).

To promote change, presidents and their administrators must bring faculty into the environmental scanning and decision-making processes, and provide transparency about budget and financial matters. As Stanley Fish (2001), dean at the University of Illinois at Chicago, puts it, "always tell the truth; tell more of the truth than you have to; tell the truth before anyone asks you to." No president can expect to have every faculty member's support all of the time, but a two-way flow of information and influence can help dispel the tendency toward suspicion and mistrust. This means that presidents must also make time for participation in faculty affairs. As noted earlier, Trow (1991, 360) believes that a strong faculty senate enhances the power of the president by providing the consultation and support without which relations would be "largely adversarial."

Some presidents elect to delegate academic responsibilities to the academic vice president. This is most likely at large universities where, increasingly, presidents must focus on legislative and donor relations. This bifurcation of responsibilities is a loss, however, since most presidents find the faculty culture as stimulating and comfortable as it is complicated. Presidents move from faculty to trustee to other constituent groups, interpreting each to the other, developing a shared story, and mobilizing support for change. To have credibility with the faculty, presidents need to identify with the academic culture, respect the shared governance structure, publicize the dedication and involvement of the faculty, and explain faculty prerogatives to trustees and business leaders. Faculty support is critical to a successful presidency. It is a necessary linchpin of change and an important element in presidential tenure. Boards tend to react, indeed to overreact, to faculty dissatisfaction with a president. At times, however, boards will "support autocratic leadership and remain indifferent over an extended period of time to opposition from faculty and others" (Birnbaum 1988, 205). Higher education has had a number of high-profile situations where the board maintained strong support of a president despite significant faculty opposition. The legitimacy and longevity of these presidents is based on the measurable improvement to their institutions' quality and reputation.

Administrators: Colleagues and Rivals

While board and faculty support are necessary for change, the senior administration is key to a president's success. No decisions are more important then the selection of a senior team that is experienced, smart, loyal, hardworking, and enthusiastic. As Steven Sample, president of the University of Southern California, writes, "Leaders rise and fall based on the performance of their subordinates" (2002, 27). A president is only as good as the top team. The errors as well as the successes of administrators are attributed to the president, and they have the power to legitimate or delegitimate the president's change agenda. Many of the presidents who responded to my survey on legitimacy affirmed this by stressing the importance of a "strong," "committed," and "loyal" senior administration team to successful change.

The president must be clear about expectations and standards for the performance and behavior of administrators. And, no matter how loyal, bright, innovative, courageous, and experienced the senior administrators are, the president needs them to coalesce into a well-functioning team, able to respond to faculty and board demands while forwarding the president's agenda. Integrating new administrators into a mutually supportive team can be a challenge. Senior administrators, if they are appointed from within the institution, often have relationships and loyalties older and stronger than with the president. This can be helpful when a consensus needs to be developed but can also be used to undermine the president. Administrators who come from other institutions are often accustomed to a different way of operating or style of management. These experiences can enhance or sabotage the development of an effective new team. Presidents also have to respond to a tendency among senior administrators to jockey for power and position. They seek the president's ear privately in order to complain about each other, to secure special favors, or to gain support for new positions or programs. Judith McLaughlin refers to this as "sibling rivalry," cautioning that presidents, like parents, be wary of appearing to have favorites (private conversation).

Senior administrators must learn not to delegate problems up to the president and to accept responsibility for unpopular decisions, except in special, agreed-upon situations. By remaining above the fray as senior statespersons, presidents can preserve their store of social capital, essential for promoting change initiatives. Successful administrators understand and value faculty culture and prerogatives along with the traditions of the institution. They also understand the differences between nonprofit and for-profit organizations. Higher education institutions have a mission of service to society even though in many ways they operate like businesses. Leaders are called upon to dedicate themselves first to the mission of their institutions and second to their careers. This means that senior administrators have the same obligation as presidents not to pursue their personal social or political agendas if doing so has negative consequences for their institutions. Academic vice presidents and deans are likely to find themselves pulled into conflicts that may arise between the faculty and the board. Academic administrators tend to identify with faculty perspectives and need their support to be effective. At the same time, trustees reflect the opinions of the larger community and the alumni body. As the final arbiters of institutional policy, their views will generally prevail. Politically savvy presidents and senior administrators prevent confrontations with the board when at all possible.

Successful administrative relationships are characterized by expertise, loyalty, and reciprocity (Bornstein 2000), all of which contribute to the social capital necessary for a well-functioning administration. Presidents can assure sufficient expertise by selecting administrators who provide the skills and knowledge they may be lacking themselves. Unlike expertise, which can be unequally distributed between a president and vice president, loyalty must exist equally and absolutely. Because of their relationships with the president's key constituents, disloyal vice presidents can delegitimate a presidency. As Freedman points out, "administrators can do you in because they become very close with the board." This is especially true of financial and development vice presidents. It undermines the president when the chief development officer says to a board member, "I wish we could get [the president] on the road more often" (Interview 2002). Administrators must be loyal to their presidents, who need to know what their constituencies are thinking, what rumors are circulating, and how administrative initiatives are being received. Presidents aware of negative constituent opinion can position themselves to take appropriate action. Loyal administrators must enthusiastically promote the president's vision and actions, share information, provide honest feedback, take responsibility for decisions, and use the president's time wisely.

Reciprocity is also essential for a well-functioning team. In return for the loyalty and good performance of administrators, the president must reciprocate with visible support, competitive compensation, and opportunities for professional development. Such support requires that a president be sensitive to the possible interest of a vice president in seeking a presidency or other position. If the interest seems inappropriate or premature, the president needs to provide counsel on professional preparation or alternative possibilities. When the timing is right, a president owes a loyal senior administrator support and encouragement to advance professionally (Bornstein 2000, 28).

All senior administrators think they understand the presidency, based on the hours they spend working with and observing the president. In fact, their primary observation of the president's functioning occurs mainly in their own domain—academic, financial, or external—and they do not see the entirety of a president's life. After a Rollins vice president was called to a presidency of his own, he e-mailed me that "having been close to you, I thought that I had a good idea of the demands on a president's time. In fact, I only knew a fraction!" Although a loss, personally and institutionally, it is a great privilege to send a senior staffer on to a presidency. In the same e-mail message, this new president concluded, "I am not complaining, though. As you noted, it is a great job!" (Edmondson 2001).

The chief academic officer is the president's most important internal colleague in the pursuit of institutional change. Without the leadership of a credible, legitimate, visionary chief academic officer, the president's academic goals have no traction. On the other hand, under the leadership of an enthusiastic internal academic leader who understands the culture and is familiar with trends in the wider academic world, the president's academic legacy is far more assured. The president and chief academic officer (CAO) must have a close and trusting relationship, and function as a team. This can be a challenging role for the CAO, who depends on close ties with the faculty. Despite this, the academic officer's main loyalty is to the president. The chief financial officer (CFO) is also a key element in a president's success or failure. A close working relationship, complete honesty, and confidentiality can help assure the financial health and growth of the institution. The CFO can also undermine the president's legitimacy by failing to consult with faculty and participate in governance processes. Operating in a more corporate mode than the other administrators, the CFO has to work especially hard to appreciate the values of the academy. An insensitive financial vice president can create serious delegitimating problems for the president.

A special relationship exists between the president and the chief advancement officer since they are involved together in numerous activities with prospects, donors, alumni, community leaders, politicians, and media representatives. They also spend considerable time together, preparing for meetings and social events. The advancement chief should weed out unnecessary invitations, delegate some functions to others, and help the president determine which events are necessary to attend, how long to stay, and whether the spouse's attendance is required. The public relations office, ideally located in advancement, is responsible for the "positioning" of the president, a key role that is not well understood or executed. Once having attained legitimacy, the president "functions as the embodiment of the institution, not simply as a representative of the institution. . . . Alumni, community members, corporate executives—all base their involvement with the institution on a belief in the president."

The advancement and public relations professionals "must believe in the president's vision and create a sense of the president's values through their introductions, conversations, and printed materials" (Bornstein 2000, 27).

The president must have a close, trusting relationship with the presidential assistant (PA). When the fit is right, the PA becomes the president's alter ego, anticipating her or his needs, preparing essential information for the endless array of events, and providing necessary feedback and cautions. PAs, if carefully selected, are indispensable to their presidents, and provide a variety of support services depending on the president's needs and preferences. In the best of circumstances, the PA develops a high level of trust among constituents who seek advice about concerns and problems and whether they should be conveyed to the president. The PA, in turn, serves as a repository and filter of information, passing along to the president that which seems essential, as well as delegating appropriate issues to others. PAs work long hours, largely behind the scenes, and must, themselves, develop legitimacy with key constituents. Having a disloyal or incompetent executive assistant is a recipe for disaster.

The administrative organization of institutions varies considerably, but, however constituted, vice presidents, deans, and directors must all coalesce into an effective unit and promote the president's change agenda. No president can be successful or legitimate without the support of a strong and well-functioning administrative team.

Students: Challengers and Builders

No faculty is ever entirely satisfied with the current crop of students. Like the Smith College faculty in the 1970s, they recall a "brighter student generation in a mythical golden past" (Conway 2001, 113). Although the admissions office may boast that an institution's selectivity has improved steadily, faculty question the veracity of the numbers and lament the preparation students have received in high school, or both. When discussing initiatives to strengthen the quality of an institution, faculties tend to focus on attracting better students.

Presidents work hard to make time to listen to and be involved with students, and find those experiences invigorating and rewarding. Many presidents revive themselves by walking around campus and talking with students; they find that such activities reconnect them with the institution's mission. However, students, individually and through their organizations, make many demands on their institutions. Experienced presidents respond to those initiatives deemed helpful and stall on others. Student concerns are mostly about immediate short-term problems; they have a fleeting attention span depending on their progress through a semester and toward graduation. Some of the demands students make must be addressed; others are unreasonable.

New rules for student behavior or activities often set off a storm of protest against administrators who may be called uncaring, insufficiently student-oriented, and unsupportive of student prerogatives. Students have the idea that there was a time at college when the atmosphere was much more relaxed and behavior unchecked. They hardly believe that there were dress codes, curfews, visitation limits, and housemothers. While some students create problems by binge drinking, hazing, and harassment, others are motivated to address significant political and social issues. The militancy and efficacy of student demonstrations in the 1960s and 1970s have provided models and impetus for protests against sweatshop conditions in multinational businesses, for "living-wage" adjustments for college and university employees, for controls on global warming, and against war. Many students are drawn to service projects in their local communities or in developing countries. There is no substitute for a service experience that transforms a student's understanding of the world and empowers that student to organize for positive social change.

Students are often responsible for innovation in academic programming and pedagogy, especially when the faculty is responsive to their changing needs, interests, and learning styles. When students first began coming to college using the World Wide Web for learning and for fun, most institutions were not prepared but quickly invested in computer technology and training. Many faculty members immediately began to incorporate technology in their classrooms, but others, especially in the humanities, resisted allowing anything to come between them and their students. However, as faculty themselves became addicted to the Internet and learned its pedagogical possibilities, they began to find ways of incorporating its use into their syllabi. We now acknowledge that technology is transforming pedagogy, scholarship, and the very meaning of college.

Undergraduate as well as graduate students can make a contribution to the planning, implementation, and assessment of change. They can also obstruct change initiatives. Because of their lack of experience, the value of their input to planning and governance processes is modest, yet the lessons they learn through their participation serve them well. Organized student opposition to change initiatives serves to alert administrators and faculty to possible problems. Protest is also a life-changing learning experience for students who, we hope, will be change agents in their own communities and workplaces.

Alumni: Gatekeepers and Hosts

The alumni constituency is one of the most critical to the president and the most vexing. Alumni see themselves as protectors of the institution's traditions and values, and woe unto any president who makes changes that appear to threaten the beloved culture. What are the changes that agitate alumni? Modernizing a long-standing curriculum requirement, banning a "harmless" hazing ritual, sanctioning a fraternity, firing a popular coach, contracting with a private company to manage a college radio station, renaming the mascot, to list a few. Changes to "the way things were" are likely to result in a flood of hostile e-mails, letters, phone calls, and visits to the president. When exercised, alumni are perfectly willing to actively interfere and protest without having all the information that led to a change. Frequently, these protests are coupled with the threat that financial support will cease, as was the case in the late 1990s with several University of Chicago alumni who were angry about curriculum changes (Bartlett 2002, A10–A11). Experienced presidents chuckle at this threat because the complainers are often modest or nondonors, and it would not derail an important change initiative.

Despite the countless examples of intrusive, intemperate, and destructive alumni behavior, presidents learn that alumni support and involvement are vital in legitimating significant change efforts. Once alumni leaders have accorded legitimacy to a president, they happily provide the institutional stories and dreams that can be woven into the president's narratives. They claim the president's vision as their own, and provide resources that will help strengthen their beloved college or university. The great danger for presidents is to take alumni support for granted and neglect this constituency after the first few years. While reining in intrusive alumni, presidents need to continuously expand the number of alumni who are involved with the institution. As with other constituencies, strong relationships and a buildup of trust will enhance the support for change.

Community Leaders: Suppliers and Buyers

Universities and colleges generally provide a plethora of opportunities for community involvement in education, culture, sports, and other activities. They also provide an arena, a "town hall," where community issues can be debated in a neutral environment. These institutions do not pay taxes on mission-driven activities, but contribute to the health of their communities in myriad ways.

Despite the acknowledged contributions of an institution to its community, local governance bodies may impede change and growth on campus. Planning and zoning standards frequently conflict with designs for new campus and commercial facilities. Town-gown relations are always fragile, but can be strengthened when the president and other administrators are active in civic affairs, serve on community boards, and participate in community service. Business and community leaders depend on local colleges and universities to help provide an economically attractive environment and to educate the workforce to meet business needs. Community opposition to campus projects can delegitimate a president's initiatives, so presidents need to build and nourish community relations. New commercial or institutional construction projects almost always occasion opposition, so the community and the town council must be educated about the benefits of the project: a commercial project will add tax revenue to the town, a parking garage will clear the streets and support local businesses, a new performing arts center will serve both the community and the university.

A well-known and successful college or university will attract top candidates for its board, and a successful president will receive many direct and indirect inquiries from community and business leaders who wish to serve. Such interest demonstrates confidence in the institution but creates pressure on the president as he or she participates in community activities.

Politicians: Givers and Takers

Today, private as well as public institutions depend on state support for a portion of their revenue. Presidents of public institutions have turned increasingly to tuition and philanthropy to augment their revenues in order to stabilize their programs against the annual uncertainty about funding and to gain more autonomy from state regulation. A number of states offer matching gift incentives to encourage fund-raising in public institutions. To increase access and the production of college graduates, some states provide a modest subsidy to residents who attend private institutions. Public university presidents also have the challenge of working with highly politicized boards that may be reconstituted after every election season. As the line between public and private institutions continues to blur, presidents in both sectors have a stake in legislative and government decision making. While relationship building is vital to the ongoing lobbying necessary to secure much-needed resources in a competitive environment, presidents struggle to resist pressure to align themselves with candidates and parties. A 1994 survey of presidents at private institutions revealed that most do not believe they should become involved in partisan politics—82 percent said that presidents should subordinate their personal views and political beliefs to the interests of their institutions, and 74 percent responded that presidents should not be involved in partisan politics. On the other hand, 55 percent of respondents said they contribute to political campaigns, 37 percent attend fund-raising events, 19 percent publicly endorse candidates, and 10 percent host political fund-raisers (Bornstein 1995, 58–59). Presidents are challenged to protect their institutions from partisan politics while building strong relationships with legislators and politicians of both major parties.

Donors: Drivers and Passengers

Alumni, parents, local residents, foundation officers, and corporate executives are the president's donor base. These relationships function much like personal friendships, and, in many cases they become friendships. But, because the president is always a fund-raiser, these relationships can be asymmetrical and freighted with ethical considerations. The prospect or donor may be eager for affiliation and attention. The development office and the president fulfill these needs through the time and care they take in numerous visits and functions. Although the prospect and the president may, under normal circumstances, have few interests in common, their connection with the institution creates the relationship. The prospect is flattered to be courted by the president and may interpret the attention as friendship, but the president's enjoyment of the relationship is based, in part, on the potential for a gift. These relationships are complicated, but often do develop into affectionate and reciprocal friendships. Ironically, the closer the friendship, the harder it may become for the president to solicit a gift.

Donors make significant gifts to presidents in whom they believe. They give to people, not institutions. Because successful change depends on new resources, it is up to the president to engage donors with his or her vision for the institution and to secure financial support. Donors take great pleasure in supporting ventures that can transform an institution. Presidents have no alternative to investing time in social activities that bring them into contact with prospects. Trustees, other administrators, and faculty can also be helpful in developing these relationships. Prospects and donors should also have opportunities to visit campus for a taste of academic life. Those who occasionally get an inside view of students and faculty at work develop an unparalleled excitement about the institution and its potential. These connections and relationships take time to develop but are the bedrock of a fund-raising campaign.

FUND-RAISING AND CHANGE
Resource Alternatives

Change requires resources, available from a variety of sources: government funds, tuition, endowment, investments, commercial ventures, patents, subsidiaries, grants, contracts, and philanthropy. In exceptional circumstances, presidents of well-endowed institutions are able to make major changes—extensive construction or renovation—by drawing funds from the endowment rather than waiting for government support or undertaking a fund-raising campaign. In the late 1990s, as endowments grew exponentially, several colleges with an exceptionally high endowment per student chose to expend a portion of their resources to enhance their campuses for the benefit of current students rather than securing gifts to underwrite the new projects and preserving endowment funds for future generations. Presidents and trustees have to decide whether to spend down their wealth or to undertake the arduous task of campaigning for new funds. Public university presidents, while increasingly dependent on philanthropic support for new initiatives, cannot neglect the inexorable annual round of lobbying for state dollars and, in some cases, for federal funding. Twenty-three percent of public institution presidents identified "relationships with legislators and policy makers as their greatest challenge" in the 2001 ACE survey (Corrigan 2002, 33). For most public institutions, the state remains a significant, though unpredictable, funding source for operations and capital projects. However, as state appropriations compose an ever-smaller proportion of the budgets of public universities, those presidents seek alternative sources of revenue: increased tuition, investments in start-up companies, commercial projects, and, above all, philanthropic support. Many public universities now have endowments close to the size of the top private institutions (Gose 2002), but, ironically, institutions that have built large endowments that generate revenue for operations may find themselves with significant budget shortfalls during market downturns.

Of the available funding sources, philanthropy provides the best vehicle for generating the funds necessary to transform a president's vision and goals into new realities. Other sources of funding, while necessary and significant, are far less within a president's control. It is the president who approves the institution's fund-raising priorities, makes the solicitations, and allocates the resources. Conway (2001, 66) notes that in her early years as president of Smith College, "since the faculty was almost fully tenured, I could change Smith's culture only by raising new resources." Stephen Trachtenberg (Interview 2002) notes that other funding sources "don't induce change; they are the result of faculty initiatives and pro-posals. A president can induce change by introducing resources. . . . Presidents leave their mark on an institution by their ability to inspire innovation, and that has to do with their ability to pay for it." Myles Brand agrees, although he notes that public institutions are less depen-dent on fund-raising and tuition than privates. But, he says, "incremen-tal resources are necessary for change and that's going to come from the federal government through competitively won grants and contracts and from fund raising. . . . Fund raising provides the incremental money for excellence" (Brand Interview 2002). Public institutions began private fund-raising programs in the 1970s, and by the 1980s had professional de-velopment offices that competed for the private sector resources they needed to fulfill their goals and aspirations (Cook 1997, 57).

Fund-raising provides presidents of all types of institutions with the slack resources they need to seed new programs, encourage promising fac-ulty, provide student programming, or invest in other initiatives without excessive consultation. Further, the vicissitudes of the economy, state funding, and student markets have made fund-raising increasingly inte-gral to an institution's strategic positioning and operations. It is also one of the factors susceptible to measurement when a board evaluates a president's performance. In view of the acknowledged importance of this aspect of the presidency, it is noteworthy that, in its 1998 survey of presi-dents, the American Council on Education found that over "50 percent of presidents of most types of institutions indicated a desire to have had more experience in [fund-raising]" (Ross and Green 2000, 27–30). Both the 1998 and 2001 ACE surveys found little difference between the "pri-mary responsibilities" of public and private institution presidents; the majority of presidents in both sectors spend most of their time on fund-raising and planning (Corrigan 2002, 34).

Fund-raising Legitimacy

Although philanthropy is a key factor in successful change, the enter-prise itself suffers from a lack of legitimacy. Fund-raising solicitations are often viewed as crude transactions tolerated because they support the lofty purposes that animate the academy. There are ongoing, although limited, efforts to elevate the legitimacy of fund-raising by grounding it in theory. Robert Payton and two coauthors (1991, 4), in "Toward a Philosophy of Fund Raising," define philanthropy as "voluntary action for the public good," essential to American democracy. They say, "The act of asking for funds is legitimate when an organization fulfills a need based on the shared values of the society or of a subsector of the society" (6). This leads to the idea of fund-raising for social purposes as "moral action" (9). The authors also emphasize the necessity of trust and trustworthiness in fund-raising, accompanied by dignity instead of shame or apology in the process (13). Gift making is a "voluntary exchange" where the contributor gets satisfaction from providing "something of value to the organization without any expectation of a material or pecuniary return" (14).

Kathleen Kelly (1998, 8) locates fund-raising in the discipline of communication and the domain of public relations, which she calls "managed communication." Her interpretation is based on a definition of fund-raising as "the management of relationships between a charitable organization and its donor publics" and calls communication the basis of donor relationships (335–36). Her theory of donor relations elevates the emerging fund-raising profession "from unexplained art to a management function grounded in the behavioral and social sciences" (387). She claims that this theoretical framework can help practitioners to increase their effectiveness and their pride in fund-raising (387). In "A Theory of Fund Raising," Bruce Cook and William Lasher (1996, 44) present a model of fund-raising as "a social exchange" between donors and institutions. They also propose a model of presidential fund-raising as "a developmental process with different decision or action points." They identify environmental, institutional, personal, and role forces that affect the president's success in fund-raising (47–48).

Paul Shervish and John Havens (2002, 225–27) take a social-psychological perspective on charitable giving. They focus on donor motivation and distinguish between demand-side and supply-side fund-raising. The "inclination model" of charitable giving focuses on a prospect's interests, experiences, and involvements. Knowing that wealth holders tend toward "hyperagency" helps fund-raisers understand these donors' interests in being actively involved in selecting or designing innovative projects and, often, lending their expertise to assure that the project meets its stated goals. Indeed, these venture philanthropists operate much like venture capitalists. Seeking to evaluate the potential of professionalization strategies to strengthen the occupation of development, Bloland and Bornstein

(1991, 119–21) draw on interviews with senior development officers and on three theoretical frameworks—functionalism, pluralist power, and institutionalization. They conclude that to become a mature profession, development must aim for three goals: high levels of effectiveness, control over their work, and legitimacy.

Four conceptual shifts must occur in order to assure the legitimacy of fund-raising: (1) fund-raising must be viewed as partnering, not begging; (2) fund-raising must move from the periphery to the center of the academy; (3) fund-raising must be integrated and seamless with other administrative functions, not discrete and disconnected; and (4) fund-raising must assure ethical practices that benefit both the donor and the institution, rather than employing self-serving practices.

Ethical fund-raising principles and guidelines have been developed within the profession, but must be adopted and monitored by the president and the chief advancement officer at each institution, and cover such issues as campaign accounting, "tainted" money, and gift restrictions. Considerable thought should be given to complex ethical issues, such as whether to accept a gift from a donor whose reputation is so tarnished that the association might injure the institution. Sometimes, proffered gifts, while difficult to refuse, are not suitable for the institution. Rollins College turned down the offer of a $1-million chair for the same reason McGill University rejected an Ayn Rand chair. The donors' restrictions on the scope of the proposed professorships made them too narrow to fit into the curricular and scholarly interests of the faculty. As McGill's president, Bernard Shapiro, said, "Our endowed chairs are 'in perpetuity,' so the subject must be sufficiently broad to sustain long-term scholarship" (Birchard 2002, A41).

Presidential Attitudes

Fund-raising seems demeaning to many presidents, especially those coming from a strictly academic career path. The fear and loathing that characterizes the way in which they view fund-raising gives rise to a vocabulary of negative expressions: "shaking the money tree," "going hat in hand," setting aside a "begging day." Gray (1998, 101), president emerita of the University of Chicago, refers to the president's "tin cup." Rhodes (1998, 16) at one point suggests that presidents "become slaves to a mendicant treadmill," although in another work (1997, xxiv) he characterizes the process differently: "To solicit funds is not to go, cap-in-hand, begging support." Here Rhodes acknowledges that instead of begging, the president is inviting a friend "to share in the privilege of the greatest partnership of all—the quest for knowledge." Most successful presidents agree with the latter interpretation of the fund-raising process.

- Soon after she became president of Smith College, Jill Ker Conway (2001, 66) found that she enjoyed her "itinerant life as a fundraiser intensely." She found the asking "fun."
- When William Tolley (1989, 53) was recruited for the presidency of Allegheny College in the early 1930s, he was told, "we don't need another scholar . . . what we need is a fund raiser . . . under the direction of a scholar, this college could go broke." And, indeed, he devoted much of his time to raising money. He found it "disagreeable . . . like washing dishes, making beds, or changing diapers," and disliked it so much "it literally made me sick." When he eventually accepted it as a necessary part of his job, he never got sick again (58).

The sociologist David Reisman (1996, 86), never a president but a long-time observer of presidents, notes that many presidents discover that fund-raising, "far from being an unhappy burden and distraction, is one of the more pleasant parts of the task." He goes on to recognize that fund-raising also brings presidents in contact with alumni, which "can be a nice antidote to coping with more individualistic faculty members, who tend to be more pessimistic."

Most presidents come to their positions lacking an understanding of the history, tradition, meaning, ethics, and organization of the fund-raising enterprise. Fund-raising has been a necessary part of a president's portfolio since the Colonial era. Fund-raising campaigns are a part of this country's great philanthropic tradition, and have played a major role in the shaping of American higher education. Since 1638, when John Harvard left half of his estate to that Massachusetts institution, gifts have been vital to the founding and the flowering of colleges and universities. Throughout the history of American higher education, philanthropy has played a significant role in building facilities, developing academic programs, recruiting students and faculty, and balancing budgets. One thing is sure: without those who asked for and those who provided financial support throughout the years, we could not have built the institutions of learning we have today.

A healthy respect for and pride in the long and honorable philanthropic tradition in American higher education will enable presidents to more confidently, and more successfully, participate in the process. Fund-raising in American society is not only associated with the nonprofit sector, but with government and business as well. Citizens seeking political office and entrepreneurs developing new businesses must also raise money. Like college presidents, they complain about the process, but their success also depends on the ability to generate support from private sources. External relations are a necessary and valued component of institutional life, making the presidency more accessible to leaders with nonacademic backgrounds. Whether presidents come to the office through the royal or a nontraditional road, fund-raising is a key factor in achieving presidential legitimacy and in implementing successful change. Carolynn Reid-Wallace, president of Fisk University, found that her successful fund-raising quieted her critics and allowed her to "push the envelope" for change (Interview 2003). Walter Massey, president of Morehouse College, notes, "I am very aware that my final legitimacy or legacy will be very much determined by how successful we are in this campaign. That's just the hard fact of life" (Interview 2003).

Presidents find that they have no real alternative to active fund-raising, despite the time it requires. Whether they like it or not, they do it. And doing it, most find they like it. The legacy of many presidents is based on their ability to secure the resources to sustain and improve their institutions. Robert Atwell puts it this way: "Talk all you want about academic leadership and vision, but in the final analysis it's all about money" (Interview 2002). Samuel Williamson agrees, "no president can long succeed without some fund-raising success. . . . I wish this were not so much the case but fund raising does dominate much of the presidential agenda" (Lecture 3 2001, 11). Despite this ambivalence, philanthropy provides the margin for excellence and the flexibility for innovation, even for those institutions whose major source of support comes from government funds. As Robert Rosenzweig (1998, 113) notes, "money is a great lubricant."

The development role of the president is, essentially, a series of conversations about the institution that ultimately lead to support for change. As Rhodes puts it, "No encounter is too brief, no event too small, no action too limited to have an influence . . . on the atmosphere of the campus" (1998, 15). Everyone is a potential donor, recruiter, and advocate for the institution. This perspective may be more natural for leaders who come to the presidency from the advancement rather than the academic route, but many academics have a gift for story telling that can capture the imagination of an institution's constituents. Creation and delivery of a narrative about the institution, its vision, mission, and goals may be the most important challenge of the presidency. Gerhard Casper, shortly after stepping down from the Stanford University presidency, said, "[Y]ou have to do a lot of educating and hope that you'll be capable of convincing people that the university's priorities should be taken seriously." He added, "[O]n the whole I have found that not to be forbiddingly difficult" (Muller 2000, 284).

It is through the telling and retelling of the institution's story that constituents from all groups become excited, challenged, and engaged. This story needs to be absorbed by staff and faculty, and retold by them as well. Too often, admissions and fund-raising staff, our primary liaisons with vital constituents, are talking about the institution from an old script. Senior faculty may also be purveying an outdated image of the school. It is important for the president to tell the story internally as well as externally. As Perlman, former president of Suffolk University, says, "redundancy of message and repetition of theme is generally desirable to get the message across" (1989, 4). This institutional story can also serve as inspiration for the campaign case statement.

A president's success in fund-raising derives from the quality of relationships developed with volunteers, donors, and staff, and the excitement of the story that weaves the institution's past into the vision for the future. In this realm, social capital, an extensive network of relationships built on trust, is vital to success. To a donor, the president must be the legitimate embodiment of the institution, serving selflessly, and faithfully interpreting the institution's storied past and golden future. To be most effective, the president must be properly positioned by advancement as the legitimate embodiment of the institution. The advancement office must believe in and promulgate the president's vision at constituent functions, as well as in published materials. According to Fisher (1989, 218), "all major gifts (gifts that have made a difference) seem to be motivated by confidence and vision—that is, confidence in the institution, particularly its current president."

Well crafted, conducted, and publicized, a fund-raising campaign enhances the quality and reputation, as well as the financial health, of an institution. A campaign provides many opportunities to tell the institution's story and enlist all constituencies in fulfilling its potential. An ambitious and successful campaign has the power to transform an institution. Financial aid dollars fuel aggressive recruiting to increase student enrollment, selectivity, and diversity. Endowed chairs and program support strengthen the faculty and curriculum. New and renovated classrooms, offices, and buildings attract both students and faculty. Beautiful landscaping enhances a sense of aesthetic pleasure, which turns out to be of great value to faculty, staff, alumni, parents, and students. All of these changes can result from successful fund-raising, lifting the morale of the campus and extending its reputation. Rhodes (1997, xix–xx) characterizes the campaign as "an institution-building activity [producing] . . . commitment, unity, confidence, and pride."

Unfortunately, the results of a fund-raising campaign are not always visible to the faculty or, if visible, seem to have supported unneeded initiatives. Often, the campaign appears not to have done anything for faculty salaries or workload. Because a sour reaction can dim the excitement of the administration, trustees, and donors, care is required to involve faculty from the beginning and throughout a campaign in setting priorities and to consult with them about ethically challenging decisions. In some situations, especially in large universities, the faculty tends to be enthusiastic about a campaign at its inception, and later to become disenchanted. There are reasons for this change. Campaigns are launched with great optimism and fanfare, invoking an institution's history and traditions, and painting a picture of the great possibilities that lie ahead—if only the resources can be garnered. Generally, the needs list contains something for everyone. It has emerged from a political process with input from every corner of the institution, and reflects many hopes and dreams.

At first, each major gift is cause for celebration, exciting the community with new possibilities, but as the campaign progresses, the excitement abates as major gifts are increasingly taken for granted. In the course of the campaign, some facilities are funded; others are not. Some professors are awarded endowed chairs; others are not. Some academic initiatives receive support; others do not. Donors may contribute disproportionately to athletic financial aid funding over merit or need. Investments in landscaping may be viewed as resources that should be assigned to a greater cause. And, with rare exceptions, campaigns do not attract funds for faculty compensation, although in a budget-relieving effort, funds can be reassigned to that purpose. In unfortunate situations, a campaign fails, leaving constituents confused and angry. Such a failure may also terminate a presidency.

The Big Hat and the Big Tent

In the end, it is the oft-despised and endless quest for private support that strengthens the traditions and values of an institution and secures the resources for its transformation. It is time for academic institutions to heal any remaining schisms among the academic, advancement, and financial sectors, and to create a thoroughly integrated and seamless enterprise. Instead of performing their work separately under different tents, all sectors can perform better working together under one tent. In like manner, instead of conceiving the presidency as a series of disparate activities requiring many different hats, presidents do better by reconceiving their work under one all-purpose hat. The metaphors of all-purpose hats and tents reflect an integrated vision of the academic, financial, and external responsibilities of the presidency and of the operations of the college. Most presidents enjoy being engaged in all aspects of college work and life. Planning, budgeting, lobbying, and fund-raising are all deeply connected to the academic purposes of the institution.

As fund-raising has gained respectability as a means of breathing life into an institution's values and aspirations, it has moved from the margin to the center of administration and, in most colleges and universities, has been integrated seamlessly into the activities of the president and the institution. This is true both literally and figuratively. The chief advancement officer used to be located with her or his staff on the periphery of campus; today, it is common to find the president's top administrators all centrally located. The advancement division used to be marginal to decision making; today, the vice president has an accepted place at the academic table and serves as a full partner in the cabinet. Presidents are well served if they structure their administration so that the core functions—academic, financial, and external—are at the decision-making and planning table. An integrated cabinet structure and a centrally orchestrated advancement operation are desirable even at institutions, mostly large publics, where donor loyalty is to particular schools or units and not to the university as a whole. Fund-raising can be integrated and demystified by inviting administrators and faculty into the process: collaboratively identifying institutional needs and sources of support, clarifying ethical and professional standards, participating knowledgeably in the cultivation and solicitation of prospects, and applying new funds. In an innovative and groundbreaking organizational restructuring, Vanderbilt Chancellor Gordon Gee assigned the advancement portfolio to his chief academic officer, thus creating the ultimate seamless integration of the areas most central to higher education. Gee calls this "a new model for higher education." "If it works, we'll be heroic," says Gee. "If not, I'll be pumping gas in . . . Utah" (Cass 2002).

This model of integration among the divisions within an institution is also developing among the divisions of advancement. Too often, public relations, publications, alumni relations, and development are only loosely related, causing them to neglect the vital interconnections of the institution and its constituents. A well-integrated advancement team can promote the institution's goals, send its key messages, and support its student recruitment and fund-raising initiatives with greater clarity and economy

Table 12.1
Change Legitimacy Rating

Factors in Legitimacy	Degree of Legitimacy	
	Low	High
Leadership Style and Change Legitimacy	Style Incompatible with Institutional Needs & Culture (e.g., Top-Down Authoritarian in an Egalitarian Culture)	Style Adapted to Institutional Needs & Culture
Governance and Change Legitimacy	Formal Processes Ineffective in Decision Making & Innovating	Formal Processes Effective in Identifying & Moving a Change Agenda
Social Capital and Change Legitimacy	Weak, Distrustful Relationships	Strong, Trusting Relationships
Fund-raising and Change Legitimacy	Marginal & Fragmented Tactics Inimical to Donors & Institution Reluctant President "Begs" for Support	Central, Integrated, & Seamless Approaches Serve Best Interests of Donors & Institutions Enthusiastic President Invites Donors to Partner

than when operating as independent silos. Without synergy among these related areas, even top professionals find themselves frustrated.

Presidents are frequently asked, "How much time do you spend on fund-raising?" This question belies ignorance about the process because everything is in some way about fund-raising, just as everything is about academic quality. There is no split, conceptually or actually, between the internal and external presidency. In order to use the bully pulpit persuasively outside of the institution, a president must be fully involved with and knowledgeable about the academic and student issues on campus. Conversely, the most effective presidents bring ideas and issues from the public arena into the internal academic discourse. Connecting internal and external communities of interest through a continuing series of conversations also enables the president to secure resources for institutional initiatives and needs. As fund-raising becomes incorporated more seamlessly into a president's life, it can be reconceived as resource development, inextricable from the president's academic goals. As a result, the development operation becomes integrated into the organizational structures of institutional life, a significant paradigm shift.

CHANGE LEGITIMACY RATING

Table 12.1, the Change Legitimacy Rating, demonstrates how each of the four factors (leadership style, governance, social capital, fund-raising) in this construct can enhance or reduce the legitimacy of change. Each of the factors and their interactions must be taken into account when contemplating change initiatives that will be accepted as legitimate. In some notable cases, not only have leaders' change initiatives been thwarted, leaders have lost their jobs, even their careers, because one or more of these factors lacked legitimacy. Presidential leadership and an institution's governance processes must be effective and mutually reinforcing for change to occur. Social capital provides the relationships of trust that allow institution-wide planning for change, and fund-raising provides the leverage for institutional transformation.

CHAPTER 13

Threats to Change Legitimacy

It is a truism that colleges and universities are slow to change. Presidents may hope to establish their legacy through a bold vision and a strategy for change. However, they need to assess the congruence of these initiatives with the institution's strengths and challenges and to be aware of the ambiguous and chaotic nature of higher education decision making. Faculties are focused on teaching, scholarship, service projects, and institutional and association politics. They tend not to follow trends in society and higher education unless they have an impact on their disciplines. Despite their tilt toward liberal politics, faculties tend to be conservative when it comes to change. By contrast, trustees usually respond enthusiastically to new trends, new employment arrangements, new programs, and new markets. They are often impatient with the slow pace of change in academe and with the president's inability or unwillingness to "get something done." Stories of failed change initiatives abound in higher education, as do stories of failed presidencies. Often these failures are linked.

I propose four serious threats to legitimate and lasting change: (1) precipitous presidential departure, (2) illegitimate process, (3) insufficient funding, and (4) homeostasis. A president's departure, even on the best terms, will impede the change process as the community becomes focused on the search for a replacement and the transition. A process considered illegitimate will fail and may well cost the president's job. Insufficient funding may not only terminate the change process, but can end the presidency. Probably the most dangerous obstacle to legitimate change is homeostasis, the tendency of organizations to overwhelm change through the power and comfort of their current equilibrium.

PRECIPITOUS PRESIDENTIAL DEPARTURE

The premature departure of the president is one of the greatest impediments to successful completion and institutionalization of a change effort. Presidential longevity and legitimacy provide the stability, consistency, and credibility that ease the path to legitimate change. This view is contrary to Birnbaum's (1992, 194–95) assertion that "there is nothing inherently beneficial about long presidential terms, and on average, institutions might be better off with shorter rather than longer presidential tenures." Birnbaum assigns far too insignificant a role to presidential leadership in the creation of change, the development of social capital, and the acquisition of resources, all of which require considerable time in office. In a 1984 publication, *Presidents Make a Difference*, the Kerr commission (65) found that the then average seven-year presidential term "is too short to serve effectively some of the major interests of an institution." Art Padilla and Sujit Ghosh (2000, 37) point out that "frequent turnover at the top ultimately results in slower change and less responsiveness throughout the institution" and that effective presidencies require "more than five or six years to manifest themselves." Another report found that innovative institutions have an average presidential tenure of about thirteen years, roughly double that of the current average (Korschgen et al. 2001, 3).

While some new presidents never gain legitimacy and are ousted within a few years of their appointment, others initiate their own departure, and, as Judith McLaughlin (1996a, 9) points out, "These early exits are costly, both to the individuals and to the institutions who suffer them." Bruce Alton and Kathleen Dean (2002, 19–23) report that each year about 450 college and university presidents leave their jobs. Of these, 40 percent retire, one in four resigns to take another presidency, 3 percent die, and another third resign for other professional positions. The latter group averaged 57 years of age and 8.4 years in office, well above the national median of 6.9 years. The authors report that presidents leave early for a variety of reasons: to take a better job, having achieved their objectives as president, inability to achieve their goals due to "intractable forces," exhaustion, resistant faculty, trustee micromanagement, political interference, and the pressure to raise money.

On July 27, 2001, *The Chronicle of Higher Education* (Basinger A22–A23) reported on a number of rapid and disruptive presidential turnovers, including the following:

- The president of Case Western Reserve University resigned after less than two years because he felt he did not have the support of the board.
- The president of Colgate University, new to college administration, left after a year because the "fit" was not comfortable.

The Harvard Business School developed a case study on leadership and governance from a well-known presidential departure in the 1990s. The president left a northeastern university for a more prominent, more selective institution after five years, despite a public pledge to stay ten years. The president announced his resignation at a time when his institution's chief academic officer position was vacant, a major community initiative underway, and a fund-raising campaign about to be announced. The case study indicates that the board chairman, with whom the president had worked closely and developed a friendship, felt betrayed and hurt, as did students and faculty. This unexpected presidential departure was seen as a setback, although the institution rallied and moved ahead with its plans (Harvard Business School 1996).

Such turnover impedes an institution's focus and momentum toward change, as it requires a renewed attention to leadership selection, a time- and energy-consuming process. McLaughlin (1996b, 16) comments, "The unfortunate consequence for higher education is that itinerant presidents are unable to provide the sustained leadership that is necessary to encourage innovation and implement change—at the very time when innovation and change are sorely needed." This consequence of unexpected turnover is corroborated by the experience of the ACE Project on Leadership and Institutional Transformation, which found that progress on change in an institution could be "significantly interrupted or even derailed" by the president's departure, especially if the effort was seen as the president's agenda and did not have widespread acceptance (Hill 2001, 8–9). While a board can look for a new president willing and able to continue the predecessor's change agenda, it will most likely have to accommodate its preferences to the new leader's vision.

Short, turbulent presidencies leave a lump in the throat of an institution that may never be digested, and rapid turnover is costly to an institution, psychologically and financially. Following a spate of presidential departures after short terms in office, Richard Ingram (2001, A22–A23), president of the Association of Governing Boards, commented that institutions can lose momentum in planning, fund-raising, and staff morale and productivity, as well as the intangible costs to institutional reputation. Change efforts can also be impeded by transition in other areas of academic leadership. Although presidential turnover is most disruptive to an institutional change effort, the loss of the direct and personal day-to-day leadership of a chief academic officer may also delegitimate or disrupt a change effort.

ILLEGITIMATE PROCESS

Unless an institution is in crisis, the academic president cannot create large-scale institutional change unilaterally and without consultation. Particularly in the areas of traditional faculty influence and prerogative, a top-down approach to change is an invitation to sabotage. Presidents have often had their change initiatives and their tenures aborted in the wake of a perceived illegitimate planning process. The academic tradition requires broad participation and consultation, along with faithfulness to the institution's culture. This is where leadership competence is necessary to manage change effectively, and where changes inimical to faculty interests may be perceived as hostile to the culture. Just as legitimacy is vital to a president's successful tenure, so, too, is legitimacy vital to the success of a change initiative. Presidents with academic careers tend to be acculturated to the need to secure support for change through faculty and trustee governance systems and structures. Those who come to their positions from nonacademic careers may find faculty governance too cumbersome and trustee governance too directive. However, they have no alternative to accepting governance input or making the desired change by fiat, an approach likely to backfire. The perceived lack of legitimacy in processing a change initiative is one of the greatest threats a president faces. It is often conflated with a perception that the president does not understand the culture and also the powerful tendency toward homeostasis. Additionally, as Trachtenberg points out, there is a "great temptation to use criticism of the process as a collateral attack on an idea. It is possible to have consulted to a fare-thee-well and still be accused of not having honored process" (Interview 2002).

- The strong actions of the Bennington board and president in response to a financial crisis were considered illegitimate by many, including the AAUP. The subsequent stabilization of the institution's financial picture quieted the dissenters. Under another scenario, such top-down initiatives may well have toppled the presidency.
- Perhaps the most extreme example of presidential failure arising from perceptions of illegitimate processing of institutional decisions has taken

place at the small experimental college in New England that has a powerful cultural tradition of participatory democracy and a higher expectation for faculty participation in institutional governance than at most schools. The faculty, because of its considerable clout with the board of trustees, has caused the turnover of seven presidents between the late 1980s and early 2001. This college culture exerts such a powerful pull toward its traditional equilibrium that it also serves as an example of the threat of homeostasis to change.

- Boards may also terminate presidents whose change agenda is not consistent with theirs. Such has been the case for several presidents of single-sex colleges who, without board consultation, have floated the idea of coeducation as a means of increasing revenue.

INSUFFICIENT FUNDING

New initiatives, whether to strengthen or to transform an institution, generally require resources. These can be reallocated from other activities, secured through private or government funds, or provided through the administration's slack resources. Since reallocation means reducing or eliminating existing programs, it is rarely the option taken to support new initiatives. Thus change is generally an increment, not a replacement. Incentives are required for people to accept new roles or responsibilities, to provide training and education, and to secure new support systems and resources. Since state funding for public universities tends to be undependable and unpredictable, presidents of these institutions must focus on securing the resources necessary to the health of basic programs. However, when contemplating significant institutional change, presidents of both public and private institutions seek to achieve their goals through the addition of philanthropic support. Increasingly, donors proffer gifts that support their own interests and not the changes planned by the institution. Presidents can work with such donors to reorient their interests but may have to accommodate their projects to secure funding. Venture philanthropists, interested in solving specific educational, social, health, or other problems, may seek considerable involvement and control over projects they fund along with institutional accountability for achieving agreed-upon goals. Corporate-sponsored research, while critical to many individual researchers and a measure used in institutional rankings, does not provide the president with the flexible funds to support system change.

Should the economy and markets be in decline, the necessary resources for change may not be immediately forthcoming. Large-scale change efforts and fund-raising campaigns may have to be deferred or scaled back. Environmental conditions may delay or defer planned change, which will be viewed as a defeat for the president. Budget deficits often put an immediate end to change initiatives as available funds are redeployed to cover basic operations. The pressures on presidents to produce significant changes and resources have caused some to develop magnificent plans, "white elephants," wholly out of scale with their institutions and missions, and hugely expensive. Examples abound of presidential grandiosity, the development of such a plan without sufficient consultation with key constituents. The threat of insufficient funding to the legitimacy of change is significant. A plan may be dazzling, but if it is out of scale or overly expensive it will be nearly impossible to garner support.

- One faith-based college ousted its president in 2002 for involving the institution in costly projects that were not funded.
- In 2000, the president of a public metropolitan institution was asked to resign because he was unable to raise the funds necessary to implement his ambitious plans. In fact, the institution faced a growing deficit and declining philanthropy.
- In 2002, after less than a year in office, a president had to resign after he had touted a $20-million gift that never materialized. The gift was to have funded an ambitious plan for extensive building renovations, exciting new programs, and financial stability.

HOMEOSTASIS

Homeostasis is the tendency of organizations to maintain relative stability. In higher education institutions things change slowly, unless spurred by a crisis. This is largely a good thing, inhibiting precipitate decisions, adoption of passing fads, and egregious error. However, when change is necessary and desirable, it is often sabotaged by provincialism, complacency, decentralization, and the diffusion of decision making. Brand calls it "inertia" (Interview 2002). Trachtenberg calls it "memory," which, he says, "is the enemy of change [and] as a university administrator, you are always fighting efforts on the part of constituencies to retain the status quo or return to the status quo ante" (Interview 2002). This tendency toward homeostasis is a force that can undermine the ambitions of even the most visionary and change-oriented leaders. Even the arrival of a new leader "creates a disruption that the system will seek to correct" by pointing out the ways in which he or she does not "fit in" (Downey et al. 2001, 37).

Unless a crisis precipitates action, stakeholders tend to be averse to change and comfortably complacent. Kotter (1996, 40) warns about the danger complacency presents to management efforts to promote change. His sources of complacency include the absence of a crisis; too many visible resources; a low-candor, low-confrontation culture; denial; and some management behavior, such as "happy talk" about the institution. Although Kotter's discussion of complacency is oriented to change in the business world, comfort with the existing equilibrium is also one of the greatest threats to change in higher education. Once an innovation is in place, it must achieve a new equilibrium, or the forces of the old equilibrium overwhelm it and people return to their customary habits and relationships. Kurt Lewin describes the three basic states of successful change in an institution as "unfreezing the present level . . . moving to the new level . . . and freezing group life on the new level" (Lewin 1961, 237). However, the forces of tradition often undermine the process of moving to and remaining at a new level. Thus, even when a community makes the hard decisions necessary to implement change through a process perceived as legitimate, there are no guarantees that the change will be institutionalized at a new level of equilibrium. A return to the previous equilibrium may occur if the innovators depart or lose interest, the naysayers gain support, or the innovation is inconsistent with the deep structure (underlying assumptions) of the system.

Systems in equilibrium are thought to react to impingements in three ways: (1) resisting the influence of the disturbance, (2) bringing into operation the homeostatic forces that restore a balance, and (3) accommodating the disturbance through achieving a new equilibrium (Chin 1961, 205). Often changes in the environment create an imbalance or instability in an organization that require modifications and alterations in its behavior. When the organization adapts to the new environment, equilibrium is restored (Cameron 1991, 284). Thus, change requires establishment of a new equilibrium within the organization in order to achieve equilibrium with a changed external environment. Unfortunately, administrators, faculties, and trustees often undertake new initiatives without knowledge about or experience in institutional change, and a limited knowledge of trends in the environment and in higher education. People tend to be comfortable with the status quo, and, wittingly or unwittingly, sabotage efforts to change their comfortable systems. The president's role is to make the rationale for the new equilibrium clear and compelling, provide incentives and rewards for change, and weave the change into

the institutional narrative and culture. Gersick's (1991) notion of punctuated equilibrium acknowledges the challenges to changing the deep
structure of an organization like a university and also the external or internal imperatives for change that arise periodically with the force to
achieve a new equilibrium if properly managed.

CHAPTER 14

Strategies for Legitimate and Successful Change

Cohen and March (1974, 203–15) make it clear that, despite careful, rational, and strategic planning, presidents have very little control over their institutions. They analogize presidential leadership to driving a skidding car. Within such an anarchic and unstable environment, they say, presidents need to develop modest rather than heroic notions about what they can accomplish. Their tactical rules for operating in such an environment are very different from those found in business-related literature: (1) "spend time"—and gain influence on decision-making activities; (2) "persist"—an idea rejected today may be accepted tomorrow; (3) "exchange status for substance"—avoid the self-esteem trap and recognize the status needs of others; (4) "facilitate opposition participation"—involve dissident groups in decision making; (5) "overload the system"—to assure that at least some projects succeed; (6) "provide garbage cans"—so that important projects are not derailed by other issues; (7) "manage unobtrusively"—small actions may be more successful than large interventions in changing an institution; and (8) "interpret history"—define what is happening and provide a context for decision making. Presidents trying to interpret history and provide a context for decision making should also heed Howard Gardner (1995, 9–10). Effective leaders, he says, communicate stories, embody those stories, and, through their example, inspire their followers. "Storytelling," writes Bateson (1990, 34), "is fundamental to the human search for meaning."

Management literature emphasizes certain leadership behaviors as necessary strategies to promote change: create a sense of urgency, develop and communicate a new vision, and institutionalize a new paradigm (Kotter 1996, 21; Tichy and Devanna 1990, 29). Eckel et al. (1999, 35–42), based on results from their long-term research project, propose a series of leadership strategies to promote campuswide change: "making a clear and compelling case, crafting a sensible and blame-free change agenda, engaging people via conversations, and making connections." The president, they say, can encourage broad participation in discussions about change and create linkages among small initiatives that can collectively have a greater impact. Conversations are seen as critical to the change process and can be managed to develop a critical mass of support for change. This approach to leadership is in stark contrast to that of Fisher (1984, 99) who believes that presidents should rarely "engage in give-and-take discussions on campus." He is also opposed to allowing any group on campus to make final decisions. Instead, everything should be recommended to the president, who makes the decisions.

There is a plethora of advice for leaders wishing to promote change. Presidents must choose the strategies for change that suit their leadership style and the culture and imperatives of their institutions. Successful presidents have developed "complex behavioral repertoires" enabling them to balance their roles as CEO, faculty colleague, institutional symbol, and public official. This cognitive complexity provides presidents with multiple lenses through which to recognize "the interactions between the bureaucratic, collegial, political, and symbolic processes present in all colleges and universities at all times" (Bensimon et al. 1989, 72).

The strategies recommended to leaders as levers for change are very much in line with Suchman's three legitimacy-building activities that I applied to the search for presidential legitimacy in chapter 8. These activities are becoming an insider in the culture, recruiting a credible group that will support some new initiatives, and creating new groups and legitimating beliefs (1995, 587).

A successful president will apply appropriate strategies to influence the four factors in change legitimacy: presidential leadership, governance, social capital, and fund-raising.

ENHANCING PRESIDENTIAL LEADERSHIP FOR CHANGE

The president's role in institutional change is neither heroic nor irrelevant. Leadership is important but must be tailored to an institution's culture and current needs. Strong, transformational leadership may be appropriate in certain circumstances, but dysfunctional, even destructive, in others. Transactional leadership can seem uninspired as presidents strengthen an institution slowly but become valued as an institution achieves its goals. Presidents need to discern the appropriate (administrative or governance) decision-making process warranted by events and acceptable to the culture and then develop strategies for promoting and rewarding change.

Once a president has gained legitimacy and identified a change agenda, a variety of strategies can be applied to engage the community in the change effort. Presidents must spend time with constituents in developing and maintaining a shared vision and consensus for change and then persist in establishing legitimate processes for design, implementation, and assessment of implementation strategies. "Garbage cans" should be established to handle the quotidian issues that inevitably surface to derail initiatives. The major roles of the president are to keep constituents focused on the institutional vision and change agenda, to keep the process moving even as it faces obstacles and setbacks, and to continually remind people of the context, rationale, and benefit of the change agenda. The president's story-telling abilities are particularly helpful in legitimating change by weaving it into the institution's history and values.

ENHANCING GOVERNANCE FOR CHANGE

Most faculty members will participate in administratively orchestrated strategic visioning and planning activities with enthusiasm if they believe the administration also values and uses faculty governance mechanisms. Faculty governance obligations tend to place significant burdens on faculty, and presidents who wish to derail attacks on the change agenda can load the formal system with issues that will absorb time and energy. At the same time, presidents must be conscious of the status needs of faculty and legitimate the voices of opposition by involving them and enabling them to influence the change process. Governance processes, by their nature, result in piecemeal decisions, and presidents need to keep faculty and board committees focused on the big picture and overarching mission and goals.

ENHANCING SOCIAL CAPITAL FOR CHANGE

Downey et al. (2001, 196–97) suggest that building influence is key to assuring a leader's assimilation into an organizational culture. By developing a network of relationships throughout the organization, the new leader can "develop a more nuanced understanding of the complex web of interrelationships . . . and enhance her [or his] credibility . . . by serving as a linking pin between areas of the organization." Assuming the success of these early efforts at gaining influence and acceptance into the culture, the president can move a change agenda through formal structures and informal networks. There is no substitute for developing and maintaining the social capital necessary to implement and institutionalize a change agenda. The relationships of trust and influence on which the president can draw constitute the capital that must be invested to assure the success of new initiatives. Presidents should seek to continually replenish the store of social capital by building and rebuilding relationships of trust. Higher education is labor intensive and without the participation of the labor force, no change can occur. Presidents must be present and visible on campus and in meetings, engaging in continuing conversations that promote the change agenda. The thoughtful exchange of ideas with individuals and groups develops the trust and networks of relationships on which a president can build.

ENHANCING FUND-RAISING FOR CHANGE

To create a seamless administrative support system for change, presidents need to bring together, under one "big tent," the academic, financial, and external sectors of the institution. Conceptually, such a system should also mean that the president's responsibilities come together seamlessly under one "big hat." In pursuit of a change agenda, the president can use fund-raising to seed and support planning efforts, new positions, new facilities, and new programs. The president takes the story of the institution, its dreams, and its strategic goals to external audiences, engaging others to support the change agenda.

CAVEATS FOR PRESIDENTS

Following is a list of caveats for presidents who seek to promote legitimate change: (1) adopt a flexible "transformative" approach to leadership, appropriate to the needs and culture of the institution; (2) use both the bully pulpit and informal conversation to make the case for change to constituents; (3) build new social capital even as existing capital erodes; (4) use all mechanisms to promote a change agenda—board and faculty governance, strategic planning, administrative action, and external support; (5) develop a positive attitude toward fund-raising; (6) do not be derailed by ambiguity, redundancy, resistance, or complacency; and (7) encourage innovation.

CHAPTER 15

A President's Quest
for Institutional Repositioning

GREAT EXPECTATIONS

When I was elected president in 1990, Rollins was a good institution with great ambitions, operating with scant resources and an aging physical plant. My challenge was to transform the college from good to great by strengthening the school's quality, reputation, and financial health. My vision for Rollins was that the institution be recognized as one of the top colleges in the nation.

To propel such a transformation, I began by working with the college's leadership to raise standards in all areas: expanding the membership and enhancing the prestige and functioning of the board of trustees, increasing the efficiency and effectiveness of the administration, making more rigorous the process and criteria for faculty evaluation, and increasing selectivity in student admissions. Tangible results of these changes include a leap in national rankings; increased student applications, enrollment, and quality; recruitment of top-quality faculty, staff, and trustees; campus beautification and expansion; successful commercial ventures; and financial stability.

To make these gains, I relied upon all of the factors involved in legitimate change: presidential leadership, governance, social capital, and fundraising. I also made a number of costly mistakes. This part of my story describes the challenges I experienced along the path to change.

Like all new presidents, I hoped to make a difference through my leadership. I was keenly aware of the great expectations people had for me and, early in my presidency, I noted in my journal: "The honeymoon period is all that its title implies. It has no firm boundaries and one doesn't know when it will end. But it's a rather extraordinary period in the life of a president. There is a tremendous sense of expectation and hope, great support from the entire community, internal and external. People seem eager to carry out your wishes—to divine your wishes—and to be co-operative and supportive in every way possible. There is a great sense of joy and hope that overrides everything. All the new president's utterances are of tremendous interest and one is scrutinized carefully to understand the meaning of behavior and action. It gives me the sense that I have to fulfill the promise that they see in me, to satisfy the expectations that have been raised so high, to produce some wonderful change or new direction for the college. It is, therefore, in many ways a burden, for, although I am riding high on this crest of enthusiasm and support, I know I have to deliver" (September 26, 1990).

I learned quickly that people listen carefully to a new president's comments and, in repeating them, weave a tapestry of interpretations purporting to reveal the future. I report in my journal that after telling a faculty leader I might engage a consultant on faculty governance, he went on to a faculty meeting and mentioned it. Of course, the group felt it should vote on the matter. It did, and the vote was fifty-fifty as to whether the president should hire a consultant. Although I was a first-time president coming from a nontraditional career path, my experiences proved un-expectedly relevant in implementing my goals for Rollins. I brought to the presidency considerable leadership experience in civic and professional settings and considered myself a change agent, having presided over several large-scale institutional change efforts. These included an innovative model of secondary school education (Bornstein 1975), a national educational equity demonstration project (Stake et al. 1983; Bornstein 1985), and designs for the systemic implementation of Title IX, the federal law prohibiting sex discrimination in schools. Because of my experiences with institutional change, both successful and unsuccessful, and my research, analysis, and publication on the subject, I was very familiar with factors in and threats to the legitimacy of change. Despite this, I made a number of serious, although not fatal, mistakes as I sought to implement change at Rollins.

I understood the importance of presidential leadership as a factor in successful and legitimate change, but believed strongly in the communal evolution of a shared vision and goals. Although I had studied the college's history and traditions before I arrived, I wanted to immerse myself in the culture, understand the community's aspirations, and assess the potential for change. At the same time, I built a strong administrative team that focused on making the college function effectively and responsively. We reviewed and strengthened administrative organization, decision making, budgeting, investment management, and trustee functioning.

Throughout my presidency, I gave priority to both board and faculty governance. I had had direct experience with the potential for governance bodies to delegitimate change: union politics slowing the pace of a school's program innovation, a fractious university faculty senate undermining administrative initiatives, and a trustee special interest group redirecting resources to support its own priorities. As a result, I invested considerable time and attention to governance. I worked with faculty to overcome the endemic suspicion of administrative objectives and actions. I learned, however, that some faculty members thrive on maintaining a schism between themselves and the administration even while promoting shared governance.

I encouraged the involvement of faculty in educational and campus life issues, but found their decision making limited by a lack of information about trends in higher education and society. Unaware of, or perhaps unconcerned about, the national scene, dedicated professors made decisions affecting students and faculty as well as the quality and reputation of the college within a narrow and very local frame of reference. I made a journal entry during my first year indicating great concern "about the way of operating that people here have. They seem to operate in a vacuum, without consultation with national bodies or a nod in the direction of the experience of other institutions" (February 11, 1991).

With the board, based on my experience at the University of Miami, I established a practice of open and frank communication on all issues. I knew that boards operate best when well informed and make better decisions when not blindsided. From the beginning, I established a clear line between the broad responsibilities of the board and the day-to-day management of the college. I sought to orient incoming board chairs and new members to the discomforts they might experience when having to defend actions or speech on campus that they or others found objectionable. I was attuned to the importance of social capital to change and invested a great deal of time generating relationships with faculty, trustees, alumni, and donors, as well as business, community, and political leaders. Because I knew that successful change requires resources, I focused on major-gift fund-raising in order to provide support for institutional change.

The year 1990 was not a promising year to take on a college presidency, especially at a significantly underfunded institution. Not only was the economy weak and the stock market shaky, but also the number of college-going students was declining. To manage responsibly during this period, we reorganized and downsized staff, which was, predictably, controversial. Each person whose job was eliminated had a constituency, which aggressively attacked the administration and board for being corporate and hard-hearted.

During this period, public trust in higher education was low, and the federal and state governments were calling for greater accountability. I was active through our state and national associations in the successful efforts to prevent excessive government intrusion into the governance of colleges and universities. Despite the external and internal challenges we faced, and their negative impact on morale, I sought to keep the campus mobilized toward developing a strategic plan for the future, developing a list of priority needs, and laying the groundwork for an ambitious fund-raising campaign. My focus was to engage the board, administration, and faculty in a major effort to reposition Rollins—its quality, reputation, and financial condition.

SEEKING THE ORACLE

From the beginning, I was advised, directly and indirectly, that good leadership called for a bold vision to mobilize our constituents. In a journal entry, I wrote, "I have been amazed to learn that, contrary to a notion one might have that there is a requirement to move in boldly and with clear, brave strategies to show how visionary and capable you are, there is a great deal of important opinion suggesting that unless an institution is in crisis, it is better to move slowly and deliberately, first getting to know the situation. This is very comforting, for Rollins is certainly not in a crisis situation" (June 21, 1990). I struggled constantly to balance the pressure to act boldly with the need to bring the college's constituencies into a more deliberative process.

In pursuit of my vision for Rollins to be recognized nationally as one of America's best colleges, I emphasized three values I had identified in my inauguration address as deeply embedded in our history and culture—excellence, innovation, and community. I attempted to keep the institution focused on those values in our planning, programming, and fund-raising. Through a combination of good people, good planning, and good luck, we were prepared to take advantage of the boom in both the economy and the college-going population that would begin in the mid-1990s.

Early in my tenure, I established and chaired a strategic planning council outside the governance structure comprising senior faculty and key administrators, very much of the type described by Keller (1983, 61, 127) and Schuster et al. (1994, 198-200). Fisher (1984, 54), who advises presidents to be accessible, but remote, would doubtless have counseled against a president serving on or chairing a committee because it locates the leader on even ground with others, thereby diminishing her or his perceived power. I found this to be true. Whatever mystique surrounded the presidency became attenuated as people worked closely with me and we struggled to define the college's future. At the same time, participating in this process helped me become a part of the institutional culture.

The Task Force on the Twenty-first Century, as we called it, drafted a mission statement, goals, and objectives. We struggled with a long-standing definitional problem: how to describe an institution known nationally as a selective liberal arts college, but having a school of continuing education offering undergraduate and master's degree programs, and an accredited graduate school of business. I promoted "comprehensive liberal arts college" as the best descriptor for an institution with disparate units surrounding a historic liberal arts core, and throughout my presidency worked, without much success, to develop lasting synergies among the units. Following this pre-planning, the task force convened an all-day, all-college planning summit to review and discuss the proposals and then made revisions based on input from every constituency. To legitimate the process, relevant sections were approved through faculty governance, and the plan was discussed and approved by the board of trustees. As part of the planning process, I invited a number of prominent consultants to campus to provide feedback on our emerging plan in the context of national trends in higher education. These consultants included Ernest Boyer, George Keller, and Robert Zemsky. With Zemsky we engaged in a "Roundtable," bringing together key faculty, staff, students, and administrators for a series of strategic conversations. The most important outcome of this process was a consensus on the goal of making Rollins the number one college choice for significantly more students. This was a salutary goal, easily accepted by faculty, administrators, and students. It enabled us to make changes in policy and procedure relating to recruitment, admission, financial aid, and curriculum that would otherwise have been difficult.

While it is unclear that strategic plans are effective in guiding an institution's programmatic, hiring, and budgetary decisions, our plan did serve as a legitimating force for action. I established a series of task forces to examine key institutional policies and practices. The Task Force on Faculty Evaluation developed a new faculty evaluation bylaw, subsequently approved through the governance system, which considerably strengthened the processes and requirements for tenure and promotion. The senior, well-respected faculty members I appointed to the task force kept threatening to disband due to disagreements about evaluation among themselves and their colleagues. I worked hard to keep the group together, and, ultimately, they performed a great service.

I also established the Task Force on Faculty Governance, which streamlined decision-making procedures and reduced the number of standing committees from eighteen to four. The restructuring was meant to streamline governance and free faculty from the excessive demands of the existing system, enabling them to concentrate on teaching and scholarship. One of the negative results of this process, which I was too inexperienced and had too little early legitimacy too prevent, was the separation of the Arts and Sciences and the graduate business faculties. I did insist that there be an overarching faculty body that I (or the faculty) could call into session when collegewide issues arose. I agonized over whether all of these initiatives would be successful in strengthening the institution. In the second semester of my first year, I wrote in my journal, "The least attractive part of the job is the worrying I do on weekends about the progress of the planning activities I have put into motion, the task forces on governance and faculty evaluation that appear to be floundering" (February 11, 1991).

After the faculty revised the governance structure and strengthened the evaluation process, I established the Curriculum Review Task Force comprising well-respected and innovative senior Arts and Sciences professors who studied the literature on change and invited community input throughout their deliberations. However, the tendency of the Rollins faculty to view such administratively appointed work groups with suspicion helped to doom the task force's report early on. A process viewed as illegitimate is one of the key threats to successful change, and I did not do all I should have to keep alive and legitimate a community-wide conversation about the report. In an embarrassing example of presidential inexperience and ineptitude, when the task force held its first public hearing on its ambitious plan for curriculum revision, I seconded a reservation that had been expressed and grounded my concern in my experience with the high school innovation. My point was good, but I was wrong to do this on several counts. First, it was my task force, and I should have discussed any concerns privately. Second, the public forum was an opportunity to test the task force's ideas. Negative comments from the president early in the conversation probably carried more weight than I realized. Third, comparisons with a secondary education change effort would not be seen as appropriate. Even though I never received any feedback on that experience, I always shudder to remember it. The proposed curriculum plan was rejected, but an innovative freshman program was rescued from the plan and approved through the governance structure. It has been very successful and remains in place.

Over the years, the Arts and Sciences faculty also had passionate, heated debates over the possible addition of programs in communications, international business, information technology, and film studies, fields that seemed to many professors to be preprofessional or technical and not in keeping with the traditional liberal arts. For market-driven initiatives to be successful, most often the dean, academic vice president, and I were all involved and depended on accumulated social capital in discussions, negotiations, and consensus building. By contrast, the faculty was more willing to experiment and innovate in the evening division, and the graduate business faculty was proactive in developing programs responsive to changing conditions and markets.

Over time, although we made significant improvements throughout the institution, we were not very successful at making change in the conceptual design of the Arts and Sciences curriculum or in defining a unique niche for the college. The concepts for niche building that I floated over the years did not energize the community as a whole, although we successfully initiated a number of innovations. In my inauguration address I had proposed a truly internationalized campus and curriculum, and we made progress over the years in increasing study- and service-abroad programs, providing foreign language instruction for faculty as well as students, and adding internationally focused academic courses and programs. These efforts were good, some quite extraordinary, but we lacked the academic leadership and vision to thoroughly internationalize the college. I also promoted the idea of a pragmatic education based on the college's historic commitment to innovative pedagogy and its focus on "the scholarship of application," recognized by Ernest Boyer (1990, 21, 63). Despite the numerous efforts I made, including written communiqués, meetings, and the national colloquy we hosted on pragmatic liberal education, our initiatives remained scattered.

My experiences, coupled with those of my presidential colleagues, taught me that, unless propelled by external forces or a crisis, faculties are not much motivated to alter the educational program, despite the urging of their presidents. For the Rollins faculty, the most powerful spurs to change were the criteria of the accrediting associations and the threat of declining enrollment. At the public university across town, state funding and enrollment patterns drove academic decision making.

CREDITS AND DEBITS

In the early years, I gave primacy to developing strong relationships with both internal and external constituents in order to build the social capital essential to strengthening the institution. I was also laying the groundwork for solicitation of the financial capital that we would need to meet our campaign goals. I was keenly aware of the importance of the board of trustees and worked with my chairs to enlarge and strengthen the membership. At my request, the board, overcoming some reluctance, applied to the state of Florida for the first ever amendment to the college's 1885 Charter, allowing us to increase the number of trustees. As a result, we recruited prominent, successful business, community, and alumni leaders to the board, and added the first trustees of color. I worked hard to build an open and honest relationship with members, and with the exception of a few shaky moments early in my presidency, the Rollins board could not have been more supportive, trusting, or enthusiastic. Each of the board chairs with whom I worked brought a wealth of experience and leadership skills that enabled the college to make some bold and innovative moves. They empowered the administration by allowing us to run the college, they secured board support for new ventures and policies, and they brought experience and expertise that complemented and extended our own strengths. I cannot overstate the importance of strong, committed, and involved board leadership. It was not until well into the presidency, however, that I developed personal friendships with trustees and their spouses and participated in social interactions with them outside of college events.

I built a strong, experienced, and focused administrative team, despite some early, and costly, missteps. I learned that when I hired for expertise over loyalty, I paid a high price for the choice. On the other hand, enthusiasm and loyalty proved no substitute for expertise. Both expertise and loyalty are essential qualities in senior administrators. The composition of my cabinet changed as vice presidents moved on, but, in part because these changes were staggered, there was a remarkable degree of continuity. Despite the negative environmental circumstances we faced in the early 1990s, we streamlined our operations and made them both efficient and customer friendly.

Each of the vice presidents played a vital role in the extraordinary transformation of Rollins. After a few years, I was fortunate to attract an experienced, competent, loyal vice president to work with me on the renovation of our facilities, the development of the campus, and the acquisition and development (commercial and educational) of property. His involvement in the community strengthened our relationships with business and community leaders, and paved the way for support and approval of our projects. My advancement vice presidents were key to the extraordinary fund-raising success we enjoyed. One of them understood better than anyone I have worked with the role of advancement in positioning and legitimating the president.

While all members of the senior team are important, the chief academic officer is pivotal to the success of a president's mission-related change agenda. A politically astute, well-connected academic officer is invaluable in assessing the faculty's readiness for change and in preparing the political ground for new initiatives. Each of the four academic vice presidents with whom I worked brought different strengths to the administration, and each had different relationships with the faculty. Rounding out my top team was a backstage, but essential, member—my executive assistant, a Rollins graduate with a Ph.D. in English. It was my great good fortune to have such a smart and loyal comrade, with great judgment, excellent editing ability, knowledge of the college's history, and an incredible work ethic. Without her, my presidency would have been a lot less successful and a lot less fun.

Because I wanted to be an academic leader, not simply the institution's chief fund-raiser, I immersed myself in academic affairs, faculty governance, cocurricular programming, and student life. I knew the importance of a president's relations with faculty in any change effort, and I was also a strong advocate of a lively scholarly life, even for a teaching faculty. Thus, I interacted with faculty about their teaching, scholarship, and other intellectual matters, a practice I continued throughout my presidency. I observed classes of senior as well as junior professors, and was always exhilarated by the quality of their teaching and their incredible devotion to students. I always read (or at least skimmed) the scholarly work faculty sent me and displayed publications on my conference table for the academic year. I wrote or e-mailed a note complimenting the professor and, if appropriate, commenting on the work itself. One faculty member's response to a note I had sent read: "Many thanks for taking the time in your busy schedule to read and respond to my article . . . such interest is one of my best incentives to continue to be a productive scholar" (April 7, 1994).

As I gained legitimacy and began to press for institutional change, the flow of memoranda from faculty with suggestions, requests, and complaints increased. I interpreted this positively as a sign of acceptance as a taken-for-granted member of the campus community, albeit one with more power. One faculty member sent a four-page memorandum with a plan for enhancing faculty compensation through budget savings, including the following: "[D]o we really need to buy gas for those leaf blowers? Couldn't we get by with brooms?" (March 12, 1993). Another professor pleaded, "I need a grounded electrical outlet in my office. . . . Would you impress the relevant people for me that this is a matter of some importance? I am obviously powerless on my own" (November 2, 1993). And there was the perennial memorandum complaining about parking, which I came to expect: "It is 7:45 A.M. and I have been unable to find a parking place in the faculty/staff parking lot . . . If I come again before 8:15 A.M. and am unable to find a parking spot . . . I will come over and park in your space (that is, if you don't beat me to it)" (May 2, 1994). Typical of a president's life, my job was to keep the institution focused on the big picture while dealing effectively with the quotidian issues that demanded attention.

I invested a great deal of time getting to know students and establishing myself as a student-oriented president. I knew well the importance of early imprinting to long-lasting perceptions, but found later that, despite my earnest efforts and genuine caring, students saw me as a corporate type. After a number of years, when my predecessor's classes had graduated, my image with students changed. I found throughout my presidency that, when I was buried in paperwork and a non-stop meeting schedule, I could always revive myself with a walk around campus and conversations with students. From my first summer, I felt that I was just going through the motions "until the students came back and I was absolutely enmeshed then in the life, the living fabric of the institution" (July 1991). I often wondered whether, as a woman president, I served as a role model for women students, and late in my presidency established a group of women campus leaders with whom I met monthly. This proved rewarding for me and for them.

During the early years of my presidency, I began to develop relationships with the college's donors, alumni, and community and business leaders. Although I was accustomed to such cultivation activities from my prior work, I found them to be far more freighted for me in my role as president. I was keenly aware that the relationships my husband and I were developing with people were different from ordinary friendships in that we were so often aiming toward a fund-raising goal. This blurred the line between friendship and institution building. Fortunately, I have always enjoyed and been curious about people. This interest and my role as president enabled me to develop a far greater openness to those whose politics and worldview differed from mine.

Because of my experience in fund-raising, I knew the importance of recording what prospects told me, following up on commitments, and finding the right moment to solicit a gift. The longer I was in the Rollins presidency and the better I knew people, the more comfortable I felt making solicitations during casual encounters. I came to call this "opportunity fund-raising." Even during holiday parties, if the moment seemed right and I had a good relationship with someone, I was comfortable in soliciting a gift. In my thirteenth year, the Orlando *Sentinel* reported on a successful $100,000 solicitation I made when a couple I knew stopped riding their bicycles on campus to talk with me.

"ON THE MOVE"

Once the strategic plan had been accepted by the board of trustees in 1992, the provost worked with the faculty to produce a needs list. This list, refined by the administration and the board, became the basis for our fund-raising campaign. Because the economy, student enrollment patterns, and our own budget were not strong, and because the college's last campaign, during the previous decade, had brought in only $43 million, I was advised to set a modest campaign goal. However, I was keenly aware that the college's small endowment, tight budget, and run-down campus would never support its ambitious goals, and I knew that people were counting on me to raise a great deal of money. In October 1996, the Rollins Board of Trustees, with considerable apprehension, approved a $100-million fund-raising campaign. I learned later that the faculty had decided the board would never agree to a goal of over $75 million; they were thrilled. Board members were energized by this new level of activity, which coincided with a decision to develop a college property for commercial use and the sponsorship of a national conference on the future of liberal education. I recorded the following comments made by trustees at this meeting: "This is the most important and enthusiastic meeting this board has ever had." "It's the best it's been, ever." "The board has never been closer together."

The campaign became the major focus of my presidency and was a great source of legitimacy for my presidency and my change agenda. I continued to be involved in academic and student life, financial matters, design and construction of new campus facilities, and development of several commercial projects. Integrating these activities (under one big hat) enabled me always to have my pulse on campus activities and bring them to the awareness of donors. I also brought external constituents into the

life of the campus. While we launched the campaign in a depressed economic environment, we soon reaped the benefits of the roaring 1990s.
We were able to fulfill most of our needs, and concluded with an unprecedented $160.2 million. With donor support we established fourteen
new endowed chairs (for a total of twenty-three, including one for "distinguished presidential leadership"), launched new academic and student-
development programs, significantly increased financial aid, and
established a number of important centers and institutes. We also secured
a $10-million endowment to support the presidency (the first in the
nation). I was especially proud that over half of the campaign came from
Rollins alumni. In the course of the campaign, I decided that a personal
gift beyond the annual fund would add legitimacy to my frequent solicitations of others for capital projects. I funded "Rita's Fountain" in the
entrance plaza to the new campus center, and, later, a lakeside gazebo,
"Harland's Haven," in honor of my husband's participation in my presidency and in the life of the college.

In large measure, the success of the campaign was attributable to an
enthusiastic and hardworking development staff with outstanding leadership. The first advancement vice president for the campaign was hired
by my predecessor and stayed on to work with me. At first, he doubted
that I could be successful in fund-raising for Rollins. However, as a newcomer to the college, I needed the guidance of someone who knew the
constituencies well. I asked him to work with me and, based on his knowledge, I made some ambitious and successful solicitations that helped
launch the campaign. His successor as vice president was smart, motivated,
and indefatigable. We had a great deal of fun together. She orchestrated
many successful solicitation opportunities for me and was herself an extraordinary fund-raiser. In fact, it was her relationship with a key donor that
resulted in establishment of a chair and endowment for the presidency.

Without question, the campaign transformed the college. Most significant were the funds that enabled us to strengthen the academic program,
recruit and retain outstanding faculty, and become more selective in student admissions. Through the campaign we also remade the campus, adding or renovating classrooms and offices, building or renovating six
facilities, and punctuating the lush landscaping with gardens, sculpture,
fountains, and gazebos. Of special significance was the gateway to the
college that we created with a gift in honor of a prior president and his
wife who had devoted their lives to Rollins and to the Winter Park community. The gateway provided a powerful sense of place and gravitas and
served as a symbolic link between the town and the college. We also

acquired nearby property for both college and commercial use and developed several lucrative, revenue-generating projects. On occasion, our historically excellent town-gown relations were strained by the perception that we were becoming too commercial. We had ongoing challenges in securing community support for our acquisition and development efforts. Although we undertook these initiatives for worthy reasons—to expand our sixty-seven-acre campus and generate additional revenue for operations—I received many negative comments and ugly letters. One man wrote, "The money-grubbing myopic request of your College administration . . . is not only deplorable but an indelible reflection on your judgement and character" (May 8, 1997). The vice president responsible for business and finance was indispensable in our efforts to overcome such negativity, spending a great deal of time with city planners, officials, property owners, and citizens. He later became chair of the local chamber of commerce, which cemented even further our relations with the city.

The vice president and I were uncompromising in our standards for design and quality. The effects of our vigilance in protecting and enhancing the special characteristics of the campus have made a difference, although they are taken for granted by most people. I am especially pleased at having protected a main pedestrian axis from the encroachment of a new facility, breaking through a fortresslike concrete barrier surrounding a new plaza, opening the stairwells of a parking garage to protect students from the dangers of concealed spaces, and assuring consistency with the historic architectural and design vocabulary of a beautiful campus.

Alumni, parents, corporate leaders, and other visitors correctly assumed that our attention to the quality and beauty of the physical plant reflected a commitment to quality throughout the college. This was an unexpected consequence of the campaign. Even early faculty digs about the "per-student cost" of the new landscaping gave way to enthusiasm for the beauty of their work environment. This is not to suggest that the campaign was without controversy. Some faculty felt that "fund-raising drives everything at this college." A faculty leader asked, "Why do we bring on trustees because they have money? Why don't we get trustees who share our values?" There were those who complained that we were not raising money for their needs or interests. And, as we became more and more successful in meeting our goals, more projects, old and new, were put before me: "If only Rita will develop a passion for this project, she will make it happen." Some trustees resigned from the board early in the campaign, suggesting that they would not be able to provide the level of support we expected. A few nondonors felt that the administration was overly focused on fund-raising.

Hamilton Holt, Rollins's legendary president, who in the 1920s and 1930s saved the college from financial ruin and reinvented the academic program, solicited money from everyone he knew or met. The college's old-timers say that the only time Holt had his hands in his own pockets was in his official college portrait. During my years as president, I often looked at that portrait hanging prominently in the college's major meeting room. When I was feeling valued only for my fund-raising prowess, I took comfort in the precedent he had set. When I reviewed the considerable change in the campus made possible through our fund-raising, I saw myself as legitimated through Holt's example. In either case, he was always a large but comforting presence.

We took advantage of the extraordinary philanthropy of the late 1990s to stabilize our finances and operations and made an early decision to make the campaign budget relieving rather than budget enhancing. Almost half of the campaign went to the endowment, which, coupled with unprecedented growth in the stock market, helped us become less tuition dependent. Both the greatly increased endowment and our commercial ventures provided much-needed additional revenue for the operating budget. By the end of the campaign, we had secured forty-five gifts of $1 million or more, and everyone had become increasingly blasé about this extraordinary largess. Early in the Rollins campaign, I convened the faculty with great excitement to announce every $1-million gift, and they were appropriately appreciative and enthusiastic, as were the trustees. In time, I no longer gathered people for these announcements and often teased faculty and trustees about their expectations for large gifts and their increasingly jaded responses. However, the campaign yielded such palpable and positive changes in quality, visibility, and financial health that the faculty was, on the whole, very enthusiastic. One expression of this enthusiasm was the resolution of thanks passed and presented to me at the campaign's conclusion in 2001, along with a standing ovation, surely unusual for faculty. The trustees were immensely proud of the campaign's success. Many of them had made significant gifts of great importance for the college. They were the backbone of the campaign; without their enthusiasm, guidance, and financial support we would never have achieved such a result.

The Campaign For Rollins, with the slogan, "Rollins, On the Move," was the engine that propelled an extraordinary transformation in all aspects of the college's quality. As a result, there was a national "buzz" about

Rollins, which, together with our new facilities and programs, generated student interest. As our reputation for quality grew, our drawing power increased. More and more students sought admission, and we increased our size while becoming far more selective. Faculty and administrators were eager to join us, and alumni and community leaders angled for membership on the board of trustees.

THROUGH A REARVIEW MIRROR

A number of tangible signs indicated that our accomplishments had gained traction. Our ranking in the *U.S. News & World Report's* annual "America's Best Colleges" report jumped from number six to number two in our category, above that of our historic rival, and remained there. The MBA program was ranked twelfth on the *Forbes* magazine list of the top twenty programs based on return on investment. The surge in the number of applicants and enrolled students, increase in our fund-raising and endowment, and the budget discipline we imposed improved the college's financial health significantly. In the process, we also greatly improved student selectivity, yield, diversity, and retention in all programs. Over the course of the 1990s, we continued to strengthen the standards and processes for faculty evaluation and increased the size and diversity of the faculty. We responded to market and student needs by adding new courses and academic majors and minors; promoting collaborative faculty-student research; and creating important service centers, such as the Christian A. Johnson Institute for Effective Teaching, the Thomas Phillips Johnson Student Resource Center, and the Philanthropy and Nonprofit Leadership Center.

Most of these initiatives were made possible by resources secured through our fund-raising campaign. We were all proud of having brought the college to a new level of achievement and recognition. I was especially gratified by a trustee's comment that my "exceptionally strong commitment to quality" has led "to the transformation of Rollins as a nationally recognized institution." The college had made great strides; the danger now was losing momentum. We faced the continuing challenge of strengthening standards; attracting students, faculty, and staff; improving compensation; reducing dependence on tuition; building the endowment; and expanding the campus.

I began warning that "One of the greatest threats to successful institutions is complacency. If we are complacent, we will fall behind and compromise the gains we have made" (memorandum to the faculty, March 2001, 3). To avoid complacency and to prepare for the next phase of development, we launched a new round of strategic planning. It was at this point, in my thirteenth year as president, that I began to contemplate the appropriate timing of my exit.

PART IV

Legitimacy in the Presidential Succession Process

CHAPTER 16

Presidential Succession and Legitimacy

INSTITUTIONAL LEGITIMACY IN THE SUCCESSION PROCESS

I have proposed a presidential cycle of three stages. The first stage is achieving legitimacy and influence with constituents, which stems from acceptance as a good leader and a fit with the institutional culture. The second stage is assuring the legitimacy and institutionalization of a change agenda, the essence of a president's legacy. The final stage in a presidential cycle is that of succession. High legitimacy in the first two stages does not guaranty legitimacy in the third (succession) stage, a period fraught with threats to the legitimacy of the exiting and the incoming presidents as well as to the institution. The management of a presidential succession can enhance or detract from the legitimacy of an institution, internally and externally.

Presidential succession is a significant moment in the academic world as it signals a college or university community's sense of itself, its mission, and its future. A poor presidential succession process may result in a diminution of legitimacy for an institution, and more than one failure will reinforce that reputation. In chapter 5, I used Hollander's definition of legitimacy as granted by constituents to an effective leader accepted as a good cultural fit. For this discussion of institutional rather than individual legitimacy, Suchman's definition seems more appropriate. He describes legitimacy as "a generalized perception or assumption that the actions of an entity are desirable, proper, or appropriate within some socially constructed system of norms, values, beliefs, and definitions" (Suchman 1995, 574). While an institution can retain its legitimacy in the face of "specific adverse acts or occurrences," it may become vulnerable after a history of such events (574). Thus, a series of mismanaged presidential transitions reflects especially poorly on an institution, although even one illegitimate succession process can traumatize an institution and create a blemish on the otherwise smooth skin of historic lore.

Because the processes of presidential search and transition are highly public, colleges and universities are especially vulnerable to a loss of legitimacy during this period. The comings and goings of higher education CEOs are of considerable interest to peers, scholars, the public, and the media. Failure, humiliation, and defeat are all fodder for those who seek to diminish the lofty pretensions of the nation's universities and colleges. There are many examples of botched successions that provide grist for these mills. The termination of a recently appointed president or the humiliation of a departing chancellor causes a loss of legitimacy for the institution, often casting a shadow over its good name for years. Because of the widespread media scrutiny of these situations, failed presidencies and the institutions that failed in managing them are well known and remembered. Some of these ruptures have been the result of good presidents being caught in political currents outside of their control, the most notorious example of which occurred in 1967 at the peak of the student demonstrations against the Vietnam War, when Governor Ronald Reagan fired Clark Kerr from the University of California for his failure to control the protestors.

Everything about a presidential succession is publicly scrutinized: the search consultant employed, the final candidates, the degree of board unanimity about the selection, the status of the departing president, representatives attending the inauguration, the departure and replacement of senior administrators, and, of course, the new president's missteps. Ideally, the succession process should be smooth, with constituents participating in ceremonies reinforcing institutional traditions while expressing gratitude to the departing leader and warmly welcoming the new president.

Rollins College offers an example of a poorly handled transition, similar to those shared by a number of institutions. In 1949, after the departure of Hamilton Holt, a transformational president who had served for twenty-four years, the college's trustees appointed a thirty-three-year-old corporate executive educated at the University of Chicago and mentored by its president, Robert Hutchins. In addition to having immediate legitimacy problems because he was not an academic, this new president inherited an unbalanced budget. Anticipating further financial problems, he acted precipitately to eliminate the football program and to downsize the faculty by one-third. The trustees, although they had approved these actions, became concerned when faculty and students mounted protests, and the retired president, although relocated to the Northeast, began to agitate against the new president, whom he had supported for the job. In fact, Holt sent the Orlando newspaper a copy of a letter urging his successor to resign. It became a front-page headline. Within eighteen months, despite his protestations and a court suit, the young leader was out of a job. The positive national media coverage garnered by his appointment rapidly turned negative (Lane Unpublished Manuscript: chapter 8). This story, with varying permutations in a wide variety of institutions, repeats itself, and leaves us wondering whether boards and faculties can do more to assure a successful transition. Although there are doubtless some people who should not be presidents, others might succeed with more support and assistance.

Many participants in the Rollins debacle argued that the young president's values, vision, and behavior were inconsistent with those of the academy and the college. They may have been right, and the situation may have been unsalvageable. I would argue that the president might have been successful if he had had a transition and assimilation plan to guide him into the culture of the college. In the end, the board replaced him with an easygoing, well-liked Rollins art professor and alumnus who helped heal the powerful rifts among and between constituents. The story of that succession failure tortures the memories of those who were participants and mars the otherwise inspiring college mythos. Many higher education institutions have similar presidential failures in their histories, often on the heels of a long-serving, successful, and charismatic leader. Max Weber (in Etzioni 1964, 55–56) asserts that "most higher-ranking individuals are dispensable; commitments are to the position, not to the incumbent." However, Weber notes an exception "upon the departure or death of the person to whom commitments are personal rather than bureaucratic." Thus, the loss of a charismatic leader may lead to a major organizational crisis, which he calls "The Succession Crisis." This was the case at Rollins when the charismatic President Holt retired, causing a great sense of loss and making a successful succession almost impossible.

To Birnbaum, presidents are generally dispensable and are of most benefit to their institutions when they arrive and when they leave. He views the succession process itself as creating "hope, excitement, and perceptions of new beginnings, as the institution renews itself" (Birnbaum 1992, 194–95, 169). I agree with Birnbaum about the sense of new possibilities that arise in transitions, but frequent turnover has the opposite effect of disheartening constituents. I also disagree that presidents are "dispensable." Such a view denies that presidential leadership is significant in strengthening and repositioning institutions, and ignores the importance of longevity to building the social capital necessary for change. Certainly, when the timing is right, the succession process provides the opportunity for an institution to renew itself. This is the time for stakeholders to consider the strengths and challenges of the institution and to identify the type of leader who would be a good fit for the next phase of its development.

RITES OF PASSAGE:
SEPARATION, TRANSITION, INCORPORATION

Arnold van Gennep studied the ceremonies celebrating the transition of an individual from one status to another within a society. I believe van Gennep's concept of the rites of passage has explanatory power for the presidential succession. The rites of passage are characterized by three phases: separation, transition, and incorporation. When individuals are in the transitional or "liminal" phase, they are in a state of suspension (limen), unstructured and ambiguous, separated from their previous status and not yet incorporated into the new one. In this phase, they may be a threat to themselves, as well as the entire group (Kimball 1968, 113).

Although the presidential transition involves two people, it represents one office within an institutional culture. In the first phase, the sitting president announces his or her departure, and begins a separation from the group. Next, following a search, a new president is appointed. However, in this "liminal" phase new presidents are especially vulnerable to rejection by the community. Victor Turner describes a rite of passage surrounding the senior chief (the highest status position) of a Zambian tribe. The chief elect during the transitional (liminal) phase is publicly humiliated and reviled to help him become a more humble, patient, and self-controlled chief. The passage from lower to higher status is through a "limbo of statuslessness," says Turner. The individual in liminality is a tabula rasa, a blank slate, on which the group inscribes its accumulated knowledge and wisdom. The ordeals and humiliations endured in the liminal state serve to break down the individual's previous status. The process also prepares the person to cope with the responsibilities of the new status and to refrain from abusing the privileges of the new status (1969, 1990, 147–51).

Turner's example and explication of the transitional, or liminal, phase of the rites of passage can usefully be applied to the experience of new presidents from the earliest candidate interviews through a lengthy period of testing that may continue well past the formal inauguration until legitimacy (acceptance into the culture) has been attained. Throughout the liminal phase, the candidate/president elect is subject to overt and covert criticisms and humiliations before being accepted into the culture and the presidency. The third phase, incorporation, can be thought of as a return to the rights and obligations of a structured position along with its customary norms and ethics (Turner 1969, 1990, 147). When we apply the incorporation phase to the presidential succession, we can conceive of it as comprising two elements: the symbolic and the actual. Symbolically, incorporation occurs in the inauguration ceremony when a new president is inducted into the institution with ceremonial pomp and circumstance, and the authority of the office is publicly transferred from the departing president. In practice, the new president is not fully incorporated until assimilated into the culture and legitimated by the community.

Harrison Trice and David Morand adapt van Gennep's rites of passage to work careers. They point out that while rites of passage are a stabilizing influence, they can also be dysfunctional. They tend to reinforce the status quo, discourage change and innovation, and to "stymie the flexibility necessary to make adaptations to a turbulent environment." However, innovative institutions socialize newcomers with rules and processes that reward innovation and by adapting the functional and dysfunctional aspects of the rites of passage to an organization's needs (1989, 413–14). This is especially applicable to the rites of passage around a presidential succession. The succession process, its rituals and ceremonies, should reflect the meaning of the change—signaling a radically new era or a continuation of the current equilibrium. This perspective allows for planned and spontaneous changes in institutional rituals and ceremonies to prepare stakeholders for the new era and to reflect the personality of the individuals involved, especially the new president.

Kathleen Manning applies the rites of passage to specific ceremonies and rituals in higher education, using a constructivist perspective rather than van Gennep's structuralist interpretation. Van Gennep describes the rites of passage as deterministic and inherent in nature; Manning observes structures and rituals as socially constructed through the action of human beings (2000, 27, 35–37). Manning adapts the rites of passage to the ceremonies and rituals of higher education (convocations, commencements, inaugurations, founders' days) that connect individuals with the institutional community through the creation of shared meaning. Manning views each ceremony as embodying all three stages of the rites of passage: separation, transition, and incorporation (10).

Table 16. 1
Rites of Passage in Presidential Succession

Separation	Transition			Incorporation	
Decision to Leave (Announcement)	Search/Selection (Anticipatory Socialization)	Testing/Assimilation	Passing the Baton (Anticipatory Nostalgia)	Inauguration	Acceptance

I take a broader approach than Manning to the rites of passage, seeing them not simply as occurring within the frame of a particular ceremonial function, but as constituting a frame for the entire presidential succession process. Thus, the announcement of the current president's planned departure signals "separation," the first rite; the period of search, selection, testing, and assimilation of the successor is "transition," the second rite; and, finally, the handoff from the exiting to the incoming president, the new president's symbolic investiture as leader during the inauguration ceremony, followed, one hopes, by acceptance into the culture, the third rite of passage, "incorporation."

RITES OF PASSAGE IN PRESIDENTIAL SUCCESSION

Table 16.1 depicts the rites of passage as I am applying them to the presidential succession process. The table shows each phase of the process connected to one of the rites of passage. Two additional ideas are included. I apply the idea of anticipatory socialization (Merton 1957) to the efforts of newly appointed presidents to identify with their new institutional cultures as quickly as possible. Anticipatory nostalgia is the concept used by Cohen and March (1974) to describe the exiting president's feelings as departure nears. The incoming president is looking ahead, the exiting president, behind.

CHAPTER 17

Factors in Succession Legitimacy

I have built the construct for legitimacy in the third phase of the presidency, the succession phase, within the context of the rites of passage as follows.

SEPARATION

The Decision to Leave

Those moving to other presidencies or positions have important obligations to the home institution. Following acceptance of another position, the president, together with the board, must communicate the timing and arrangements of the succession process in a way that reassures constituents about administrative continuity. Such communication is also critical for presidents stepping down to retire or to take another role in the same institution. In the case of a president asked to leave because of one of the threats to legitimacy outlined in chapter 7 (poor management, lack of cultural fit, misconduct, erosion of social capital, inattentiveness, or grandiosity) or some other reason, trustees must be especially vigilant to reassure the community about the stability of the institution. Trustee involvement and leadership is crucial to the success of a presidential succession process.

Although some long-term presidents have successfully reinvented their presidencies and maintained their own enthusiasm and constituent support for several decades, those who have served for ten years or more must contemplate the discontents that can torpedo a presidency. In the late stage of a presidency, incumbents may delude themselves into thinking they deserve more recompense than they receive. They may find that their relationships with constituents have begun to fray, or that they have become bored with the day-to-day demands of the position and increasingly turn responsibilities over to others. They may have begun to act on behalf of their constituents with less and less consultation. There is folklore about a presidential slump that may occur after five to seven years on the job, but after a decade or so, certainly when there is a legacy of which to be proud, a president should begin the process of considering the timing for a graceful exit. Long-term presidents generally leave for four reasons: They are asked to leave, they take another presidency, they take another position, or they retire. Unless misconduct is involved, it is important both to the individual and the institution to assure a smooth exit and a legitimate postpresidential status. A long-term presidency with a sour ending is hard for an institution to digest, and the incumbent, who has dedicated his or her life to the institution for a period of time, is alienated from a beloved home. An institution suffering a lack of legitimacy due to the behavior of the president will need to reclaim its reputation.

Flawn (1990, 196) advises a presidential tenure of between five and ten years. "Do not leave," he says, "before you have made a solid record of accomplishment; do not stay too long after you have made the record. . . . It is better to take early retirement as a successful president . . . than to stay for a 'few more years' and see the institution get away from you." Alton and Dean (2002, 23) report that in the last thirty years the number of presidents who serve to age sixty-five has increased by 25 percent and the number who serve in two or more presidencies has doubled. Their research on presidential turnover shows that apart from retirement, the two most important factors influencing departures are the opportunity for another position and the belief that one's objectives have been accomplished. When has a president accomplished enough? There are always changes awaiting leaders. Should the next phase be left to the successor? How does a president know when to leave? What are the options for the postpresidency? The question of timing is subtle, and many presidents have difficulty relinquishing the challenge, prestige, and perquisites of the position.

In 2001, the average presidential tenure was 6.6 years—6.3 at public institutions, 7.1 at privates (Corrigan 2002, 2, 38). However, just about all respondents to my interviews and 36 percent of the respondents to my survey on legitimacy indicated that ten years is the optimal period for a successful presidency. After ten years, presidents "burn out or have done what they can do and they're hanging on. . . . Institutions evolve and the person who was the right fit at the beginning of a presidency may no longer be right" (Breneman Interview 2002). Brand says that in large public research universities presidents do their best work between five and eight years. While it is "almost impossible to be effective in less than five years," after eight years it is also "difficult to be effective. . . . The transformational president has the difficulty of balancing multiple constituencies," and, in time, "they get tired of us" (Interview 2002).

Fisher believes "six to ten years in a particular office is about the maximum for effectively exerting charismatic power" because that mystique is diminished with familiarity. Further, he says, presidents should leave if they lose interest in what they are doing (Fisher 1984, 49, 46). Often, presidents are criticized for staying too long. Trachtenberg, president of two institutions for a total of twenty-five years, says, "People know in their hearts when it's no longer fun. Universities are wonderful indulgences. . . . It's hard to think of a more enjoyable way of earning your livelihood, even under the most dire and challenging circumstances." But he points out that a number of people, mainly "legacy academics," report feeling "burned out and exhausted after four years" (Interview 2000). On the other hand, Father Hesburgh, president of the University of Notre Dame for thirty-five years, told a *Chronicle* reporter: "You can argue about how long the tenure of a president should be, but I think I was a much better president 20 or 30 years down the line than when I began" (Hesburgh chronicle.com 2001). After considerable study, my own view is that a successful president achieves legitimacy, moves a legitimate change agenda, and then moves on. The cycle takes from eight to fifteen years (with ten years as a good guidepost) and, although some presidents have reinvigorated themselves and their constituents for another cycle, most have completed their objectives and need to pass the baton.

Presidents considering retirement from the presidency face the challenges embedded in each of the rites of passage: separation (when to leave), transition (anxiety and uncertainty), and (incorporation) a meaningful postpresidential life, work, or retirement. Many presidents have great difficulty making the decision to leave. After a decade or more of successful stewardship, they have become embedded in the campus culture. Their lives and relationships are woven around their institutions, and they are addicted to the challenges and opportunities of the presidency. Those who lose their personal identity in the presidency have a great deal of trouble letting go (Moore and Burrows 2001, 34–35). There seems to be general agreement that it is important to leave a presidency before legitimacy erodes. In the last months of a nine-year presidency, Mohrman (2002) wrote: "It's always better to leave a little too soon than a little too late. When a president remains in office too long, not only does the individual suffer, but also the institution. A kind of paralysis sets in: new initiatives are unlikely, morale may drop, and the uncertainties about when a new leader will be coming may provoke anxiety." Professors often experience the same dilemma about the appropriate time to leave or retire. In a letter to the editor of the *Chronicle of Higher Education*, Gilbert Fite (2002, B21–B22) asks, "Did I want to be remembered at the height of my career, or as a doddering old fuddy-duddy bothering people around the history department and the university?"

This is not a subject for presidents to discuss with their boards until they are sure of their timing and needs. Most presidents make their decisions without any professional guidance, although informal advice and experience are shared anecdotally among presidential colleagues. At a 2002 seminar for presidents, two recently retired presidents expressed strong opinions about three elements of departure:

1. Do not stay too long, things can unravel quickly and negatively.
2. Do not give too much notice because the lame duck period is very difficult and people ignore you or take over.
3. Move out of town, preferably for good, but for at least a year. If you stay, the following will occur: if your successor is doing well, you will feel jealous; if she or he is doing poorly, people will try and suck you into discussions about how badly things are going (Private conversation, March 2002).

On the other hand, when Roscoe Brown stepped down from the presidency of Bronx Community College after sixteen years, he noted that the general prescription to take six or so months off from any professional responsibility does not work because it is too abrupt a transition from the hectic life of the presidency. He advises that it is better to do something professional while contemplating longer-term possibilities. In "An Exit Checklist for Presidents," he includes a reminder for presidents to review their papers and files, and decide what should be preserved and what discarded (Brown 1996, 44). I would add that most of those papers and files should be forwarded to the library archives as part of the precious historical documents of that presidential era. This material will play a role in preserving the president's legacy.

When asked in an interview whether a departing president should leave town, one retired president responded, "For a year, certainly. Otherwise, it's awkward for a new president, who may want to let go of some people, not support certain things that the former president cared about. And, the comparisons are inevitable. You're either not as good a speaker, or you're a little better. To have the other person there highlights the comparisons and makes them even more stark" (Freedman Interview 2002). There are many jokes about the successor paving over the predecessor's accomplishments or blaming everything on the predecessor. This is largely out of the control of the exiting president. But, says David Warren, "The incoming president needs to figure things out without the filter created by the predecessor." Presidents should "pass the baton and move on. In cases where a president does stay around, with a new title, often in fund raising, mostly I hear frustration and dissatisfaction. Some don't know when to leave the stage" (Interview 2002).

- After a decade as president of Smith College, Conway resigned for a variety of reasons, including a desire to spend more time with her husband and to write. She describes her fears as follows: "[I]t hit me that I was leaving, and that it was going to be harder than I'd thought. . . . When I looked to the future, I still had moments of sheer panic. What if it turned out that I couldn't manage much in life without a sheltering institution? . . . What would I do with myself without the discipline of the inexorable schedule?" (Conway 2001, 136, 138).

- In 1974, when James McNaughton Hester exited the presidency of New York University after thirteen years, it was also with mixed feelings. Although he took on an exciting new opportunity, he had conflicting feelings: "[I]t was clearly nearing time for me to turn NYU over to someone else. I had had ample opportunities to contribute what I could to the philosophy, organization, and resources of NYU. . . . And so I ended my great experience as president of NYU. . . . This was, of course, a deeply emotional experience for me because I had been so closely identified with NYU and its evolution for so many years. One inevitably feels some guilt in leaving an institution when many problems are yet to be solved. But I decided that there is never a moment when all problems are solved, and except for a few inevitable qualms, I have felt right about leaving NYU when I did" (Hester 1996, 116–17).

- After twenty-one years as president of the University of Chicago, Robert Hutchins accepted an invitation to become part of the newly formed Ford Foundation. He left the university in 1951 with a serious budget deficit, unsuccessful fund-raising results, tuition increases, staff unionization, and educational innovations that failed to become institutionalized there or elsewhere. Given his luminous reputation among the giants of education, it is sobering to note that at his farewell address to the faculty, Hutchins declared his administration a moral failure because there was no "notable progress being made towards the creation of a dedicated community" (McNeill 1991, 163–64).

Kauffman (1983, 7) reminds us that just as there is no clear career path to the presidency, a "temporary role rather than a profession," there is no clear career path beyond the presidency. This is not an issue for those who yearn for the life of a retiree, freed from the shackles of professional responsibility. But for others, this is the most vexing piece of the puzzle: how to find a meaningful way to make a contribution and preserve one's status and legitimacy following retirement from a presidency. For most college presidents, "the presidency is the capstone of their careers. . . . It is the best job they ever have had, or ever will have" (Cohen and March 1974, 186). Those who reach this career pinnacle too early have difficulty facing the need to exit. There is no comparable position awaiting them, unless they are not too old to secure another presidency. Many return to the classroom. Cohen and March (191–92) identify three phenomena presidents experience as they face exit. They experience "anticipatory nostalgia" about the presidency. They make departure more tolerable by focusing on the unpleasant aspects of the job. And they worry about no longer being seen as the president and about making a serious mistake before they exit. Freedman (Interview 2002) comments that, while he was still president at Dartmouth, every president he knew "worried that they might be ambushed . . . that something would happen and you would leave ignominiously. . . . You want to leave when they still like you."

A college president's fears about retiring from office are not much different from those of a corporate CEO or, indeed, a U.S. president. John Adams, according to David McCullough in his prize-winning biography, was afraid of becoming "irrelevant," and wrote, "The only question remaining with me is what shall I do with myself? . . . Something I must do, or ennui will rain upon me in buckets" (2001, 568). The uncertainties and anxieties that both exiting and incoming presidents experience are also experienced by constituents. The current president's departure announcement, followed by the processes of search and selection, set in motion a period of ambiguity, uncertainty, and testing—the transition (liminal) phase. Terrance Deal and Allan Kennedy (1982, 157–58) have observed that change, even, or especially, a change in leadership, threatens a culture: "People form strong attachments to heroes, legends, the rituals of daily life . . . all the symbols and settings of the workplace." Change leaves employees confused, insecure, and angry.

TRANSITION

Search and Selection

In preparing for a change of leadership, constituents will be most anxious that the search be thorough and inclusive. The status and influence of constituencies are reflected by their representation on the search committee, and a search must be perceived as legitimate for a new president to get off to a good start. A search firm is not always necessary, but can protect a board's independence and shield it from criticism. A search firm should work with the institution to develop a legitimate search process, and assist in identifying, filtering, and presenting the best candidates. In 2001, search firms were used to recruit over half of new presidents, up from 16 percent before 1985 (Corrigan 2002, 3). However, as David Warren indicates, to assure the legitimacy of the process, the firm must support, not lead, the search committee. A committee representative of the institution's key constituents must drive the process and make the decisions, especially about the finalists and their presentation to the campus (Interview 2002). During this period, even in a closed search process, regular communication with the candidates and with constituents is reassuring.

The search process is the candidate's opportunity to gain an understanding of an institution's history, values, and goals. Through the interview process the candidates develop an understanding of the expectations constituents have of a new president and can express their own expectations of trustees, faculty, alumni, and students. The most successful process is one where everything on both sides is on the table, so that there are no surprises later. The candidate selected will very likely have a different style of leadership from the predecessor and promote a new vision and change agenda for the institution. He or she may also assemble a new leadership team. As addressed in chapter 6, the early legitimacy accorded a new president is enhanced immeasurably by a search process considered inclusive and thorough—one that results in a unanimous and enthusiastic choice by the committee and the board. An open and honest series of conversations about the institution will prepare the chosen candidate to gain legitimacy and prepare constituencies to accept the new president.

From the moment of contact with the search committee until arrival on campus, the candidate experiences what Merton calls "anticipatory socialization"—adopting the values of a group to which a person aspires but does not belong. This process eases adjustment when the person becomes a part of that group (Merton 1957, 265). In a study of the factors in the succession and socialization of school principals, anticipation, or "anticipatory socialization," was the first stage followed by encounter (the arrival stage) and then stabilization (the final stage) (Hart 1991, 458–61). Another study of leadership succession also indicates that the "prearrival events" that occur before the successor takes over the position are "an integral part of the succession process" (Gordon and Rosen 1981, 240–41). I believe that anticipatory socialization is also characteristic of the higher education succession process as candidates seek to absorb the culture of the new institution.

The legitimacy of the succession process may be compromised when presidents follow a highly successful predecessor. In July 1997, when Barry Munitz announced that he was leaving the chancellorship of the California State University system to become president of the J. Paul Getty Trust, a newspaper headline read, "Munitz Leaving Tough Shoes to Fill." How often a new president hears that there are big shoes to fill. Max Weber suggests that smaller shoes may also be hard to fill: "Even fairly limited differences between a successor and his predecessor are believed to be a source of difficulties" (in Etzioni 1964, 55–56). It can be an asset to a new president's quest for legitimacy to be very different from a well-liked predecessor. Some institutions seek new presidents with strengths in areas in which the predecessor was weak. Faculty, especially, expect a new president to solve all the problems they blame the previous president for not handling (Birnbaum 1992, 84). Sometimes, after a transformational president leaves, institutions seek a conservator to maintain and preserve what has been accomplished, or, following a period of good stewardship, an institution builder will be sought.

The succession process provides an important opportunity for constituents to evaluate their college or university's strengths, challenges, and opportunities, and to identify the characteristics important in the next president. "Although the normative process suggests the need to identify organizational goals before the search, in practice it may be the search itself that defines the organizational goals. . . . It is the process of discussing the apparent differences between candidates that permits the committee to enact its values. It decides from among all the rhetorical requirements which are truly the most important ones." The process itself helps the committee to better clarify its goals and expectations (Birnbaum 1988, 498–99, 504).

Testing and Assimilation

The trials of the testing period were discussed briefly in chapter 6, in the section on institutional legitimacy. In the context of the rites of passage, this period is freighted with special vulnerability and ambiguity as the newcomer is criticized and humiliated little differently from Turner's Zambian chief. Observers of a new college president are on the lookout for mistakes and for violations of "our culture." They make negative comparisons with the predecessor president, even though they may have had problems with her or his leadership. The new president must pass through Turner's "limbo of statuslessness" and be acculturated into the ways of the new community.

Donna Shalala, new in the University of Miami presidency but with two presidencies and a cabinet post behind her, was asked to comment on the "rocky start" of Lawrence Summers in the Harvard presidency. She said, "It's called 'gotcha.' They're [constituents] looking for everything. Fundamentally, they're wondering, 'Who is this person and what do they care about?'" (Lindsay 2002). Freedman suggests that when it is your first presidency, "people are really looking. We may have made a mistake and you may have made a mistake. You may think you want this, but you don't have the endurance or the skills or whatever to do it." In a second presidency you have a track record and "it's more a question of whether you are a fit for this place, do you understand it?" (Interview 2002).

One of the reasons the testing period for new presidents is so vicious in academe is that we generally hire people from other institutions who do not know the culture of the new organization. This is one of those deeply embedded cultural differences between academic and corporate culture. Corporate leaders engage in serious succession planning and the grooming of future CEOs. Academic communities, on the other hand, tend to believe that an outsider will take the institution to a new level of quality and reputation. They yearn for a visionary leader with star quality who will add luster to their institution and enhance its quality and reputation. In the fractious political world of academe, insiders suffer from familiarity and accrued grievances that translate into a lack of trust and confidence. Fisher (1991, 32–33) explains this by pointing out that insiders lack charisma with their colleagues, who are familiar with their "doubts, uncertainties, and limitations." It is much more likely for an outsider to develop charisma than it is for a well-known insider.

In the corporate world, as reported in chapter 7, there is only a 50 percent chance that when an outsider takes a job at a new company, he or she will remain with the company for more than two years (Downey et al. 2001, 3). Dan Ciampa and Michael Watkins (1999, 96–97) point out that the transition period begins before entry and present a series of prescriptions for new corporate leaders. They advise a transition process of overlapping learning and planning, and the creation of early momentum for change by focusing on a few priorities. They suggest becoming oriented to the culture, developing a compelling personal vision of the organization's future, and building supportive coalitions (114). Finally, they remind new leaders to manage their emotions and avoid isolation by developing a network of advisers and counselors who can offer technical, political, and personal help. They point out that interpersonal skills and maturity are critical in the transition period because early impressions are difficult to reverse: "Initial impressions can easily become self-fulfilling prophecies. . . . Once such impressions have hardened, there is virtually nothing the new leader can do in the short term to alter them" (273–74).

An "executive coach," a new type of corporate consultant, reports that nearly 20 percent of CEO failures become apparent within a few months after appointment. Unless there is a wrong fit, once the early warning signs are observed and the problem identified, corrective action is "neither costly nor difficult" and will often save the incumbent. She advises that prompt action with a coaching plan can avoid 60 percent of terminations (Soder 2002, 6). Downey et al. (2001, 1) suggest that assimilation begins as soon as a new leader is hired and is complete when the individual "becomes a full contributor and is no longer considered an outsider."

Downey et al. (2001, 28–29) propose a model for the "assimilation" process. They conceive of the assimilation of a new leader as a reciprocal process where both the individual and the organization are transformed. The model has a series of stages, designed to help new leaders avoid falling into "cultural potholes" (34). Moore and Burrows (2001, 48–53) apply this idea to higher education boards, that after appointing a new president, leave her "to fend for herself." The absence of "comprehensive transition management" during the first year in office may result in an unsuccessful presidency. The board should work with the incoming president on plans for orientation and professional development.

At colleges and universities, as in corporations, the process of assimilation should be planned as part of the transition and not be taken for granted. The sooner the new president achieves legitimacy and influence, the more quickly constituents will be ready to embrace change. Several higher education institutions have successfully experimented with a formal assimilation process.

- Stephen Weber succeeded a successful twenty-year president at San Diego State and went through a "New President's Assimilation" program adapted from a corporate model. After his first year, President Weber reflected on the process and said it "has made Cabinet members more self-confident and willing to risk telling me things I might not be eager to hear. My own learning curve was certainly accelerated" (Krinsky and Weber 1997, 11–13).

- At Susquehanna University, the search firm recommended that a presidential transition committee be established as soon as a selection was made. The committee, composed of members of key constituencies, communicated with the institution, recommended a schedule of meetings with individuals and groups for the president's first months, provided key information to their new leader, and served as a confidential sounding board for him. The committee was also sensitive to the importance of celebrating and thanking a long-time employee who had served as acting president. Like many high-profile ad hoc committees, the group had to deal with suspicion regarding its purposes and actions (Robertson 2001, 20–24).

I would extend the planning to involve the departing president in developing plans for a graceful exit and meaningful postpresidency. This planning is especially important since exiting presidents suffer from "anticipatory nostalgia" (Cohen and March 1974, 192) and know they will miss the challenge and stimulation of the job, the relationships, the opportunity to be influential, the status and prestige, the perks and support staff, and the students (Moore and Burrows 2001, 33).

INCORPORATION

Passing the Baton

The departing president, especially one leaving under positive conditions, has an obligation to assist the new president's search for legitimacy, most importantly in the language and comments used with constituents eager for gossip. The new president would do well to consult with the departing president, who may be able and willing to provide information no one else can or will. Assuming that some important decisions have been left for the new president, he or she may ask for advice before acting. The departing president can assist the new leader by pointing out institutional crevasses and the strengths and weaknesses of people and processes. Such information is especially important in regard to the president's administrative and office staff members, who are inevitably unsettled by the uncertainties of the transition. Although the competence and loyalty of the staff may have been invaluable to the prior administration, new presidents often wish to appoint colleagues with whom they have worked before. On this, as on other issues, the new president will want to test the information provided by the exiting president before taking any action, but an open relationship eases the way toward legitimacy. The departing president gains legitimacy by being valued as a source of advice and information while the incoming president wants to display independence from the predecessor and competence in meeting all challenges. In general, new presidents ask for very little advice from their predecessors.

Most departing presidents, now "lame ducks," keep their heads down and prepare for their next position or retirement. They try not to obstruct the new president's ability to connect with the institution and its constituents. The new president is both separating from a former life and seeking legitimacy in the new one. The relationships between the two presidents and between each of them and their overlapping constituencies are fraught with uncertainty and mistrust that often continues until the exiting president is ensconced in a new situation and the incoming president has been legitimated. The degree of consultation and contact between the two presidents is in the hands of the newcomer. A new president may seek a close, amiable relationship or may prefer to consult with and seek advice from others than the predecessor. Some new presidents express their satisfaction with their predecessors as "inversely correlated with the frequency of interaction" (Moore and Burrows 2001, 56–57).

A well-planned and successful transition provides both the incoming and outgoing presidents with legitimacy.

- For example, Wilson College followed a successful search with a "smooth and dignified presidential transition." As soon as the new president was appointed, a transition team was established comprising representatives from all constituencies. The close working relationship between the two presidents during the period of transfer, roughly six months, helped to assimilate the newcomer and allowed the retiring president to remain effective during the lame duck period (Edmundson and Jensen 2002).

Inauguration

The inaugural ceremony is set within the context of an institution's culture, history, and traditions. It connects the future to the past, and symbolizes the new president's incorporation into the culture. It is the major opportunity for new presidents to communicate their vision, values, and goals to the internal and external constituencies of the institution. Three models of inaugurations have been identified, emphasizing stability, change, or innovation. Planned around one of these themes, the inauguration becomes a platform for the new leader and lifts it from the realm of the ordinary to make it "a launch pad for campus initiatives" (Ficklen 2002, 38, 41).

The tone of the inauguration, of course, is established by the style and content of the program and the new president's address. This is the moment for the president's vision to be revealed and a challenge laid out for the constituencies to consider. Freedman notes, "More people listen to your inauguration address than any other. . . . It's really important in that inauguration to say: 'Here's what I hope to address in my time, here are the goals that I hope we will achieve together'" (Interview 2002). Inauguration ceremonies reaffirm the meaning and power of the shared mission of participants. They should excite the imagination with reminders of the unique institutional history and traditions. The academic regalia and procession lend the event the magic, weight, and context of history, and the inclusion of a range of constituent voices signifies welcome and hope. It is a time when the institution embraces its new leader (even when the leader is an insider), while paying homage to the institution's history and former presidents. The event is, above all, symbolic of a new era. If we consider the presidential succession process an institutional rite of passage, the rituals and symbols of the inauguration invest the president as primary representative of the institution, indeed, as symbol of the institution itself. This ceremony represents incorporation of the new president into the institutional culture, but the perils of the transitional (liminal) period are not over until assimilation has occurred and legitimacy is conferred.

Acceptance

Discussed at length in Part II, legitimacy must be achieved before a new president is fully incorporated into the fabric of the new institutional culture. Even an appointee from within must gain legitimacy in the presidency. Acceptance is the final step in the rites of passage that characterize the presidential succession process. Unfortunately, the succession process is generally unplanned, exposing both the exiting and incoming presidents, and the institution, to unnecessary hazards.

SUCCESSION LEGITIMACY RATING

Table 17.1, Succession Legitimacy Rating, portrays the succession legitimacy process in the context of the rites of passage. This construct

Table 17.1
Succession Legitimacy Rating

Factors in Legitimacy	Degree of Legitimacy	
	Low	High
Separation		
Decision to Leave	Poor Timing (Overstay, Leave Too Soon, Campaign in Progress, Weak Administrative Team)	Good Timing (Campaign Completed, Goals Completed, Strong Administration in Place)
Transition		
Search/Selection	Non-representative Process Candidate Not a Good Fit	Representative Process Candidate a Good Fit
Testing/Assimilation	Sink or Swim	Assimilation Plan
Incorporation		
Pass the Baton	Lack of Transparency, Candor, or Sensitivity to Each President's Needs	Planned Process for Handoff Supportive of Both Presidents
Inauguration	Inadequate Ceremonies	Ceremonial Pomp Reflecting New Presidency
Acceptance	Constituents Resist New President's Influence	Constituents Open to New President's Influence

indicates that there may be high or low legitimacy in each of the factors involved in the presidential succession process. The degree of legitimacy of each factor and the relationships among the factors may change over time.

CHAPTER 18

Threats to Succession Legitimacy

As threats to the legitimacy of the succession process, I propose the following: (1) Pandora's box, 2) intrusive predecessor, and 3) inattentive governing board. To facilitate legitimacy, all constituents must understand the delicate nature of the rites of passage in the succession process, especially the transition (liminal) phase, and participate sensitively in making it successful. Both the exiting and incoming presidents are experiencing major discontinuities and require thoughtful support and assistance to legitimate them and the process. Each of the following threats is common and, with preparation, avoidable.

PANDORA'S BOX

In the ancient myth, Pandora's curiosity impels her, against instructions to the contrary, to open a box, inadvertently releasing all the ills of the world. And so it is that new presidents may encounter a Pandora's box of serious problems that have been hidden from sight during the search process. In 2001, one in five presidents reported that they had not received a "full and accurate disclosure" of the institution's financial condition. A number said that the board failed to make its expectations clear to them (Corrigan 2002, 46). Some presidents are recruited to fulfill a specific charge or direction, but arrive to find that not all major stakeholders support this charge. When presidents lack information, they may fall into any number of crevasses, unknown to them. An off-the-cuff answer to a question arising from a deep-seated controversy can cause havoc. A solution proposed to bring closure to an issue may be inconsistent with prior agreements. And so on. Other crevasses awaiting new presidents result from knowledge and history that have been withheld—a shortfall in the budget, a poor recruiting year, mismanagement of the endowment, angry donors, irritated legislators, a divided board. The possibilities are vast and grave.

On the other hand, the new president may have secrets from the board that emerge unexpectedly later on. These can include misrepresentations regarding academic preparation, career path, scholarship, or personal life. The president, in an eagerness to secure the position, may also have suppressed concerns about the institution's mission or culture. Surprises that emerge after a president's selection can pose serious threats to legitimacy.

INTRUSIVE PREDECESSOR

Like the ghost of Hamlet's father, a predecessor president can haunt the successor, shackling him or her with unresolved grievances and making it difficult to chart a new course. Boards seeking dignity and legitimacy for a departing president often make the mistake of establishing a new role as chancellor, quasi administrator, or board member. Even when not rewarded with such a role, many former presidents stay on as faculty members and remain active in the community. A chancellor's role often carries responsibility for managing relationships with a few of the institution's top prospects, and little else. On the other hand, some boards, grateful to their departing presidents, grant them significant continuing authority.

- When John Silber was appointed chancellor after twenty-five years as president of Boston University, he had "an unusual amount of executive responsibility . . . including overseeing long-range planning and venture-capital operations, and advising the president on hiring and tenure decisions." His authority made it unclear how much of the university leadership had been transferred to the new president. Further, when the president who followed him resigned, Chancellor Silber stepped back into the presidency and indicated that he would have "an advisory role" in the search for a replacement ("Silber Resumes Presidency" 2002). The problem for an incoming president is establishing legitimacy when a successful predecessor with "big shoes" is so visible and involved.

- In 1968, the Brandeis University board of trustees appointed seventy-year-old Abram Sachar, completing twenty years as president, to the new position of chancellor. Sachar, the university's founding president and a "living legend," continued to reside in the president's mansion through the administrations of subsequent presidents and "to make every aspect of college business his business, to the dismay—and often to the detriment—of his successors," most of whom he reportedly drove from office (Simurda 1992, 47).

- The president of a Southern liberal arts college, leaving office in the late 1960s after eighteen years on the job, was awarded an appointment as chancellor and made chairman of the board of trustees. His young successor viewed his predecessor's positions as an impediment to his own quest for legitimacy, and the two never reconciled their differences.

Such an arrangement is a greater impediment to legitimacy for an in-experienced than for an experienced president. For example, in the early 2000s, a newly appointed president of a southern university was unfazed by the chancellorship of her predecessor because she was in her third presidency and not intimidated by his presence. Based on her impressive career, this president brought considerable legitimacy with her, but, as in all cases, she had to develop acceptance and legitimacy as a good fit with the new culture.

There are myriad examples of intrusive presidential predecessors who, wittingly or unwittingly, interfere with their successors' ability to achieve and maintain legitimacy and to make change. Some presidents maintain a highly visible presence on their campuses. Many collect their mail in the president's office.

- One president, with a high salary for the first five years out of office, also charged vacation travel to the college.
- One sitting president continued to vacation with trustees from the college where he was previously president, without the knowledge of his successor.

The permutations of these continuing involvements and relationships of a former president may be harmless to the successor president if the new leader can establish and maintain legitimacy. If there are problems, the visibility and intrusiveness of the predecessor can delegitimate the new president.

INATTENTIVE GOVERNING BOARD

As noted in the discussion of the threat of "inattention" to presidential legitimacy in chapter 7, all the constituents connected to an institution have numerous demands on their attention. Attention, in fact, is a scarce resource that people allocate to fulfill their obligations (Cohen and March 1974, 4). Once a search is completed, board members will turn their attention to their other responsibilities, some of which may have been neglected during this time. This redirection of attention is not mean spirited, but reflects both the heavy demands on board members and the limited time they can allocate to volunteer activities.

Once the board has made a presidential selection, it assumes that this person will know how to manage the transition. Most boards do not see the necessity of getting involved in the ongoing care and feeding of their presidents. They are inattentive to a president's need for support in the transition into the institution, during change, in crises, and at exit. Presidents are loath to ask for support and direction, not wishing to appear inadequate to the task. Some boards, on the other hand, are demanding, directive, and intrusive, and inattentive to the president's need for independence and flexibility. Things are off to a bad start when, after a search, the board remains divided on the new president's appointment. "When a board appoints a president, it accepts the responsibility of being—and being perceived to be, both on and off campus—solidly behind that president." Any reservations should be resolved "behind closed doors" (Fisher 1991, 96).

At one well-known university, a split over the appointment of a president reflected a serious schism over the direction of the institution. By failing to address and resolve the problem, when the president's contract came up for renewal, the board split again. The trustees failed to keep their differences behind closed doors and embarrassed the president by going public. This kind of inattention to the importance of a solidly supportive board undermines the president's ability to be seen as legitimate by both internal and external constituents.

A board should also help to script the postpresidency to both dignify the exit and clear the field for the successor. A retiring president is dealing with a seismic shift in career status and is also facing the major upheavals of physically vacating the office and home. Just as boards need to take responsibility for the successful assimilation of the new president, they also need to assist the exiting president during this traumatic period of loss and change.

CHAPTER 19

Strategies for Succession Legitimacy

Constituents perceive a presidential succession process as a loss or an opportunity for renewal or both. Indeed, both loss and renewal are involved, which a successful transition acknowledges. According to Ciampa and Watkins (1999, 33), in the corporate world "there is no single best way to manage a leadership transition. New leaders' approaches will inevitably be shaped by the situations they face, their prior experience, and their leadership styles." They point out that the transition period represents the beginning of a new era, bringing changes "that will permanently affect both the company's performance and its culture."

Despite the chaotic and anarchic nature of academic institutions and the endemic resistance to change among some constituents, I propose the following strategies to enhance succession legitimacy: ceremonies and rituals, transition planning, and legacy planning. Successful handling of the rites of passage of the presidential succession process provides legitimacy to the people involved and to the institution.

CEREMONIES AND RITUALS

Ceremonies place an institution's culture "on display" and "keep values, beliefs, and heroes" in the "minds and hearts" of constituents (Deal and Kennedy 1982, 63). The presidential succession process should be suffused with ceremony, ritual, symbol, and style. Departure of a president, even when it is time for new leadership, may give rise to feelings of loss and anxieties about change. Several of the presidents I interviewed described the president as a parental symbol-laden figure with emotional freight well beyond the customary employer-employee relationship. Deal points out that a "deep sense of individual and collective loss and grief . . . lurks below the surface of cultural change" and that collective cultural rituals can assuage deep fears and "mend tears in the fabric of shared meaning." Change, he says, is loss, and ritual serves as respite or repair. Failure to mark important changes can "unravel the fabric" holding an institution together (1985, 296–97). Deal suggests that, in businesses, until the loss of the exiting CEO is recognized or resolved, "the new CEO's ability to move the company ahead will be severely constrained" (309). Often a key figure has become a hero or heroine, and those who look up to these figures feel a great sense of loss. Both planned and spontaneous rituals can help people to "come to grips with the ambiguity and loss that change produces" (317).

Retirement rituals recognize the achievements of the departing president and, at the same time, reaffirm the values and traditions of the culture through the symbolic gifts and the stories that mark the end of an era. The institution's heroes and legends are recalled as background for the coming era. As part of the departure ritual, institutions often memorialize a president by naming endowed chairs, student scholarships, lecture series, programs, and/or buildings. These rituals serve as a summing up and an early attempt to define the departing president's legacy in the context of the institution's history. Rituals provide "the place and script" with which employees can experience meaning; they "bring order to chaos" (Deal and Kennedy 1982, 62).

Appropriate departure rituals provide meaning for both the exiting president and the campus constituents. They help relieve the anxieties of the transition or liminal period and prepare the institution to accept and incorporate the new president. This is also a period of great optimism and hope that the unfulfilled aspirations of the institution may, at last, be met. Here, too, symbols and ceremonies, from the departure announcement through the inauguration (discussed earlier), are important markers of change. One of the "Ten Commandments of Transition," developed by the incoming and outgoing presidents of Wilson College, reads, "Give equal attention to the new and the old, taking time to mourn what is passing and think creatively and innovatively about what is to come" (Edmundson and Jensen 2002). This advice addresses the importance of recognizing through ritual the cultural changes represented by a transition.

TRANSITION PLANNING

A successful transition process requires a plan for the smooth handoff of the baton of leadership from one president to another. It requires an assimilation plan for the new president and a plan for the postpresidency of the departing president. Each of these plans should be initiated or assisted by the board and guided by the presidents. Following a search considered legitimate by constituents, the board's introduction of the new president is met with excitement and great expectation. By this time, planning for the next phase of the departing president's career should be well under way, and this is the point at which the assimilation plan (described earlier) for the new president and the handoff plan become operative. This is also the time to assist senior administrators in transferring their loyalty to the new president or in securing new positions elsewhere. To enable the exiting president to continue to be effective during the lame-duck period, the board should authorize her or him to continue providing leadership and making decisions. Pierce, preparing to leave the presidency of the University of Puget Sound after eleven years, secured that authority from her board and told her senior administrators, "If anyone treats me like a lame duck, they're fired" (Pierce Interview 2003).

If the departing president is not going on to another position and eschews retirement, he or she is probably in need of some legitimating role or activity. Pierce says, "I don't want to walk away from everything I've cared about all my life or that I've learned" (Interview 2002). For many, moving from the challenges and prestige of the presidency to an unknown circumstance is depressing. Some presidents arrange a temporary perch for the year following their departure with one of the higher education associations, universities, or centers that provide such opportunities, generally to teach or conduct research. Other presidents are invited to serve on boards, and many move into consulting, writing, and volunteering. Some are called to interim presidencies. Sitting presidents are well advised to develop the connections that may be helpful later on. Board members can make recommendations for volunteer and corporate board service; they can also assist in securing a legitimate but nonintrusive position at the institution. However, if the departing president is taking another position or going into retirement, nothing more is required of the institution except a smooth transition, appropriate farewell celebrations, and subsequent invitations to institutional ceremonies and important events.

University and college presidents tend to be unusually energetic, intelligent, and people oriented, with a need for challenges and problems to solve. Even those who accept another position face a sense of loss and an unpredictable new environment. A new position means learning a new culture, new constituents, and a new job. Always, there is the possibility of being blindsided by unknown situations. Those retiring from the activity and involvement of the presidency to a situation lacking in status and without the stimulating context of an organization may be anxious about the prospect. For others, retirement is welcome.

- In 1969, William Pearson Tolley retired after twenty-seven years as president of Syracuse University and a prior twelve years as president of Allegheny College. Thoughtfully, he left the centennial anniversary of the university, the following year, to his successor: "I felt that a new Chancellor should be at the helm for the centennial celebration." He writes, "Despite my love for my work, I did not dread retirement. I was in excellent health. I was enjoying tennis more and more. I was also anxious to have a more active life of scholarship" (Tolley 1989, 202).

Although the planning for a smooth transition has many complex dimensions, if well handled it enhances the legitimacy of all of the parties and, most particularly, the institution.

LEGACY PLANNING

College and university constituents tend to talk about their institution's history in terms of presidential eras. David Whetten and Kim Cameron, after conducting a series of interviews, report being "impressed with the tendency of faculty and administrators to demarcate their institution's history into presidential eras. . . . Their recollections of what transpired on campus during each term was strongly colored by their overall evaluation of the effectiveness of each president." The authors suggest that administrators "periodically examine their actions from the point of view of a future historian" (1991, 463). Former U.S. president Bill Clinton, in his last few years in office, reputedly spent considerable time worrying about his place in history and creating a significant postpresidential life. What is the role of a departing president in creating the story of that presidential era? U.S. presidents establish libraries to preserve their legacies as they interpret them and to establish a legitimate postpresidential mission.

In publishing a memoir of her Smith College presidency, Conway (2001, 137) constructs an interpretation of those years that will color all subsequent historical reports. She asserts, for example, "[M]y legacy to Smith, least visible to outsiders, was a professional fundraising organization and the professional investment process that had been instituted to make the best use of the capital we raised." Breneman (Interview 2002) comments that a president's legacy "is in the quality of the people re-cruited, hired, and promoted" and the quality of trustees recruited. Some believe that just as each institution has its own myth, successful presidents have their own myths and stories. This sentiment was expressed during a discussion of women in the presidency. "[P]residents who are doing well create their own mystique by projecting energy and cultivating a sense of presence. . . . For some, the path to success is pragmatic; for others, it is more spiritual" (Brown et al. 2001, 13).

Birnbaum (1986, 384) asserts that presidents tend to overestimate their influence and effectiveness and to believe that they have overcome the weaknesses of their predecessors and that during their own tenure the institution has made significant strides. He cautions that presidents and those who study presidents may be "misled into overestimating presiden-tial responsibility for institutional outcomes." This tendency to give presi-dents too much credit for institutional successes burdens them with expectations of heroic leadership (393–94). Cohen and March (1974, 119) observe that presidents are more likely to overestimate their power in the early years than they do later on when they recognize the limita-tions of the office.

My survey on legitimacy revealed that most presidents believe they are successful and that they have achieved legitimacy, although they are keenly aware of how others have lost it. Doubtless, some excessive self-congratulation exists, but presidents do try to acknowledge and build on the achievements of their predecessors and often bring strengths that compensate for weaknesses of the past. In this way, institutions do make progress toward their goals and presidents do make a difference.

CAVEATS FOR PRESIDENTS

This book tracks a presidential cycle from entrance to exit while ac-knowledging that some presidents, rather than resign or retire, propose a new vision for change and secure the legitimacy necessary to initiate an-other cycle. Inevitably, however, there is a succession process in which the sitting president departs and a new president takes over. Both presi-dents and the institutional community experience these rites of passage from different perspectives.

Following is a series of caveats to enhance the success and legitimacy of the presidential succession process:

1. Both the incoming and departing presidents should be attuned to the need of constituencies for ritual and ceremony to mark the transition.

2. The departing president should disengage from the search process for a successor, assisting, if asked, only in identifying possible search firms and candidates.

3. When the new president is named, the departing president should be enthusiastic, attend to welcoming ceremonial touches, and work out a smooth transition.

4. The board should establish an assimilation process for the new president and a postpresidential planning process for the departing president.

5. The departing president should maintain a positive, enthusiastic demeanor to reassure constituents.

6. The board should attend to important institutional symbols and rituals for the departing president such as a portrait, honorary degree, emeritus title, and an appropriate farewell party.

7. The incoming president should seek information and advice from predecessors and include them in inauguration festivities.

CHAPTER 20

A President's Exploration of the Timing, Grace, and Legitimacy of Exit

LETTING GO

My own search for the appropriate timing for an exit from the presidency occurred simultaneously with the writing of this book. This was a private deliberation, confined to my own thoughts and numerous discussions with my husband and children. My husband, Harland G. Bloland, had retired early from his professorship at the University of Miami in order to serve with me at Rollins. He was a great companion throughout my presidency and, because his field is higher education administration, a wonderful sounding board for critical issues and an insightful reader and critic of my scholarly work. Harland's faculty status and scholarship also helped to legitimate me with the Rollins faculty, and his charm helped convert many prospects into donors. Harland knew before I did that it was time to move on, but he willingly spent many hours discussing the options. My children were also incredibly supportive during this time of deliberation about my exit. They knew how much the position meant to me and participated in many discussions about next steps. One of my granddaughters did not want me to leave the presidency because then "you won't be important anymore."

While Harland and I were discussing the timing of an exit and the contours of a postpresidential life, we received much advice from trusted presidential colleagues who were also contemplating a move or had made an exit. Much of it did not comport with our own needs. This exploratory period lasted several years; it began with anxiety and concluded with acceptance, even peace. During this time, several presidential colleagues lost their jobs after long and successful tenures. I noted in my journal: "Having witnessed their ignominious endings, I am aware that this job is completely unpredictable. There are many constituencies and forces that can turn against a good president, and there is the potential after a long tenure to forget the importance of consultation and personal involvement. If we begin to worry about getting the boot at the end of the presidency, it will mirror our worries of the first few years. Is there no time of certainty in this job? I think not" (June 25, 2000). Several times, the process slowed as a result of college events. For example, when a $10-million endowment for the presidency along with a professorship in "distinguished presidential leadership" was announced at the campaign finale, I learned that the donor hoped the gift would induce me to stay on at Rollins. His gift provided a powerful incentive for me to do so. When two of my vice presidents were recruited to positions that greatly advanced their careers, I felt I had to stay on to conduct the searches, stabilize the administration, and reassure the faculty and the board. In recruiting a board member for the chairmanship and another the vice chairmanship, I was asked to commit to staying on. I was into my thirteenth year when I acknowledged to myself that there would always be problems, needs, and challenges seeking my attention, but that they could await a new leader. I began to consider an appropriate timeline for an exit, beginning with a private talk with the board chair and focusing on a postpresidential career that I began trying to concretize. While I began developing exit scenarios, exploring postpresidential options, and looking at postpresidential housing, I continued to work hard at my job and find time to write. Although I had negotiated for a summer sabbatical and never taken one, I was loath to give up any of my working life in the last years. This made the writing of this book extraordinarily challenging since I had to fit it into the interstices of a complex and busy life.

My husband and I were conflicted about remaining in Central Florida, comfortable for us but possibly too close for the comfort of a successor. Many of our closest friends were in Miami, where we had lived for years. I worked and reworked the timeline, identifying the order in which I would release the news of my departure. Inconveniently, the post–September 11 stock market decline reduced our retirement nest egg, and I began to consider working a few more years although it was apparent that my era was about over and my presidency should come to an end soon. I was also concerned about a number of other matters: avoiding a leak of the news, thereby losing control of my announcement; preparing a press release and memorandum to my constituencies; remaining active and involved during the "lame duck" period; and whether I and the new president would both be better off if I left town. In the process of informing my staff, I became aware of the impact my decision would have on their lives. Their concern and anxiety were immediately palpable, and while I knew they felt a sense of loss, they were also facing an upheaval in their lives.

As I contemplated my exit, I began thinking about my legacy, as presidents tend to do toward the end of their tenure. How would I be remembered? How would the history of my presidency be recorded? Did my efforts truly make a difference? Was Rollins a better place as a result of my presidency? Had I made a worthwhile professional contribution to the field of higher education? From the beginning, I was aware of the importance of preserving presidential materials for archival research, having used those of my predecessors often. To build on the efforts of those who came before us and keep them a living part of the institution's story, good records of the presidency are essential.

In the last few years of my presidency, I received some wonderful awards and recognitions from national and local organizations. Among the most meaningful was the "Bornstein Award for Faculty Scholarship" established by the board of trustees. The award honors scholarly achievement includes a $10,000 stipend and is announced at commencement. As I wrote to the board chair, the award "is the most extraordinary tribute a president could have [and] will forever promote the values of excellence that I have tried to instill in every aspect of our work. No college is better than its faculty; this award is a testament to the board's recognition of the faculty's importance" (letter, May 28, 2002). Among the many generous sentiments expressed after I announced my intention to step down, I especially treasure these from a senior faculty leader: Rita will "always be a part of Rollins because of her tremendous legacy—not just in buildings and endowment, but also in the principles of excellence that she's championed. . . . [Her] accomplishments will keep her present to us and her words will continue to itch in our ears—perennially nudging us to higher and higher levels, prodding us always to be better, to do more—even while assuring us, as she always does, that we're wonderful just as we are."

RECALLING THE RITUALS OF ENTRANCE

As I prepared for my transition out of the presidency and sought to develop a legitimate and gratifying postpresidential career, I also tried to prepare for a smooth entrance for a new president. I remembered my own experience in the search process, as recorded in my journal: "an extraor-dinary series of interviews and tests, which really stretched me and pressed me and were very, very difficult. . . . And that I came out on the other side of them, victorious, so to speak, was a great, wonderful feeling . . . having gone through the search process empowered me to go on and be the president because in some way, as I went through it, I began to have the feeling that I could do it . . . that I could think like a president. . . . The process gave me the courage to do it" (July 14, 1991).

As I considered the details of the succession process, I was mindful of the thoughtfulness of my predecessor following my election as president. He assisted in a smooth and successful transition by attending to many symbolic gestures designed to generate acceptance and to incorporate me into the culture. As soon as the trustee vote was announced, he had the chapel bell rung. Later, he and his wife hosted a party at their home to introduce us to friends of the college. He invited me to participate in his last commencement where he introduced me. He also invited me to the last trustee executive meeting of his tenure. Throughout my presidency, he provided enthusiastic feedback on my public addresses, written communiqués, fund-raising and other triumphs. Like most presidents, I was eager for feedback on my work and appreciated my predecessor's approval.

For a new president, the ultimate moment of symbolic incorporation into the culture of an institution is the inauguration. Over the years, some of my colleagues decided to forego or foreshorten the ceremony for finan-cial or political reasons, but this ritual, held in the spring of my first year, was a high point in my presidency. It was well planned and well attended and made me feel accepted as institutional leader. My journal reveals my considerable anxiety about writing and delivering a worthy speech: "One of the agonies I live with daily now is that of writing an inaugural address. Suddenly, this task lies before me as a big mountain needing to be climbed, preoccupying my thoughts and taking up whatever vacant moments there are. . . . Of course, I lust to disgorge an artful, memorable, appropriate piece of work. . . . This places a particular burden on me for a speech of distinction as opposed to a merely competent speech, which I am sure I can write. This adds to the stresses of the winter and spring terms because on top of a jammed schedule, always there is hanging the nagging sense that I should be working on The Speech" (January 7, 1991). The follow-ing month I added, "[T]he writing of an inaugural address hangs over me like a dreaded albatross. I feel as though I ought to have lofty thoughts,

artfully expressed, in memorable cadences, to be bound later in a book-
let for all to read throughout the generations to come. This is an incredible burden for me, especially as I consider my prose competent but only
occasionally inspired" (February 11, 1991).

I was exhilarated by the pomp and ritual that characterized the
institution's approach to my inauguration as to its other ceremonies. I recall emerging from the robing room and looking over the campus green
around which stretched what seemed an endless line of faculty in full regalia. My heart thumped with excitement, and I enjoyed every moment of
the event. My address, after months of research into the college's history
and endless rewriting, was well received. I had wanted my remarks to be
worthy of the institution and was delighted when a senior physics professor said that the speech "fired me up; I am ready to go" and the provost
called it "a firecracker of an address." Not only did the college's constituents now feel connected to me, I felt powerfully invested in the community. I noted in my journal, "I felt really bonded through the experience with
the internal and external Rollins communities" (April 1991). Little did I
know then that the community's acceptance of my leadership was still fragile
and that I had yet to achieve true legitimacy as president. I hope I can apply what I have learned to creating a successful and legitimate transition
for my successor. In part, my comfort with the process will depend on my
enthusiasm for the postpresidential work and personal life I will have created
with the assistance of the board of trustees.

"TO BE OF USE"

As I came to terms with the fact that I had met my goals for the college and needed to pass the leadership baton to someone ready to com-
mit for another cycle, I had to script a useful life for the postpresidency.
Having already had an extraordinary opportunity to make a difference in
the world, I had difficulty discerning how I could continue to make a
contribution. My life had been animated by the need to be useful, and I
maintained my optimism in this time of separation by designing possibilities for good work. My primary interests were in strengthening the
governance and leadership of higher education and other nonprofit organizations, and in expanding government, business, and public awareness of the contributions and importance of the nonprofit sector. I wanted
to continue writing for publication, serving as a consultant to presidents
and boards, and strengthening the Philanthropy and Nonprofit Leadership Center at Rollins.

I was sensitive to the danger of continuing a professional association with the college. As noted earlier, my predecessor's ubiquity on campus was vexing to me at first. I felt that the active participation in college life of a well-liked, avuncular, student-oriented predecessor interfered with my ability to establish myself as the legitimate president. This became less and less of an issue as I established my legitimacy and initiated change. It was impossible to doubt or resist his ebullient and wholehearted support of my presidency. Because he reveled in having meaningful work to do and loved undergraduates; I felt he deserved a place in campus life. My own plan would take me to the periphery of campus life where I would stay out of the way as a new president carried the baton. Because of my need for a continuing professional connection to Rollins as well as our sense of Orlando as home, my husband and I decided to remain in the area.

I began the personal story of my presidency with my challenging quest for legitimacy, followed by my focused drive to reposition the institution by strengthening its quality, reputation, and financial health. I conclude with the final stage of the presidential cycle, the succession, characterized by the challenges I faced in the separation and transition processes leading, I hope, to the incorporation of both parties into our new roles. Letting go of the presidency has been difficult. Each step in the process, from my initial conversation with the board chair on, has been emotional. I was unprepared for the outpouring of disbelief, grief, and affection that followed my announcement. For the most part, once I had made the decision I did not waver, although, on occasion, I admit to having second thoughts, especially when someone importuned me to stay longer for one good reason or another. With the help of my executive assistant, I crafted and followed a plan and timeline for informing internal and external constituents.

Most of us called to academe are motivated by the desire to transform the world through education and discovery. We wish especially "To be of use," as powerfully depicted in the poem of that title by Marge Piercy (1990, 106), a paean to people "who strain in the mud and the muck to move things forward." My years in education enriched my life and provided extraordinary opportunities to contribute to society. I am proud to have been part of the struggle for equal educational opportunities and to have participated in significant innovative efforts to improve education at both the secondary and postsecondary levels. Although progress is always subject to backsliding and revised priorities, I believe that these initiatives have made a difference in the lives and achievements of

Americans. Above all, I have prized the unexpected opportunity to serve as president of a high-quality, nationally known comprehensive liberal arts college surrounded by dedicated faculty and staff, wonderful students, ambitious trustees, loving alumni, and a supportive community.

APPENDIX A:
Interview Schedule

INTERVIEW SCHEDULE ON LEGITIMACY
IN THE ACADEMIC PRESIDENCY

- Name some factors involved in a president's coming to be accepted by constituents.
- Comment on the following as facilitators of or impediments to legitimacy: search process; president's background and identity characteristics; role of predecessor; board governance structure, practices, and relationships; faculty governance structure, practices, and relationships; cultural fit; external environment; president's vision; management style (distant or collegial); and fund-raising success.
- What are the conditions necessary for institutional change?
- How is presidential success measured?
- Roughly how long does it take to gain legitimacy with key stakeholders?
- Is gaining legitimacy easier in a second presidency?
- Once achieved, is legitimacy maintained or does it wax and wane?
- Identify the major factors in presidential failures.
- Are the majority of presidents transformational or transactional?
- How would you characterize yourself?
- How are you defining these terms?
- Is there an optimal number of years for a successful presidency?
- How important is presidential longevity to an institution?
- How should presidents decide when to leave?

APPENDIX B:
Survey Instrument, Cohort, and Responses

LEGITIMACY IN THE ACADEMIC PRESIDENCY

These questions focus on factors that can facilitate or impede a president's (chancellor's) legitimacy. Legitimacy is acceptance by key stakeholders as a good fit with the institutional culture and an effective leader. Your responses and comments will be helpful in understanding the role of legitimacy in presidential effectiveness. Thank you.

1. How long have you served as president of your current institution? _____ Total years as a president? _____

2. Did the search process that brought you to your institution facilitate or impede the legitimacy of your presidency?

   ❏ Facilitated   ❏ Impeded   ❏ No effect

   Comments:

3. Did your academic preparation and career path facilitate or impede the legitimacy of your presidency?

   ❏ Facilitated   ❏ Impeded   ❏ No effect

   Comments:

4. Did your identity characteristics (gender, ethnicity, religion, etc.) facilitate or impede the legitimacy of your presidency?

   ❏ Facilitated   ❏ Impeded   ❏ No effect

   Comments:

5. If your predecessor(s) remained in the community or stayed actively involved with the institution, did this facilitate or impede the legitimacy of your presidency?

   ❏ Facilitated   ❏ Impeded   ❏ No effect

   Comments:

6. Have the structure and functioning of the governing board facilitated or impeded the legitimacy of your presidency?

   ❏ Facilitated   ❏ Impeded   ❏ No effect

   Comments:

7. Have the structure and functioning of the faculty governance system facilitated or impeded the legitimacy of your presidency?

   ❏ Facilitated   ❏ Impeded   ❏ No effect

   Comments:

8. Have the structure and functioning of the alumni organization facilitated or impeded the legitimacy of your presidency?

   ❏ Facilitated   ❏ Impeded   ❏ No effect

   Comments:

9. Have external factors (e.g., economy, college enrollment trends, community issues) facilitated or impeded the legitimacy of your presidency?

   ❏ Facilitated   ❏ Impeded   ❏ No effect

   Comments:

10. Has your degree of success in fund-raising facilitated or impeded the legitimacy of your presidency?

❏ Facilitated ❏ Impeded ❏ No effect

Comments:

11. Has your leadership style facilitated or impeded the legitimacy of your presidency?

❏ Facilitated ❏ Impeded ❏ No effect

Comments:

12. Do you consider yourself more of a transformational (bold, visionary, inspirational) or a transactional (collegial, interactive, collaborative) president?

❏ Transformational ❏ Transactional

13. Do you consider the leadership style of most presidents as more transformational or more transactional?

❏ Transformational ❏ Transactional

14. Roughly how long did it take you to gain legitimacy?

❏ 1 year ❏ 2–3 years ❏ 4–5 years
❏ more than 5 years ❏ Still working on it

15. If you have held a prior presidency, would you say your attainment of legitimacy was:

❏ Easier this time ❏ About the same ❏ More difficult this time

Comments:

16. Identify the factors necessary for successful institutional change.

17. Identify some reasons that presidents lose their jobs.

18. What is the optimal number of years for a presidency at one institution?

19. Additional comments:

   INSTITUTION _____

   ❏ PUBLIC   ❏ PRIVATE   ❏ FAITH-BASED

SURVEY: LEGITIMACY IN THE ACADEMIC PRESIDENCY
Survey Methodology: Population

- 2000 Carnegie Classification
  - Doctoral/Research Universities—Extensive: 151 Institutions
  - Doctoral/Research Universities—Intensive: 110 Institutions
  - Master's Colleges and Universities I: 496 Institutions
  - Baccalaureate Colleges—Liberal Arts: 226 Institutions

Survey Methodology: Sample

- There were 377 institutions randomly selected to participate in this study (about 38 percent of the population).
- There were 182 surveys returned (48 percent), and 42 percent were from public institutions, 39 percent were from private institutions, and 19 percent were from faith-based institutions.

Survey Findings: Descriptive

- On average, respondents have served at their current institutions as presidents for eight years and have held the title of president across institutions for nine years.
- 36 percent of respondents indicated that ten years is optimal for a presidency at one institution.

Survey Findings: Impediments

- Collectively, 11 percent of the responses from presidents indicated that one or more factors impeded their legitimacy. The impeding factors most often selected were:
  - External factors (economy, college enrollment trends, community issues)
  - Structure and functioning of the faculty governance system
  - Predecessor(s) remaining in community and staying actively involved with the institution

Survey Findings: Leadership Style

- 49 percent of the presidents identified themselves as transformational leaders. Among these presidents, 71 percent indicated that the leadership style of most presidents is transactional.

- 28 percent of the presidents identified themselves as transactional leaders. Among these presidents, 88 percent indicated that the leadership style of most presidents is transactional.

- 23 percent of the presidents identified themselves as both transformational and transactional leaders. Among these presidents, 74 percent indicated that the leadership style of most presidents is transactional.

- Therefore, regardless of how presidents evaluated their leadership style, they were more likely to indicate that most presidents are transactional leaders.

Survey Findings: Legitimacy

- Three out of four presidents indicated that they achieved legitimacy within three years.

- 14 percent of the presidents indicated that they are still working on legitimacy.

- 23 percent of the presidents have served as president at more than one institution. Among these presidents, 50 percent indicated that legitimacy was easier this time.

BIBLIOGRAPHY

Alton, Bruce T., and Kathleen Lis Dean. "Why Presidents Think the Grass Is Greener." *Trusteeship* 10, no. 3 (May/June 2002): 19–23.

Arendt, Hannah. *The Jew as Pariah*. New York: Grove Press, 1978.

Arenson, Karen W. "Like Harvard and Brown, Princeton Is Losing Its President." *New York Times*, September 23, 2000.

Astin, Helen S., and Carole Leland. *Women of Influence, Women of Vision: A Cross-Generational Study of Leaders and Social Change*. San Francisco, CA: Jossey-Bass, 1991.

Atwell, Robert H. "Inside the College Presidency: Interview." *Educational Record* 77, nos. 2, 3 (spring/summer 1996): 6–11.

Barnett, Ronald. "Managing Universities in a Supercomplex Age." In *Chaos Theory & Higher Education: Leadership, Planning, & Policy*, edited by Marc Cutright, 13–32. New York: Peter Lang, 2001.

Barr, John W., and Susan P. Borden. "Reality Bites Back." *Trusteeship* (January/February 1995): 8–14.

Bartlett, Thomas. "The Smearing of Chicago." *Chronicle of Higher Education*, June 28, 2002, pp. A10–A12.

Basinger, Julianne. "When a President Quits Early, the Damage Can Linger On." *Chronicle of Higher Education*, Money & Management, July 27, 2001, pp. A22–A23.

Basinger, Julianne. "Casting a Wider Net." *Chronicle of Higher Education*, Money and Management, December 13, 2002, pp. A32–A33.

Bass, Bernard M. *Leadership and Performance Beyond Expectations*. New York: Free Press, 1985.

Bateson, Mary Catherine. *Composing a Life*. New York: Penguin, 1990.

Bennis, Warren, and Burt Nanus. *Leaders: The Strategies for Taking Charge*. New York: Harper & Row, 1985.

Bensimon, Estela Mara. "Five Approaches to Think About: Lessons Learned from Experienced Presidents." In *On Assuming a College or University Presidency: Lessons & Advice from the Field*, 1–12. Washington, DC: American Association for Higher Education, 1989.

Bensimon, Estela M. "The Social Processes through which Faculty Shape the Image of a New President." *Journal of Higher Education* 62, no. 6 (November/December 1991): 637–60.

Bensimon, Estela Mara. "A Feminist Reinterpretation of Presidents' Definitions of Leadership." In *Women in Higher Education: A Feminist Perspective*, ASHE Reader Series, edited by Judith S. Glazer, Estela M. Bensimon, and Barbara K. Townsend, 465–74. Needham Heights, MA: Ginn Press, 1993.

Bensimon, Estela M., Anna Neumann, and Robert Birnbaum. *Making Sense of Administrative Leadership: The "L" Word in Higher Education*. ASHE-ERIC Higher Education Report No.1. San Francisco: Jossey-Bass, 1989.

Bensimon, Estela M., Anna Neumann, and Robert Birnbaum. "Higher Education and Leadership Theory." In *Organization and Governance in Higher Education*, 4th ed., ASHE Reader, edited by Marvin W. Peterson, 389–98. Needham Heights, MA: Ginn Press, 1991.

Berdahl, Robert O. "Shared Governance and External Constraints." In *Organization and Governance in Higher Education*, 4th ed., ASHE Reader, edited by Marvin W. Peterson, 217–224. Needham Heights, MA: Ginn Press, 1991.

Bess, James L., and Paul Goldman. "Leadership Ambiguity in Universities and K-12 Schools and the Limits of Contemporary Leadership Theory." *Leadership Quarterly* 12 (2001): 419–50.

Birchard, Karen. "McGill U. Rejects Ayn Rand Chair." *Chronicle of Higher Education*, August 16, 2002, p. A41.

Birnbaum, Robert. "Leadership and Learning: The College President as Intuitive Scientist." *Review of Higher Education* 9, no. 4 (summer 1986): 381–96.

Birnbaum, Robert. "Presidential Searches and the Discovery of Organizational Goals." *Journal of Higher Education* 59, no. 5 (September/October 1988): 489–509.

Birnbaum, Robert. *How Colleges Work: The Cybernetics of Academic Organization and Leadership*. San Francisco, CA: Jossey-Bass, 1988.

Birnbaum, Robert. *How Academic Leadership Works: Understanding Success and Failure in the College Presidency*. San Francisco, CA: Jossey-Bass, 1992.

Birnbaum, Robert. "The President as Story-Teller: Restoring the Narrative of Higher Education." *Presidency* 5, no. 3 (fall 2002): 32–39.

Birnbaum, Robert, and Paul D. Umbach. "Scholar, Steward, Spanner, Stranger: The Four Career Paths of College Presidents." *Review of Higher Education* 24, no. 3 (spring 2001): 203–17.

Bloland, Harland G. "On Strategizing the 'Strategic Planning' Plan." *PEN–Postsecondary Education Network* (September 1987): 6–7.

Bloland, Harland G., and Rita Bornstein. "Fund Raising in Transition." *Taking Fund Raising Seriously*, edited by Dwight F. Burlingame and Lamont J. Hulse, 103–23. San Francisco, CA: Jossey-Bass, 1991.

Bloland, Harland G. Creating the Council for Higher Education Accreditation (CHEA). Phoenix, AZ: American Council on Education/Oryx Press, 2001.

Bornstein, Rita. "An Historical Analysis of the Dynamics of Innovation in an Urban High School." Ph.D. dissertation, University of Miami, 1975.

Bornstein, Rita. "Ambiguity as Opportunity and Constraint: Evolution of a Federal Sex Equity Education Program." *Educational Evaluation and Policy Analysis* 7, no. 2 (summer 1985): 99–114.

Bornstein, Rita. "Back in the Spotlight: The College President as Public Intellectual." *Educational Record* 76, no. 4 (fall 1995): 56–62.

Bornstein, Rita. "A President's Guide to Fund-Raising Success: Relationships Are Key." *Presidency* 3, no. 2 (spring 2000): 25–29.

Bornstein, Rita. "Public Diary on Ethical Issues, January 8–19." *Journal of College and Character.* CollegeValues.org, 2001.

Bourdieu, Pierre. "The Forms of Capital." In *Handbook of Theory and Research for the Sociology of Education*, edited by John G. Richardson, 241–58. New York: Greenwood Press, 1986.

Boyer, Ernest L. *Scholarship Reconsidered: Priorities of the Professoriate*. Princeton, NJ: Carnegie Foundation for the Advancement of Teaching, 1990.

Brand, Myles. "The Engaged President: Changing Times, Unchanging Principles." *Presidency* 5, no. 3, (fall 2002): 26–30.

Breneman, David W. "For Colleges, This Is Not Just Another Recession." *Chronicle of Higher Education*, June 14, 2002, pp. B7–B9.

Brown, Gladys, Claire Van Ummersen, and Judith Sturnick. *From Where We Sit: Women's Perspectives on the Presidency*. Washington, DC: American Council on Education, 2001.

Brown, Roscoe C., Jr. "Moving On: Advice for Departing Presidents." *Educational Record* 77, nos, 2, 3 (spring/summer 1996): 43–47.

Burns, James McGregor. *Leadership*. New York: Harper & Row, 1978.

Cameron, Kim S. "Organizational Adaptation and Higher Education." In *Organization and Governance in Higher Education*, 4th ed., ASHE Reader, edited by Marvin W. Peterson, 284–299. Needham Heights, MA: Ginn Press, 1991.

Cass, Michael. "Fund Raising Added to New Vanderbilt Provost's Duties." *Tennessean.com*. Local News, January 22, 2002.

Casteen, John T. III. "Presidential Leadership: Intellectual Vocation, Moral Mandate." *Presidency* 5, no. 3 (fall 2002): 20–25.

Caudron, Shari. "The Looming Leadership Crisis." *Workforce.com/archive* 78, no. 9 (September 1999): 72–79.

Chait, Richard. "Colleges Should Not Be Blinded by Vision." *Chronicle of Higher Education*, July 22, 1993, pp. B1–B2.

Chin, Robert. "The Utility of System Models and Developmental Models for Practitioners." In *The Planning of Change: Readings in the Applied Behavioral Sciences,* edited by Warren G. Bennis, Kenneth D. Benne, and Robert Chin, 201–14. New York: Holt, Rinehart and Winston, 1961.

Ciampa, Dan, and Michael Watkins. *Right from the Start: Taking Charge in a New Leadership Role.* Boston, MA: Harvard Business School Press, 1999.

Clance, P. R. *The Imposter Phenomenon: When Success Makes You Feel Like a Fake.* Toronto, Canada: Bantam, 1985.

Clark, Burton R. *The Distinctive College.* New Brunswick, NJ: Transaction Publishers, 1992.

Clayton, Mark. "More Women Are Climbing to the Top of the Ivory Tower." *Christian Science Monitor,* September 19, 2000, p. 14.

Cohen, Michael D., and James G. March. *Leadership and Ambiguity: The American College Presidency.* New York: McGraw-Hill, 1974.

Cohen, Michael D., and James G. March. "Attention and the Ambiguity of Self-Interest." In *Ambiguity and Choice in Organizations,* edited by James G. March and Johan P. Olsen, 38–53. Bergen: Universitetsforlaget, 1976.

Coleman, James S. "Social Capital in the Creation of Human Capital." *American Journal of Sociology* 94 (1988): S95–S120.

Collins, Jim. *Good to Great: Why Some Companies Make the Leap and Others Don't.* New York: HarperBusiness, 2001.

Conway, Jill Ker. *True North.* New York: Knopf, 1994.

Conway, Jill Ker. *A Woman's Education.* New York: Knopf, 2001.

Cook, W. Bruce. "Fund Raising and the College Presidency in an Era of Uncertainty: From 1975 to the Present." *Journal of Higher Education* 68, no. 1 (January/February 1997): 53–86.

Cook, W. Bruce, and William F. Lasher. "Toward a Theory of Fund-raising in Higher Education." *Review of Higher Education* 20, no. 1 (fall 1996): 33–51.

Cooper, William. Letter to the Editor. *Chronicle of Higher Education,* May 31, 2002, p. B16.

Corrigan, Melanie E. *The American College President: 2002 Edition.* Washington, DC: American Council on Education, 2002.

Couto, Richard A. "The Transformation of Transforming Leadership." In *The Leader's Companion,* edited by Thomas Wren, 102–8. New York: Free Press, 1995.

Deal, Terrence E. "Cultural Change: Opportunity, Silent Killer, or Metamorphosis?" In *Gaining Control of the Corporate Culture,* edited by R. Kilmann, M. Saxton, and R. Serpa, 292–331. San Francisco, CA: Jossey-Bass, 1985.

Deal, Terrence E., and Allan A. Kennedy. *Corporate Cultures: The Rites and Rituals of Corporate Life.* Reading, MA: Addison-Wesley, 1982.

Die, Ann H. "Going the Distance: Reflections on Presidential Longevity." *Presidency* 2, no. 3 (fall 1999): 32–37.

Dill, David D. "The Management of Academic Culture: Notes on the Management of Meaning and Social Integration." In *Organization and Governance in Higher Education*, 4th ed., ASHE Reader, edited by Marvin W. Peterson, 182–194. Needham Heights, MA: Ginn Press, 1991.

Downey, Diane, with Tom March and Adena Berkman. *Assimilating New Leaders— The Key to Executive Retention*. New York: American Management Association, 2001.

D'Souza, Dinesh. *Illiberal Education: The Politics of Race and Sex on Campus*. New York: Free Press, 1991.

Dyson, Dave, and Ralph Kirkman. "Presidential Priorities." *AGB Reports* (March/ April 1989): 6–11.

Eakin, Emily. "On the Lookout for Patriotic Incorrectness." *New York Times*, November 24, 2001, p. A15.

Eckel, Peter D. "The Role of Shared Governance in Institutional Hard Decisions: Enabler or Antagonist?" *Review of Higher Education* 24, no. 1 (fall 2000): 15–40.

Eckel, Peter, Madeleine Green, Barbara Hill, and William Mallon. *Taking Charge of Change: A Primer for Colleges and Universities*. Washington, DC: American Council on Education, 1999.

Edmondson, Charles. E-mail message. February 13, 2001.

Edmundson, Lorna Duphiney, and Gwendolyn Evans Jensen. "The Ten Commandments of Presidential Transition." *Chronicle of Higher Education Career Network*, on-line, February 26, 2002.

Edmundson, Mark. "Bennington Means Business." *New York Times Magazine*, October 23, 1994, pp. 42–75.

Elfin, Mel. "The Age of Scarcity." *America's Best Colleges*. U.S. News & World Report, College Guide, 1992: 4.

Etzioni, Amatai. *Modern Organizations*. Englewood Cliffs, NJ: Prentice-Hall, 1964.

Ficklen, Ellen. "Presidency as Platform." *CASE Currents* 28, no. 5 (May–June 2002): 38–41.

Fish, Stanley. "The Unbearable Ugliness of Volvos." In *There's No Such Thing as Free Speech and It's a Good Thing, Too*, 273–79. New York: Oxford University Press, 1994.

Fish, Stanley. "The Golden Rule." *Chronicle of Higher Education*, Archive, September 21, 2001.

Fish, Stanley. "Reading the Morning Mail." *Chronicle of Higher Education*, chronicle.com, July 19, 2002.

Fisher, James L. *Power of the Presidency*. New York: American Council on Education/MacMillan, 1984.

Fisher, James L. "The Historical Importance of Major Gifts." In *The President and Fund Raising*, edited by James L. Fisher and Gary H. Quehl, 212–20. New York: Macmillan, 1989.

Fisher, James L. *The Board and the President*. New York: American Council on Education/Macmillan, 1991.

Fisher, James L. "To the Editor." *Chronicle of Higher Education*, Archive, October 13, 1993.

Fisher, James L. "Reflections on Transformational Leadership." *Educational Record* (summer 1994): 54, 60–65.

Fisher, James L., and James V. Koch. *Presidential Leadership: Making a Difference.* Phoenix, AZ: American Council on Education and Oryx Press, 1996.

Fisher, James L., Martha W. Tack, and Karen J. Wheeler. *The Effective College President.* New York: American Council on Education/MacMillan, 1988.

Fite, Gilbert C. "Moving Away from Academe after Retirement." *Chronicle of Higher Education,* January 25, 2002, pp. B21–B22.

Flawn, Peter T. *A Primer for University Presidents: Managing the Modern University.* Austin: University of Texas Press, 1990.

Freeman, Sue J.M. "Women at the Top: 'You've Come a Long Way, Baby.'" In *Women on Power: Leadership Redefined,* edited by Sue J.M. Freeman, Susan C. Bourque, and Christine M. Shelton, 27–60. Boston, MA: Northeastern University Press, 2001.

French, John R.P., Jr. and Bertram Raven. "The Bases of Social Power." In *Studies in Social Power,* edited by Dorwin Cartwright, 150–67. Ann Arbor: University of Michigan, 1959.

Fukuyama, Francis. *Trust: The Social Virtues and the Creation of Prosperity.* New York: Simon & Schuster, 1995.

Gamson, William A. *Power and Discontent.* Homewood, IL: Dorsey Press, 1968.

Gardner, Howard, with the collaboration of Emma Laskin. *Leading Minds: An Anatomy of Leadership.* New York: BasicBooks, 1995.

Gersick, Connie J.G. "Revolutionary Change Theories: A Multilevel Exploration of the Punctuated Equilibrium Paradigm." *Academy of Management Review* 16, no. 1 (1991): 10–36.

Glazer-Raymo, Judith. *Shattering the Myths: Women in Academe.* Baltimore, MD: Johns Hopkins University Press, 1999.

Gleick, James. *Chaos: Making a New Science.* New York: Viking, 1987.

Goleman, Daniel. *Emotional Intelligence.* New York: Bantam Books, 1995.

Gordon, Gil E., and Ned Rosen. "Critical Factors in Leadership Succession." *Organizational Behavior and Human Performance* 27 (1981): 227–54.

Gose, Ben. "The Fall of the Flagships: Do the Best State Universities Need to Privatize to Thrive?" *Chronicle of Higher Education,* July 5, 2002.

Gray, Hanna H. "On the History of Giants." In *Universities and Their Leadership,* edited by William G. Bowen and Harold T. Shapiro, 101–15. Princeton, NJ: Princeton University Press, 1998.

Greenberg, David. "The College President as CEO." *Washington Post,* July 26, 1998, pp. 1, 18–21.

Greenstein, Fred I. *The Presidential Difference: Leadership Style from FDR to Clinton.* Princeton, NJ: Princeton University Press, 2000.

Gregorian, Vartan. "Interview with Norman Atkins." *Rolling Stone* (March 21, 1991): 63–67.

Guest, Larry. "Who, If Anyone, Minds the Store at Rollins?" *Orlando Sentinel,* 1991, C-4.

Hahn, Robert. "Getting Serious about Presidential Leadership: Our Collective Responsibility." *Change* (September/October 1995): 13–19.

Hall, Ellen W. "Virtual Reality in Academic Life." Paper presented at the 1993 Fall Conference of South Carolina Women in Higher Education Administration, Furman University, December 6–7.

Hart, Ann Weaver. "Leader Succession and Socialization: A Synthesis." *Review of Educational Research* 61, no. 4 (winter 1991): 451–74.

Harvard Business School, Case N9-397-068. *Trinity College*. Boston, MA: Harvard Business School Publishing, 1996.

Heilbrun, Carolyn G. *Writing a Woman's Life*. New York: Ballantine Books, 1988.

Hesburgh, Rev. Theodore M. "The Public Role of College Presidents: a Discussion with the Rev. Theodore M. Hesburgh." Colloquy Live, *chronicle.com*, January 31, 2001.

Hester, James McNaughton. "Adventure on Washington Square: Being President of New York University 1962–1975." Unpublished manuscript, 1996.

Higgins, James M. *The Management Challenge: An Introduction to Management*. New York: Macmillan, 1991.

Hill, Barbara, Madeleine Green, and Peter Eckel. *What Governing Boards Need to Know and Do about Institutional Change*. Washington, DC: American Council on Education, 2001.

Hogan, Robert, Robert Raskin, and Dan Fazzini. "The Dark Side of Charisma." In *Measures of Leadership*, 343–54. Greensboro, NC: Center for Creative Leadership, 1990.

Hollander, Edwin P. "College and University Leadership from a Social Psychological Perspective: A Transactional View." Presented at the Invitational Interdisciplinary Colloquium on Leadership in Higher Education, Teacher's College, Columbia University, 1987.

Hollander, Edwin P. "The Essential Interdependence of Leadership and Followership." In *Current Directions in Psychological Science*, American Psychological Society, Cambridge, UK: Cambridge University Press, 1992: 71–75.

Hollander, Edwin P., and James W. Julian. "Studies in Leader Legitimacy, Influence, and Innovation." In *Group Processes*, edited by Leonard Berkowitz, 115–51. New York: Academic Press, 1978.

Hollinger, David A. "Faculty Governance, the University of California, and the Future of Academe." *Academe/aaup.org* 87, no. 3 (May–June 2001).

Honan, W.H. "At the Top of the Ivory Tower the Watchword Is Silence." *New York Times*, July 24, 1994, p. E5.

Ingram, Richard T. "When a President Quits Early, the Damage Can Linger On." *Chronicle of Higher Education*, July 27, 2001, pp. A22–A23.

Jablonski, Margaret. "The Leadership Challenge for Women College Presidents." In *Women in Higher Education: A Feminist Perspective*," 2d ed., ASHE Reader, edited by Judith Glazer-Raymo, Barbara K. Townsend, and Becky

Ropers-Huliman, 243–251. Boston, MA: Pearson Custom Publishing, 2000.

Johnson, Kevin. "University of S.C. 'idol' hit with new indictment." *USA Today*, November 9, 1995, p. 8A.

Kantrowitz, Barbara, with Carolyn Friday, Mark Starr, Daniel Glick, John Taliaferro, and Patricia King. "Wanted: Miracle Workers." *Newsweek*, April 8, 1991, pp. 48–49.

Karp, Mitchell, Karp Consulting Group, Inc. E-mail, September 6, 2001.

Kauffman, Joseph F. "Commentary on 'Examining the Myths of Administrative Careers.'" *AAHE Bulletin* 35, no. 9 (May 1983): 7–8.

Kauffman, Joseph F. "Strategies for an Effective Presidency." In *On Assuming a College or University Presidency: Lessons & Advice from the Field*, 29–42. Washington, DC: American Association for Higher Education, 1989.

Keats, John. Letter to George and Tom Keats, 13, 19 January 1818. In *The Letters of John Keats*, 1814–1821, edited by Hyder Edward Rollins, 1:204. Cambridge, MA: Harvard University Press, 1958.

Keller, George. *Academic Strategy: The Management Revolution in American Higher Education*. Baltimore, MD: Johns Hopkins University Press, 1983.

Kelly, Kathleen S. *Effective Fund-Raising Management*. London: Lawrence Erlbaum, 1998.

Kerr, Clark. "A Report of the Commission on Strengthening Presidential Leadership." *Presidents Make a Difference: Strengthening Leadership in Colleges and Universities*. Washington, DC: Association of Governing Boards of Universities and Colleges, 1984.

Kerr, Clark. *The Great Transformation in Higher Education: 1960–1980*. Albany: State University of New York Press, 1991.

Kerr, Clark, and Marian L. Gade. *The Many Lives of Academic Presidents: Time, Place & Character*. Washington, DC: Association of Governing Boards of Universities and Colleges, 1986.

Kets de Vries, M.F.R. "Organizational Paradoxes." In *Bass & Stogdill's Handbook of Leadership*, 3d ed., edited by Bernard M. Bass, 158. New York: Free Press, 1990.

Kezar, Adrianna. *Understanding and Facilitating Organizational Change in the 21st Century: Recent Research and Conceptualizations*. ASHE-ERIC Higher Education Report 28, no. 4. San Francisco, CA: Jossey-Bass, 2001.

Kezar, Adrianna, and Peter D. Eckel. "The Effect of Institutional Culture on Change Strategies in Higher Education." *Journal of Higher Education* 73, no. 4 (July/August 2002): 435–60.

Kimball, Solon T. "Gennep, Arnold Van." In *International Encyclopedia of the Social Sciences*, Vol. 6, edited by David L. Sills, 113–14. New York: Macmillan Company, 1968.

Kirp, David L. "Hurricane Hugo." *Lingua Franca* (April 2001): 40–49.

Klein, Joe. *The Natural: The Misunderstood Presidency of Bill Clinton*. New York: Doubleday, 2002.

Koehane, Nannerl O. "More Power to the President?" *Presidency* 1, no. 2 (fall 1998): 12–17.

Korschgen, Ann, Rex Fuller, and John Gardner. "The Impact of Presidential Migration." *ASHE Bulletin* (February 2001): 3–6.

Kotter, John P. *Leading Change*. Boston, MA: Harvard Business School Press, 1996.

Krinsky, Ira W., and Stephen L. Weber. "'New Manager Assimilation' Process." *AAHE Bulletin* 49, no. 9 (May 1997): 11–13.

Lane, Jack C. Unpublished manuscript, on the history of Rollins College.

Leatherman, Courtney. "President's Hair Style, Clothing, Marriage, and Handling of 'Moral Issues' Rile Older Alumnae of Converse College." *Chronicle of Higher Education*. December 16, 1992, p. A17.

Leatherman, Courtney. "Survey Finds College Officials Preoccupied with Finances." *Chronicle of Higher Education,* July 28, 1993, p. A16.

Leatherman, Courtney. "New York Regents Vote to Remove 18 of 19 Adelphi U. Trustees." *Chronicle of Higher Education*, Archive, February 21, 1997.

Levao, Richard A. "Board Politics: Pulling the Pieces Together." *Presidency* 5, no. 1 (winter 2002): 34–39.

Levin, John S. "Presidential Influence, Leadership Succession, and Multiple Interpretations of Organizational Change." *Review of Higher Education* 21, no. 4 (summer 1998): 405–25.

Levine, Arthur. "Higher Education's New Status as a Mature Industry." *Chronicle of Higher Education*, Archive, January 31, 1997.

Levine, Lawrence W. *The Opening of the American Mind: Canons, Culture, and History*. Boston, MA: Beacon Press, 1996.

Lewin, Kurt. "Quasi-Stationary Social Equilibria and the Problem of Permanent Change." In *The Planning of Change: Readings in the Applied Behavioral Sciences*, edited by Warren G. Bennis, Kenneth D. Benne, and Robert Chin, 235–38. New York: Holt, Rinehart and Winston, 1961.

Lindsay, Jay. "Controversies Abound in the Ivory Tower as New Harvard President Tangles with Faculty." *Seattletimes.com*, January 16, 2002.

Lively, Kit. "Giving to Higher Education Breaks Another Record." *Chronicle of Higher Education*, May 5, 2000, p. A41.

Lohr, Steve. "He Loves to Win. At I.B.M., He Did." *New York Times*, Money & Business, March 10, 2002, pp. 1, 11.

Manning, Kathleen. *Rituals, Ceremonies, and Cultural Meaning in Higher Education*. Westport, CT: Bergin & Garvey, 2000.

Marchese, Theodore J. "Boards and Presidential Transitions." *Trusteeship*. September/October 2001: pp. 34–35.

McCullough, David. *Truman*. New York: Simon & Schuster, 1992.

McCullough, David. *John Adams*. New York: Simon & Schuster, 2001.

McLaughlin, Judith Block. "Entering the Presidency." In *Leadership Transitions: The New College President*, edited by Judith Block McLaughlin, 5–13. San Francisco, CA: Jossey-Bass, 1996a.

McLaughlin, Judith Block. "The Perilous Presidency." *Educational Record* 77, nos. 2, 3 (spring/summer 1996b): 12–17.

McLaughlin, Judith Block, and David Reisman. "The President: A Precarious Perch." In *Higher Learning in America, 1980–2000*, edited by Arthur Levine, 179–202. Baltimore, MD: Johns Hopkins University Press, 1983.

McMillen, Liz. "More Colleges Tap Fund Raisers for Presidencies." *Chronicle of Higher Education*, September 11, 1991, pp. A35–A36.

McNeill, William H. *Hutchins' University: A Memoir of the University of Chicago 1929–1950*. Chicago: University of Chicago Press, 1991.

McPherson, Mary Patterson. "Two Afternoons on the Job." In *Against the Tide: Career Paths of Women Leaders in American and British Higher Education*, edited by Karen Doyle Walton, 153–64. Bloomington, IN: Phi Delta Kappa Educational Foundation, 1996.

Mercer, Joye. "The Fund Raiser as President." *Chronicle of Higher Education*, September 15, 1995, pp. A35–A36.

Merton, Robert K. *Social Theory and Social Structure*. Glencoe, IL: Free Press, 1957.

Michaelson, Martin. "What Does It Take to Be a Great Trustee?" *Trusteeship* 10, no. 3 (May/June 2002): 37.

Mohrman, Kathryn. "A Lame Duck President Looks Back." *Chronicle of Higher Education Career Network*, April 25, 2002.

Moore, John W. with Joanne M. Burrows. *Presidential Succession and Transition: Beginning, Ending, and Beginning Again*. New York: American Association of State Colleges and Universities, 2001.

Mortimer, Kenneth P., and T. R. McConnell. "Process of Academic Governance." In *Organization and Governance in Higher Education*, 4th ed., ASHE Reader, edited by Marvin W. Peterson, 164–74. Needham Heights, MA: Ginn Press, 1991.

Mossberg, Barbara. "Leadership's Natural Ally: Applying Chaos and Complexity Theories to Academe." In *Chaos Theory & Higher Education: Leadership, Planning, & Policy*, edited by Marc Cutright, 203–48. New York: Peter Lang, 2001.

Muller, Henry. "I Have at Least Nine Jobs." *Fortune*, October 16, 2000, pp. 275–88.

Munitz, Barry. "Leaders: Past, Present, and Future." *Change* 30, no. 1, Archive (January/February 1998).

Murphy, Mary Kay, ed. *The Advancement President and the Academy*. Phoenix, AZ: American Council on Education and Oryx Press, 1997.

Naipaul, V.S. "Our Universal Civilization." In *The Writer and the World: Essays*, 503–17. New York: Knopf, 2002.

Neumann, Anna. "Making Mistakes: Error and Learning in the College Presidency." *Journal of Higher Education* 61, no. 4 (July/August 1990): 386–407.

"New Harvard President Has a Rocky Start." *Associated Press*, CNNfyi.com, January 30, 2002.

Northouse, Peter G. *Leadership: Theory and Practice*. Thousand Oaks, CA: Sage, 2001.

Orrill, Robert, ed. *Education and Democracy: Re-imagining Liberal Learning in America*. New York: College Entrance Examination Board, 1997.

Padilla, Art, and Sujit, Ghosh. "Turnover at the Top: The Revolving Door of the Academic Presidency." *Presidency*, 3, no. 1 (winter 2000): 30–37.

Payton, Robert L. "The Ethics and Values of Fund Raising." In *The President and Fund Raising*, edited by James. L. Fisher and Gary H. Quehl, 33–42. New York: Macmillan, 1989.

Payton, Robert L., Henry A. Rosso, and Eugene R. Tempel. "Toward a Philosophy of Fund Raising." In *Taking Fund Raising Seriously*, edited by Dwight F. Burlingame and Lamont J. Hulse, 3–17. San Francisco, CA: Jossey-Bass, 1991.

Perlman, Daniel H. "Paradoxes of the Presidency." *AAHE Bulletin* (October 1989): 3–6.

Pfeffer, Jeffrey. *New Directions for Organization Theory: Problems and Prospects*. New York: Oxford University Press, 1997.

Piercy, Marge. *Circles on the Water*. New York: Knopf, 1990.

Plante, Patricia R. with Robert L. Caret. *Myths and Realities of Academic Administration*. New York: American Council on Education/MacMillan, 1990.

Powers, Scott. "Bornstein, Rollins Mark 10 Years as Fruitful Duo." *Orlando Sentinel*, June 4, 2000, pp. B1, B4.

Pusser, Brian, "AGB-UVA Symposium on Research and Scholarship in Higher Education." *Occasional Paper No. 41*. Washington, DC: Association of Governing Boards of Universities and Colleges, September 2000.

Putnam, Robert D. "The Prosperous Community: Social Capital and Public Life." *American Prospect* 4, no. 13, Archive (March 21, 1993): 1–7.

Rasinski, Kenneth, Tom R. Tyler, and Kim Fridkin. "Exploring the Function of Legitimacy: Mediating Effects of Personal and Institutional Legitimacy on Leadership Endorsement and System Support." *Journal of Personality and Social Psychology* 49, no. 2 (1985): 386–94.

Reisman, David. "Afterward: Reflections on the College Presidency." In *Leadership Transitions: The New College President*, edited by Judith Block McLaughlin, No. 93, Spring 1996, 85–87. San Francisco, CA: Jossey-Bass.

Renewing the Academic Presidency: Stronger Leadership for Tougher Times. Washington, DC: Association of Governing Boards of Universities and Colleges, 1996.

Rhodes, Frank H.T. "Introduction." In *Successful Fund–raising for Higher Education: The Advancement of Learning*, edited by Frank H.T. Rhodes, xvii–xxiv. Phoenix, AZ: American Council on Education/Oryx Press, 1997.

Rhodes, Frank H.T. "The Art of the Presidency." *Presidency* 1, no. 1 (spring 1998): 14–18.

Riley, Richard. "A Fond Farewell." *Presidency*, 4, no. 2 (spring 2001): 7.

Robertson, Betsy Koons. "Raising the Roof: Introducing a New President Requires Taking Giant Steps around Campus." *CASE Currents* (September 2001): 20–24.

Rollins College Adventure in Common-Sense Education, The. Winter Park, FL: Trustees of Rollins College, 1929.

Rosener, Judy B. "Ways Women Lead." *Harvard Business Review* 68, no. 6, (November–December 1990): 119–25.

Rosenzweig, Robert M. *The Political University: Policy, Politics, and Presidential Leadership in the American Research University.* Baltimore, MD: Johns Hopkins University Press, 1998.

Ross, Marlene, and Madeleine F. Green. *The American College President.* Washington, DC: American Council on Education, 2000.

Rusaw, A. Carol. "Achieving Credibility: An Analysis of Women's Experience." *Review of Public Personnel Administration,* archive. Columbia, SC: 1996.

Sample, Steven B. "Unlocking the Power of Contrarian Leadership." *Presidency* 5, no. 2 (spring 2002): 25–27.

Schuster, Jack H., Daryl G. Smith, Kathleen A. Corak, and Myrtle M. Yamada. *Strategic Governance: How to Make Big Decisions Better.* Phoenix, AZ: American Council on Education/Oryx Press, 1994.

Shalala, Donna E. "Miami Is the World: Miami Es el Mundo," Inaugural Address, University of Miami, November 2, 2001.

Shapiro, Harold T. "University Presidents—Then and Now." In *Universities and Their Leadership,* edited by William G. Bowen and Harold T. Shapiro, 65–99. Princeton, NJ: Princeton University Press, 1998.

Shervish, Paul G., and John J. Havens. "The New Physics of Philanthropy: The Supply-Side Vectors of Charitable Giving." *CASE International Journal of Educational Advancement* 2, no. 3 (March 2002): 221–40.

Silber, John. *Straight Shooting: What's Wrong with America and How to Fix It.* New York: Harper & Row, 1989.

"Silber Resumes Presidency of Boston U. after His Successor Resigns Abruptly." *Chronicle of Higher Education,* Archive, July 11, 2002.

Simurda, Stephen J. "The Impossible Presidency." *Lingua Franca* (November/ December 1992): 44–51.

Smothers, Ronald. "Carolina Educator: Bold Leader or Big Spender?" *New York Times,* Education, July 4, 1990, p. 16.

Soder, Dee. "CEO Selection and Evaluation Today: What Directors Say." *Director's Monthly* 26, no. 10 (October 2002): 1–6.

Stake, Bernadine Evans, Robert E. Stake, Laura Morgan, and James Pearsol. "Final Evaluation Report of the National Sex Equity Demonstration Project." Chicago: University of Illinois, September 1983.

"Statement on Government of Colleges and Universities." In *Organization and Governance in Higher Education,* 4th ed., ASHE Reader, edited by Marvin W. Peterson, 157–63. Needham Heights, MA: Ginn Press, 1991.

Suchman, Mark C. "Managing Legitimacy: Strategic and Institutional Approaches." *Academy of Management Review* 20, no. 3 (1995): 571–610.

Sweeney, P. "Teaching New Hires to Feel at Home." *New York Times*, February 14, 1999, p. 15.

Tavris, Carol. "Are Girls Really as Mean as Books Say They Are?" *Chronicle of Higher Education*, July 5, 2002, pp. B7–B9.

Tichy, Noel M., and Mary Anne Devanna. *The Transformational Leader*. New York: John Wiley & Sons, 1990.

Tierney, William G. "Why Committees Don't Work: Creating a Structure for Change." *Academe/aaup.org*, May–June 2001.

Tolley, William Pearson. *At the Fountain of Youth: Memories of a College President*. New York: Syracuse University, 1989.

Topping, Mary E. H., and Ellen B. Kimmel. "The Imposter Phenomenon: Feeling Phony." *Academic Psychology Bulletin* 7 (summer 1985): 213–26.

Trice, Harrison M., and David A. Morand. "Rites of Passage in Work Careers." In *Handbook of Career Theory*, edited by Michael B. Arthur, Douglas T. Hall, and Barbara S. Lawrence, 397–416. Cambridge, UK: Cambridge University Press, 1989.

Trow, Martin A. "Comparative Reflections on Leadership in Higher Education." In *Organization and Governance in Higher Education*, 4th ed., ASHE Reader, edited by Marvin W. Peterson, 355–68. Needham Heights, MA: Ginn Press, 1991.

Trustees & Troubled Times in Higher Education. Washington, DC: Association of Governing Boards of Universities and Colleges, 1992.

Turner, Victor. "Liminality and Community." *The Ritual Process*. Chicago: Aldine, 1969. Reprinted in *Culture and Society: Contemporary Debates*, edited by Jeffrey C. Alexander and Steven Seidman, 147–54. Cambridge, UK: Cambridge University Press, 1990.

Whetten, David A., and Kim S. Cameron. "Administrative Effectiveness in Higher Education." In *Organization and Governance in Higher Education*, 4th ed., ASHE Reader, edited by Marvin W. Peterson, 459–69. Needham Heights, MA: Ginn Press, 1991.

Williamson, Samuel R. Four Lectures Given at the Virginia Theological Seminary, spring 2001. Unpublished.

Yoder, Janice D., Thomas L. Schleicher, and Theodore W. McDonald. "Empowering Token Women Leaders: The Importance of Organizationally Legitimated Credibility." *Psychology of Women Quarterly* 22 (1998): 209–22.

Yukl, Gary A. *Leadership in Organizations*. Englewood Cliffs, NJ: Prentice-Hall, 1989.

INDEX

About the Author

RITA BORNSTEIN is President of Rollins College. She was previously Vice President at the University of Miami. In 2001, she was awarded the George D. and Harriet W. Cornell Chair of Distinguished Presidential Leadership.